TAKE A
WALK ON
THE
DARK S

ROCK A
MYTHS,
AND CURS

R. GARY PATTER

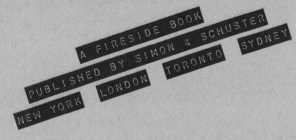

A FIRESIDE BOOK

PUBLISHED BY SIMON & SCHUSTER

NEW YORK   LONDON   TORONTO   SYDNEY

Ruby M. Hunt

For you, Mom:

Mom, this one is for you! Thanks for loading up our car with all my friends and taking us to the drive-in to watch three horror films back to back on Friday nights. Thanks for buying me those Rolling Stones concert tickets when I was fourteen years old and waiting over six hours until the Stones flew in from New York and finally performed. Most of all, thanks for your unconditional love, guidance, and support and for being the person you are.

CONTENTS

INTRODUCTION

WHO CREATED ROCK AND ROLL? Was it given life at an obscure country crossroads by a young Robert Johnson willing to sacrifice his soul for the power of the blues? Was it the rhythmic gospel beat found in the southern backwoods churches that gave it a pulse? Or was the part-time delivery boy who stopped in at Sun Records to record a song for his mother the one who breathed life into its body? Pinpointing the origins of rock and roll is an arduous task. Rock and roll, by its very nature, is difficult to define, and even harder to explain.

There may never be one clear-cut, universally accepted theory as to the origins of rock and roll music. One thing, however, is clear: Rock and roll has had a turbulent history. Rock and roll is a living, breathing body, constantly expanding its horizons and pushing its limits. Danny and the Juniors once boasted, "Rock and roll is here to stay, it will never die." While that may be true, rock and roll has had its share of close calls. From its inception, rock and roll has been peppered with myth, folklore, legend, rumor, and fact. Perhaps no other field in pop culture has had so rich a history. Musicians' untimely deaths. Lives filled with excess. Bizarre, unusual coincidence. Poignant, prophetic lyrics. Chilling, gripping circumstances.

Rock and roll is an enigmatic body of culture. *Take a Walk on the Dark Side: Rock and Roll Myths, Legends, and Curses* involves two distinct facets of rock history—fact and irony. *Take a Walk on the Dark Side,* however, is a different sort of rock history; it is an account of fact, fiction, myth, rumor, and legend.

This combination makes *Take a Walk on the Dark Side* a labor of love. It combines the two things that fascinate me most—rock and roll music and its history, and that which is bizarre and unexplainable.

My love for rock and roll is easy to explain. I grew up on rock and roll music. Much as it did with contemporary American culture, rock and roll took hold of me. The songs that I grew up with are like old friends. They are a part of my childhood, my memories, my life, and part of me.

My interest in the bizarre and unexplainable is probably best credited to human nature. Many individuals throughout history have been influenced by fate, happenstance, or chance. This allows humanity a glimpse of its own mortality. Public tragedies allow us to experience this vicariously. Some of us, however, have come far too close to the clutches of circumstance. In July 1996, I was in Paris with a group of family and friends. I remember all too well the icy sensations of horror that swept across me as I learned that TWA Flight 800 had exploded off the New York coastline. My return tickets were a grim irony: TWA Flight 802. Flight 800 had left JFK airport in New York and was destined for Charles de Gaulle airport in Paris. We were leaving Charles de Gaulle and flying into JFK in New York that evening. The incident was chilling yet fascinating.

Rock and roll has had a profound effect on me. On one hand, rock and roll's pulsating rhythms and poignant lyrics make me feel alive, yet rock and roll's bizarre coincidences and riveting circumstances serve as a dramatic reminder of my own mortality.

I think the Grateful Dead aptly described the history of rock music when they sang "What a long, strange trip it's been." How it began, where it started, what caused this thing called rock and roll music is an enigma. Rock and roll is constantly changing and ever-expanding.

In any event, it is clear that rock and roll was created in the American rural South. To some degree its very creators have struggled with the age-old question of whom the music actually serves. The self-proclaimed originator of rock and roll, Little Richard, who many of the British invasion groups believed to be bigger than Elvis, was ordained a minister in the Seventh Day Adventist Church. This conversion occurred in October of 1957, after Little Richard became alarmed that his chartered plane, with part of the fuselage on fire, would crash somewhere over Australia. Richard remembers the event: "I gave up rock and roll for the rock of ages! I used to be a glaring homosexual until God changed me!"[1] To seal his pact with God, Little Richard promptly threw thousands of dollars' worth of jewelry into the Tasman Sea after he safely landed in Sydney. Strangely, the Australian tour included Gene Vincent and Eddie Cochran. Cochran would die in an automobile accident on April 17, 1960, and Vincent would be injured in the same accident. Gene Vincent would die of a hemorrhaged ulcer on October 12, 1971. In this event Little Richard definitely made the best decision. Today, Little Richard has finally been recognized for his contributions to rock and roll and has been inducted to the Rock and Roll Hall of Fame in Cleveland, Ohio. But he hasn't retired from performing, and he still manages to present the conflict between the infectious beat of rock and roll and his religious upbringing.

Perhaps the strangest conflict within an early rock and roll innovator occurred in the case of Jerry Lee Lewis. Even his birth was accompanied by the unusual: "On that day, September 29, 1935, at an hour more dark than light, Mamie Lewis heard the first scream of her newborn child. A dog no one had ever seen had been howling outside the window near the bed. Her sister Stella had thrown stones to chase it away, but it had come back. Now, finally, it went off into the brush toward Turtle Lake, and Stella Calhoun never saw it again."[2] I was first introduced to the southern lore involving a howling dog at night when I was a student at Tennessee Technological University in Cookeville, Tennessee. My roommate, Steve, his girlfriend, and I were sitting up late one night watching a movie when we heard the sound of a howling dog. The sound was chilling. Steve's girlfriend calmly looked us both in the eye and whispered, "Someone close to one of us will die tonight." At first I laughed but then she looked seriously at me and exclaimed, "Ever since I was a little girl in Columbia

[Tennessee] and heard a dog howl at night someone close to me has died." At that time I was glad she was Steve's girlfriend and not mine. "But," I demanded, "I hear dogs bark at night all the time!" Giving me a knowing glance she simply responded, "Barking is normal, but how many times have you heard a dog howl?" I had to admit that she had me there. As I slept that night I paid little attention to our conversation about the nocturnal habits of howling dogs. However, just before dawn, the high-pitched ringing of the phone awakened me. Steve answered the phone and then became very quiet. I asked him, "What's up? Who's calling us at this hour?" I'll never forget the haunted look in his eyes when he explained to me that his mother had just called. It seemed that she wanted to notify him of the death of his uncle. According to his mother, his uncle had died at approximately the same hour we heard the howling dog outside our apartment.

The reference to the dog outside the Lewis home may have signaled a run of incredible bad luck for the rock and roll giant who became known as the Killer. Jerry Lee Lewis's career was practically destroyed when the media discovered that he had married his thirteen-year-old cousin, Myra. To complicate matters more, this marriage took place before his divorce from his second wife was final. The marriage to Myra ended in divorce in 1970. In all, Lewis has been married six times. "His fourth wife, Jaren, drowned in 1982 while awaiting terms of the final settlement of their divorce. He married his fifth wife, twenty-five-year-old Shawn Michelle Stephens, in 1983; after less than ninety days she was taken from his home dead of an overdose of methadone . . . Both of his sons have died untimely deaths: one, Steve Allen Lewis, named for the television host and announced enemy of rock and roll, drowned in a swimming pool at age three in 1962; the other, Jerry Lee Lewis Jr., died in an auto accident at age nineteen in 1973. Lewis's older brother Elmo died when he was still a boy."[3]

At times Lewis followed in the footsteps of Little Richard

and would preach in the local Pentecostal churches. It appeared that in his family the choice was usually music or the ministry. One of Jerry Lee Lewis's cousins, Mickey Gilley, made a career for himself as a country singer. Another cousin, Jimmy Swaggart, became a famous televangelist. It may very well be left to the individual to decide which force each of the three cousins serves. In some cases this has become a continuous internal struggle between faith and fame.

Lewis had one such struggle during the recording of "Great Balls of Fire." After Lewis and the session players got to drinking, Jerry Lee became filled with the Holy Ghost, and he decided that the song "Great Balls of Fire" was of the devil and that to sing it was to sin. Sam Phillips (owner of Sun Studios) argued against Jerry Lee's stand. Following a long period of time filled with mutual quoting from the Scriptures by Phillips and Lewis, the rock classic was finally cut between midnight and dawn. Perhaps it was appropriate that the recording would occur around the very witching hour of night. In a recent interview Lewis said he still believes that his music may have served the devil. When his daughter reprimanded him over that comment, Lewis commented something to the effect that "If my music hadn't served the devil, then I sure gave him a good shoeshine." Jerry Lee Lewis may well have believed that on the night of his birth Robert Johnson's legendary hellhound had found him and led him down a path of self-destruction.

When rock and roll legends are discussed there are mentions of doomed bands and bizarre coincidences that reach from beyond the grave. One of the most incredible coincidences concerns the tragic legacy of Buddy Holly. Holly was one of the first white artists to take the black man's music and adapt it to a more diverse audience. When he and his band the Crickets were signed to their first label, Brunswick, the record executives had first thought that the band was a black group. Little did they know that an all-white southern band from Texas would take the legendary all-black Apollo Theater in New York by storm. Did this diffusion of musical styles help lead the country to denounce the Jim Crow laws and lay the first foundation for the establishment of the Civil Rights movement? Maybe; this is a point that could be well argued. When Holly appeared on stage and on national television wearing his trademark black horned-rimmed glasses, he gave other musicians, including a very nearsighted John Lennon, the courage to appear naturally on stage wearing glasses and not be hung up promoting a cool stereotypical image. As a matter of fact, Buddy Holly's look was the epitome of cool!

If the cultural acceptance of Buddy Holly was important, even more so was his music. The secret to his songs was primarily the clever wordplay and an infectious beat. Holly's playing did more to promote the Fender Stratocaster guitar than any other artist (notwithstanding Jimi Hendrix, of course). In a time filled with the terrible uncertainty of the Cold War, Buddy Holly and his music provided a much-needed reprieve. After Holly's marriage to Maria Elena Santiago, he became a solo artist and booked himself into a series of winter rock and roll shows. It was at this time, on February 3, 1959, that the music died.

The pilot, Roger Peterson, was twenty-one years old and was not instrument certified to fly in the conditions that that fateful night demanded. (One of the most interesting rumors concerning the plane was that its name was *American Pie*. This namesake was said to serve as Don McLean's inspiration for his "American Pie," an ode to Buddy Holly and the day the music died. Unfortunately, this concept of "American Pie" is just an unfounded urban legend. There is no documentation that the plane was christened with a name; this has become yet one more instance of rock and roll folklore.) Shortly after 1:00 A.M. Eastern time in the early morning hours of February 3, 1959, the small

Beechcraft Bonanza airplane crashed into an open field. All the plane's passengers were killed, as well as the pilot. Holly died at the age of twenty-two, the Big Bopper at twenty-eight, and Ritchie Valens at seventeen. The untimely death of these three young stars has played a major role in rock and roll mythology.

It seemed that tragedy would continue to pursue other associations with Buddy Holly. His birthplace in Lubbock, Texas, was condemned for demolition on February 3, 1978, the nineteenth anniversary of Holly's tragic death. Another coincidence that concerned Buddy Holly involved the Who's drummer, Keith Moon. Moon had long been known as a wild man of rock. His drinking and other madcap exploits were legendary. The last album Moon made with the Who was *Who Are You,* released in 1978. On the album cover Moon was shown sitting in a chair that is labeled "Not to Be Taken Away." The dramatic irony of the chair's statement was reinforced with the announcement of Keith Moon's death. According to published reports, Moon had attended the London premiere of *The Buddy Holly Story* with Paul McCartney and some other friends. After the premiere, Moon and his girlfriend returned home, where he took his medication and went to bed. A few hours later Moon awoke and took some more pills. This was to be a fatal mistake. The large meal had slowed the reaction of the first pills. When the second dosage was taken an accidental overdose occurred. Keith Moon was dead at the age of thirty-one. The incredible irony in Keith Moon's death was not only in the fact that his last public appearance was at *The Buddy Holly Story,* but that he died on September 7, 1978. You see, September 7 was Buddy Holly's birthday! Another strange coincidence involving Keith Moon concerns the suite in which he died. The flat belonged to Harry Nilsson, and four years earlier Cass Elliot of the Mamas and the Papas had died in the same room from a heart attack (and not from choking to death on a ham sandwich!).⁴ Maybe this gives a new meaning to "Heartbreak Hotel."

Many DJs claimed that rock and roll would never die, but in the late 1950s the music was placed on temporary life support. For instance, it was in 1957 that Little Richard became an ordained minister and cut back on his devotion to rock and roll. Nineteen-fifty-seven was also the same year that Jerry Lee Lewis married his thirteen-year-old cousin. This scandal made headlines early the next year in 1958 and effectively, but thankfully temporarily, pulled Lewis's music from the airwaves and Lewis's presence from the concert stages. Also in 1958, Elvis Presley was drafted into the army. When he returned he played the role of a pop singer and movie star but finally rediscovered his rock and roll roots in 1968. The next year, 1959, saw the deaths of Buddy Holly, the Big Bopper, and Ritchie Valens, as we have noted. At the conclusion of this year, Chuck Berry would be arrested and imprisoned on a morals charge. At the very moment that rock was reeling from the deaths and seclusion of its most brilliant performers, the U.S. Congress began the payola scandals. "Payola" referred to bribes being given to certain disk jockeys to play certain artists' recordings on the air. Of course this would result in hit records. The central figure of this investigation was none other than Cleveland, Ohio's own Alan Freed, the man who coined the term "rock and roll" and its first promoter. Sadly, Freed was blackballed by the very industry he helped create. He died indigent on January 20, 1965, at the age of forty-two.

It is my sincere hope that the material presented in *Take a Walk on the Dark Side* might make you see things in a different light. Perhaps some of the references will make your pulse race a little faster. Maybe you'll find yourself glancing over your shoulder when you are alone in the room. Perhaps you will never listen to one of your records or CDs in the same way. Please remind yourself that some of these stories are simply myths and legends;

the others? Well . . . you be the judge of that, but above all, enjoy the book.

In compiling my sources I would like to thank my publisher, Fireside Books, at Simon & Schuster, and especially my editor, Brett Valley, for his guidance and assistance. I would also like to thank Matt Walker, my former editor, who is now at Yale working on his Ph.D. My very special thanks goes to Lisa Lyon, producer of *Coast to Coast AM* and the Premiere Radio Network, as well as to Barbara Simpson (the Princess of Darkness) and to Ian Punnitt, two of the best interviewers anywhere. I'd like to thank Anne Devlin from *Anne Online,* and my attorney Norman Gillis; and Connie Loy for being there and believing. There are several other individuals who have made a difference in my professional life. I'd like to thank Jeff Cohen of Richmond, Virginia, Allan Handelman, J. Fox and Dave Bolt of the ABC Radio Network, and the hundreds of DJs across the country who sit with me and discuss these incredible tales. Indeed, "Music is our special friend." Special thanks also goes out to the incredible Susan Vargas, my favorite television producer in Hollywood. Susan, I'm sure we will do more incredible series together. As for my ultimate source of strength, I would like to thank my family, especially my mom, who guided me with unconditional love, and my daughter, Shea, who is growing up way too fast. I know that this work would not have been possible without all of their combined efforts. I would also like to thank Derek Davidson at Photofest, Jon R. Hichborn at royaltytracking.com and Delta Haze, and Yvette Reyes at AP/ Wide World Photos for their much appreciated assistance.

In some cases you must realize, as I have done during my research, that some of these are simply myths that have made their way up the ladder to accepted legend. For example, I get tired of the Yoko bashings that I have heard from some unknowing fans. Isn't it ironic that the woman some Beatle fans accuse of breaking up the Beatles in the first place is the same person who made it possible for the three surviving Beatles to reunite and give their fans the three Anthologies? Maybe some individuals seek only the negative.

I would also especially like to thank all the fans, who always offer me more strange coincidences to consider. If you know of some other strange facts in which I would be interested, please contact me at Fireside Books. As always I appreciate your input!

For the record, I do not believe that a listener can be possessed by listening to music that is said to contain backward messages. Rather, an individual can become obsessed and spend his life listening to the garbled backward sounds of mixed phonemes. In many ways the backward sounds resemble splatters of paint thrown haphazardly on a wall. Sometimes the actual problem may be in the viewer and not the creator. But if you enjoy discussing these messages, you'll learn about them here. Just remember that any sound can have more than one interpretation. It may be a good idea to listen to a track first without looking at someone's comment on its hidden meaning. With this in mind I hope you enjoy your journey into this offering. We'll begin as together we walk down a deserted rural highway in Mississippi. The full moon is shining palely down upon one solitary figure holding a guitar standing by a crossroads. The time? It is shortly after midnight. Come. Let me introduce you to Robert Johnson . . .

I. WAITING AT THE CROSSROADS

I went down to the crossroads and fell down on my knees,
Asked the Lord up above for mercy, save poor Bob if you please.
— Robert Johnson, "Crossroads Blues"

You may bury my body down by the highway side
So my old evil spirit can get a Greyhound bus and ride.
— Robert Johnson, "Me and the Devil Blues"

WHISPERS FROM THE CROWD followed him throughout every roadhouse in Mississippi. This solitary, gaunt, black bluesman spun pentatonic riffs and moaning slide guitar lines to accompany a hoarse voice filled not only with the well-known pain of the blues, but also a voice that seemed to hint that his worst pain would certainly await him after death. Members of the crowd had heard the legend. This was Robert Johnson. The same man who had waited at the crossroads and made his pact with Satan himself. In exchange for the ability to play the blues, and enjoy the adoring company of women, whiskey, fortune, and fame, Robert Johnson would offer up his tormented soul as his only escape from the cotton fields in which he had made his own hell. This was a bargain that would allow him a reprieve from the poverty into which he had been born.

As with any legend, it is difficult to separate fact from fiction. It appears that Robert Johnson was born in Hazlehurst, Mississippi, on May 8, 1911. His birth was a result of an extramarital affair between his mother, Julie Ann Majors, and a farmworker whose name was Noah Johnson. Robert Johnson's "legal" father, Charles Dodds Jr., had earlier deserted his young wife to live with his mistress in Memphis, Tennessee. By 1927, Robert Johnson was working in the cotton fields and had utilized several aliases, Robert Sax and Robert Spenser among others. Johnson later stated to other bluesmen that he used the aliases in case a murder happened while he was in town, so that the police would be unable to pin it on him.

Biographers state that Robert Johnson was married twice. His first wife was Virginia Travis, who in 1930 died tragically in childbirth; death claimed both mother and child. He later married Callie Craft and started to pursue his musical release through the blues. Johnson's first musical instrument was the harmonica but he later changed to the guitar, an instrument that would allow him to become known as a blues innovator and the father of modern rock and roll. Local blues legends like Willie Brown, Son House, and Charley Patton would politely let the young Johnson sit in with them as they played the roadhouses. At first they were not impressed with Johnson's playing and avoided any contact with the young want-to-be bluesman. It was at this time that Johnson disappeared for six months. Some say that he went in search of his natural father, while others say that this was the time that Robert Johnson, armed with a black cat's bone, waited at the crossroads and made his bargain.

The Robert Johnson myth concerns the reaction of the older blues players to Johnson's return and his new complete mastery of the guitar. According to legend, it was Son House who stated that "He [Johnson] sold his soul to play like that." The actual crossroads encountered by Robert Johnson was that of superstition and religion. Throughout the early Puritan church doctrine Christians believed that God gave man an inner light that would multiply his acts of goodness. This was a sign that the true believer was one of the chosen, the elect, whose crops would always grow taller, and that success would follow him throughout each of life's challenges. He was marked by the community as a tribute to his Christian ideals and virtues, which represented obedience to God's commandments and living a life to be emulated that would transcend a life filled with suffering. Just so, the old field spirituals helped the black worker cope with the horrors of the cotton fields and slavery in general. These ballads gave each individual hope, a hope that there was an afterlife where suffering would end and eternal bliss in paradise would await each true believer. It was in this world that a man's good works and faith would allow him to find eternal Providence. In Robert Johnson's case, this would prove to be the opposite. The lifestyle of the blues dictated a life filled with whiskey, loose women, and gambling. These were not the golden virtues patterned in the southern churches to lead man to salvation, but instead a pathway to pain and damnation.

Johnson's guitar instructor was said to be Ike Zinnerman. This was a peculiar name for a bluesman, since the great performers all had legendary nicknames such as Blind Lemon Jefferson, Sonny Boy Williamson, Muddy Waters, Son House, and Howlin' Wolf. Even stranger than his name was the method of his instruction. It seemed that he claimed to have learned to play the guitar at night, sitting in old country churchyards, with his only companions being the tombstones of the dead and an eager pupil, Robert Johnson. Some claimed Zinnerman to be the devil, and most of the area bluesmen had no problem in accepting this explanation. With this as his origin, Johnson inspired whispers of his legendary pact throughout the cheap blues joints where his music became popular.

The use of the crossroads as a symbol of Satan's presence comes from the concept of being the final resting place for suicides and those unworthy of being buried in hallowed ground. As the bodies were buried, stones and other objects were tossed upon the corpses to show Christian contempt for their selfish deaths. After the burial, the only memorial those poor souls' graves would contain would be the well-beaten footpaths of unsuspecting travelers who unknowingly, with each heavy footfall, would help obliterate the memory of the unfortunate remains sequestered within their narrow cells underneath the crossroads. Crossroads were also supposed to be the site where witches held their gatherings. Many readers familiar with the works of Nathaniel Hawthorne will remember that Young Goodman Brown keeps his appointment with the devil at a crossroads. Perhaps this scene drawn from Hawthorne's "Young Goodman Brown" may well parallel that of another meeting at a crossroads, a meeting involving a young Robert Johnson:

He had taken a dreary road, darkened by all the gloomi-
est trees of the forest, which barely stood aside to let the

narrow path creep through, and closed immediately behind. It was all as lonely as could be; and there is this pe-
culiarity in such a solitude, that the traveler knows not
who may be concealed by the innumerable trunks and the
thick boughs overhead; so that with lonely footsteps he
may yet be passing through an unseen multitude; . . . and
he glanced fearfully behind him as he added, "What if the
devil himself should be at my very elbow!" His head being
turned back, he passed a crook of the road, and, looking
forward again, beheld the figure of a man, in grave and
decent attire, seated at the foot of an old tree. He arose at
Goodman Brown's approach and walked onward side by
side with him. "You're late, Goodman Brown," said he.

Hawthorne well knew the superstitions associated with
witchcraft and the devil's black arts. It was his ancestor, John
Hathorne, who had never repented of the execution of witches at
Salem village. Young Goodman Brown and his wife can be considered allegorical characters associated with the struggle between
good and evil. Hawthorne allows his protagonist to securely
reestablish his faith in God through the devotion and love of his
wife. Of course it is fitting that in this allegory Young Goodman
Brown wife's name is Faith. Though Young Goodman Brown dis-
avows his fellowship with the devil and wakes to find himself all
alone in the deserted forest, the story's ending hints of newfound
tragedy, in some ways very much like the legend of Robert Johnson. Goodman Brown's life changes completely. He is haunted
constantly by his visions of the witches' ceremony, turns from
his wife, and now looks at each pious figure in his village with
complete misgiving. This is how Hawthorne describes Goodman
Brown's burial: "And when he had lived long, and was borne to
his grave a hoary corpse, followed by Faith, an aged woman, and
children and grandchildren, a goodly procession, besides neigh-

bors not a few, they carved no hopeful verse upon his tombstone, for his dying hour was gloom."

An illustrative discussion of Christian burial occurs in Shakespeare's *Hamlet*. After Ophelia's questionable death, which many readers believe to have been a suicide, Laertes asks the priest, "What ceremony else?" The priest replies, "Her obsequies have been as far enlarg'd/As we have warranties; her death was doubtful;/And, but that great command o'ersways the order,/She should in ground unsanctified have lodg'd/Till the last trumpet; for charitable prayers,/Shards, flints, and pebbles should be thrown on her." The doctor answers the grieving Laertes, asserting, "We should profane the service of the dead/To sing a requiem and such rest to her/As to peace-parted souls" (5.1.200–212). Of course in *Hamlet,* the king forces a Christian burial for Ophelia against the precepts of Church doctrine.

Most of the old bluesmen were well aware of mojo hands, and charms made with graveyard dust. The term "mojo" comes from African language and refers to magical powers that could be summoned to help the initiate achieve his will. Remember, blues great Muddy Waters sang of having his "mojo workin'," and in "Hootchie-Cootchie Man" he lists a number of talismans to aid him in his love life, one of these charms being none other than a "black cat's bone." The black cat's bone relates as one of many superstitions dealing with the use of supernatural power to aid the bearer in his quest for fame, love, and fortune. One legend states that a black cat should be boiled until only the bones remain. The bones should then be placed in a running stream of water. The superstition also states that one bone will float upstream and away from the others. With this bone the bearer will be given the power to cast spells, and perhaps, as in the case of Robert Johnson, the ability to summon the devil.

The legendary concept of selling one's soul to the devil at a lonely country crossroads actually precedes that of Robert Johnson. It had been hinted that another early bluesman, Tommy Johnson (no relation to Robert), had earlier waited at a deserted crossroads and made a pact with Satan. LeDell Johnson, Tommy Johnson's brother, related this description of the supposed event in Francis Davis's *The History of the Blues:* "If you want to learn to play anything you want to play and learn how to make songs yourself, you take your guitar and you go to where a crossroads is. A big black man will walk up there [at the stroke of midnight] and take your guitar, and he'll tune it." [1] Tommy Johnson and the crossroads are mentioned in the 2000 film *O Brother, Where Art Thou?* In one scene Everett, Delmar, and Pete pick up a young black man at a deserted crossroads. After introducing himself as Tommy Johnson he informs his fellow passengers that he had just sold his soul to the devil. A few minutes later the group records "I Am a Man of Constant Sorrow." After the paid session Everett turns to Tommy and says, "Damn, Tommy, I do believe you did sell your soul to the devil."

In African folklore, "the guardian of the crossroads" was a god called Èsù by the Yoruba and Légba by the Dahomey. This deity "interpreted the will of the gods to man and carries the desires of man to the gods." [2] As Christian missionaries brought the new faith to the African tribes, it would only be appropriate to associate any ancient pagan god with the devil. In this case the crossroads became a spiritual symbol of tribal traditions counterbalanced by the acceptance of a new faith in a new God. In 1986, producer-director Walter Hill attempted to bring the Robert Johnson story to film. In his *Crossroads,* the film begins with one of Robert Johnson's recording sessions. The film then shifts into the story of Eugene, a young classical guitarist who finds the legendary Willie Brown in an old folks' home in New York and helps Brown escape back to the Delta to break his pact with Old Scratch. What is interesting is that the mysterious black man at the crossroads is called Légba (obviously Hill had done his homework). The role of Eugene was played by Ralph Macchio (*The Karate Kid*), who obviously is better at "wax on, wax off" than spinning blues riffs from his beat-up Fender Telecaster guitar, but there is one memorable moment when Willie Brown and Eugene fight for their souls in a "head cutting" contest in a juke joint from hell. "Head cutting" was a term used for blues men to prove their worth in a musical duel. It determined who had the best licks. The devil's champion was Jake Butler, played by guitar virtuoso Steve Vai (obviously the devil still doesn't play fairly). In a smoldering jam Eugene (his bag of guitar tricks provided by legendary guitarist Ry Cooder) and Willie Brown defeat the forces of darkness and win back their immortal souls. *Crossroads* was one of the first films to introduce the Robert Johnson legend.

After Robert Johnson began to achieve his exemplary fame as a first-rate guitarist, he would travel throughout the South rambling from town to town, jumping freight trains with just a moment's notice. In 1936, at the insistence of a Jackson, Mississippi, music store owner, Robert Johnson began his short recording career with Ernie Oertle, a Columbia records salesman. Within one year Johnson had recorded each of his legendary songs and may have received as much as $100 for the total effort. Having a bad reputation seemed to help pack the blues joints in which Robert Johnson performed. There was just something about his appearance. He had a cataract in one eye that many superstitious fans claimed to be the "evil eye" that could help send an innocent onlooker into the burning flames of hell. Some of the local musicians noticed that Johnson turned his back to the audience when he performed. This they took as sign that he had something to hide. Actually, he was hiding his guitar licks from the other players. When Eddie Van Halen first emerged in the music world and demonstrated his proficiency on the guitar, he also would often turn his back to the audience during his trademark "Eruption" solo. This was to keep his newfound technique a

closely guarded secret. Johnson also experimented with open tun-
ings, which eerily brings back LeDell Johnson's story of waiting at
a crossroads and at the stroke of midnight "a big black man comes
and tunes your guitar."

As with every legend, the circumstances of Johnson's death
are shrouded in mystery. Though it is evident that he was murdered, there are many variations to his tragic death. Some sources
say Robert Johnson was stabbed or shot to death by a jealous
girlfriend or by one of his many lovers' avenging spouses. The legendary account of his death hints of Johnson being poisoned
by a jealous husband shortly before the other musicians arrived
to begin their performance. It was suggested that wood alcohol
or strychnine may have been the method of poisoning. Johnny
Shines and other musicians claimed that Robert Johnson died
after three days of intense, excruciating pain. On the day he died,
August 16, 1938, Johnson was said to have fallen to his knees and
barked and howled like a dog shortly before his untimely death at
the age of twenty-seven. The legend also states that Johnson's
family may have buried his body in an unmarked grave, and—as
many followers of the legend believed—in unhallowed ground.
In this case Johnson may very well have gotten his wish in "Me
and the Devil Blues": "Early this morning when you knocked
upon my door/And I said, 'Hello, Satan, I believe it's time to go.'"
Johnson's grave can be visited in the Zion Church graveyard just
off Highway 7 in Morgan City, Mississippi. The headstone was
provided by Sony Music and contains a listing of Johnson's
twenty-nine songs. Then again in a cemetery near Greenwood,
Mississippi, there is another grave said to contain the mortal body
of Robert Johnson. The headstone was donated by rock band ZZ
Top. Many visitors place guitar picks as a tribute to the blues great
when they visit this site. To make this even more confusing, in
2000 another gravesite was found and documentation provided
to say that this was the actual resting place of Robert Johnson.

WAITING AT THE CROSSROADS

This unmarked grave is located at Little Zion Missionary Baptist Church in Greenwood, Mississippi. According to Mrs. Rosie Eskridge, she saw her husband bury a body said to be that of Robert Johnson at this very site sixty-two years ago. Of course, for the more adventurous, the notorious crossroads where Robert Johnson's pact was made is said to be found near the center of Clarksdale, Mississippi, where Highway 61 intersects Highway 49.

The emergence of Robert Johnson's music is due to the many cover versions by his 1960s blues disciples. Elmore James and supergroups such as Cream, Led Zeppelin, and the Rolling Stones have each recorded at least one adaptation of a Johnson blues classic. Sadly, many performers have also duplicated the tragic element of Johnson's life as well as in his music. One of the strangest parallels with Robert Johnson concerns the birth and rise to fame of Elvis Presley. Presley was born in Tupelo, Mississippi, just 126 miles north of Greenwood, Robert Johnson's final resting place. Presley proved to be a sensation as he adapted the infectious beat of black rhythm and blues to the taste of a southern white audience. Elvis's ascent to fame from his very humble origins was very comparable to the path taken by a young Robert Johnson—showing the power of the blues!

Elvis Presley's meteoric rise as a pop icon was found to be somewhat disturbing by the conservative white audiences throughout Presley's native South. Rock and roll was considered to be Satan's music. Many radio stations went as far as banning the playing of all rock-and-roll records. Curiously, Elvis enjoyed singing gospel songs and went as far as releasing an album dedicated to his favorite songs of faith. Whereas these gospel ballads hinted at a singer who was at peace with God, Elvis seemed to be fascinated with the occult. He studied reincarnation, UFOs, and Eastern religious practices. Like Robert Johnson, Presley was the by-product of southern poverty whose only hope for a better life was grounded in his deep-rooted faith. It was said that Elvis Presley stated that he would not live to be older than his mother; ironically, Elvis Aaron Presley died at the age of forty-two. His mother lived to be forty-six.

Elvis has become even more popular in death, with many obsessed fans reporting "Elvis sightings" across the country. Others insist that there are many cryptic messages that hint that Elvis has not left the building after all! These clues include: the mysterious misspelled name upon his tombstone, his Tennessee driving license still being valid, his million-dollar life insurance policy not being claimed, and discrepancies in his autopsy report. Even in the psychic world at least one clairvoyant has claimed to have received messages from Elvis, who, after passing over into the afterlife, has finally developed into a first-rate songwriter: According to some sources, a European psychic is in search of a recording contract to bring Elvis's "new" songs to his long waiting fans.

The strange coincidences that surrounded the paths of Elvis Presley and Robert Johnson came full circle with the date of Elvis's death, August 16, 1977. Both men died on the same day, in the same month, thirty-nine years apart.

2. THE BUDDY HOLLY CURSE?

"EVERY DAY'S A HOLLY DAY"

> The snow was snowing, the wind was blowing when the world said, "Good-bye, Buddy."
> —Mike Berry, "Tribute to Buddy Holly"

will forever be known as "The Day the Music Died." Shortly after 1:00 A.M. Eastern time, during what was considered to be a routine flight, three of the brightest stars in the rock and roll heavens came plunging back to the earth in a comet of fire and distorted, twisted metal. When the solemn news quickly spread across AM radio airwaves, the victims were identified as Buddy Holly, twenty-two; J. P. Richardson, "The Big Bopper," twenty-eight; and Ritchie Valens, seventeen. These three young musicians were not the first to be sacrificed upon the altar of musical stardom, but such a cataclysmic loss of life at such an early age foreshadowed countless others who would follow in their tragic path.

Today, more than forty years since the crash, the events of that terrible night and the strange sequence of coincidences that have followed have become the very substance of urban legend. Many rumors, as well as conspiracy theories, have continued to swirl about the events that have now defined rock and roll's first great catastrophe, in some ways painting a mental image much like the squall that encased the downed Beechcraft Bonanza in a light shroud of freshly fallen snow as the splintered aircraft lay broken and embedded in the frozen earth just nine miles outside Clear Lake, Iowa.

Several documented accounts have stated that all three performers had some sort of premonition of the calamity that would befall them. The Big Bopper had served as a DJ for radio station KTRM in Beaumont, Texas, as he continued to develop his rock and roll career both as a songwriter and performer. As a DJ, the Bopper's zany radio antics included a sleepless Disc-A-Thon in 1957. The Disc-A-Thon was a popular gimmick that required the station DJ to stay awake and on the air for as many days as possible playing record after record until he collapsed from the terrible weariness. Curious onlookers would rush to the studio to watch the radio personality and silently wonder how long he could possibly last until he succumbed to exhaustion.

Jerry Boynton, who served as radio announcer for KTRM, remembered the Disc-A-Thon and a near-exhausted Richardson who had been awake for slightly more than three straight days. Richardson asked, "Jer, you think I'm going to die?" And Boynton replied, "J. P., I think you are. [Laughs]." [1] During the course of the day several breaks were arranged to help refresh the DJ and keep him going just a little longer. Cold towels, hot coffee mixed with adrenaline, and an iron will kept the Big Bopper continuing his spectacular sleepless production. Finally, after setting a new record of 122 hours and eight minutes (just over five days) without sleep and constantly being on the air, the Big Bopper was carried out of the station by an ambulance. During the sleepless marathon he had begun to hallucinate. In one hallucination he told of foreseeing his own death, later reporting that "the other side wasn't that bad." [2]

For Ritchie Valens, the very thought of flying was terrifying. Donna Fox, subject of Ritchie Valens's hit song "Donna," recalled, "He would have nightmares about that [flying]. He just had a horrible fear of small planes, and planes in general. He indicated that he would never fly. He just would never fly." [3]

That horrible fear began on January 31, 1957. This day was the funeral of Ritchie's grandfather. Ritchie had missed school that day to attend the funeral service. Shortly after the family returned to the Valenzuela home, a deafening explosion shook the earth. When Ritchie and his older brother Bob Morales looked into the heavens, they saw a plane plummeting from the sky totally engulfed in flames.

Quickly, the family members jumped into a car and followed in the general direction of the now crimson sky. Almost like children searching for the pot of gold at the end of the rainbow, the Valenzuela family found the wreckage of the doomed aircraft. Ironically, the crash site was the playground of Ritchie's school, Paicoma Junior High School. The school ground resembled a battlefield, with pieces of contorted, burning metal intermixed with playground equipment. The scene created a ghastly paradox of childhood innocence and untimely death. Horribly, three students were killed and ninety others injured. One of the students killed was Ritchie's best friend. Every day Ritchie would sit on these same playgrounds playing his guitar while his fellow students would gather around him. He was convinced that if he had not attended his grandfather's funeral he would have been one of the victims lying on that pockmarked school ground. But malevolent fate had other plans; two years and three days later he would be at the scene of another plane crash, as one of three rock and roll stars lying sprawled upon the snow-covered grounds of Albert Juhl's farm just outside Clear Lake, Iowa.

When Ritchie's career took off like a shooting star he realized that he would have to overcome his fear and dread of flying. With the release of "Come On, Let's Go," "Donna," and "La Bamba," Ritchie Valens was very much in demand. He had a cameo role in the film *Go, Johnny, Go!* with fellow rocker Eddie Cochran and was asked to join Buddy Holly on the Winter Dance Party. Just before Valens was to catch his flight to join the tour he attended church services with a friend: "On his final night in Los Angeles, he'd gone to the Guardian Angels church on Laurel Canyon Boulevard with his friend Gail Smith and prayed for a safe journey. He was afraid of airplanes, he told Gail, . . . but he was getting used to them and might even take one at some point during the Winter Dance Party. Gail warned that it was snowy and storming in the North and asked, 'What'd you do if you crash?' 'I'll land on my guitar,' Ritchie said."[4] Strangely, Ritchie Valens's mother was also said to have had a premonition concerning the death of her son on that fateful tour. She had refused to say anything to him because she didn't want to interfere in his career.

The center of the rock and roll universe was Buddy Holly. The other stars would orbit around his presence during the Winter Dance Party tour. Though Holly had the reputation based on his many past hits, the hottest star in this galaxy tour was Ritchie Valens, who was shooting straight up the charts with "Donna" and "La Bamba." Holly's last two compositions, "Heartbeat" and "It's So Easy," had failed to make a splash on the charts. He was determined to get back to the top as a solo artist since his split with the Crickets. In a deal worked out with his producer and cowriter Norman Petty, the Crickets—Jerry "J. I." Allison and Joe B. Mauldin—would retain the rights to the band's name and would continue to perform without Buddy. In another sense of irony, both Jerry and Joe had tried to contact Buddy the night of the plane crash in hopes of reuniting the band. Sadly, this was not to be.

For the Winter Dance Party tour, Holly had hired longtime friend and protégé Waylon Jennings to be the bassist. According to Jennings, Buddy purchased a new electric Fender bass guitar and told Jennings he had two weeks to learn to play the instrument. For backup guitar, Holly chose Tommy Allsup. With the addition of these two fellow Texans, the band was complete.

The chief reason for Holly's agreement to do the Winter Dance Party was to generate enough income to support his new wife, Maria Elena, who was also pregnant with the couple's first child. The income would also help support Buddy's new publishing company. Though he hated to go in the dead of winter—the midwestern winters could be brutal and unbearable in early February—he had no choice. In recalling their first date, Maria mentioned that Buddy proposed to her then and there. When she asked that just maybe Buddy should get to know her a little better, he smiled and replied, "I haven't got the time." Perhaps this was a premonition that Holly had, that he would have a short life, and so he had decided that he should find all the happiness to fill his tragically numbered days.

Shortly before leaving for the Winter Dance Party tour, both Maria Elena and Buddy were shaken by disturbing but strangely prophetic dreams. Maria was awakened suddenly from a nightmare in which she was standing in a vast open area, much like a farm: "I didn't know where I was or how I got there. And then all of a sudden I could hear noises, like shouting, and it got closer and closer in the distance. I could see all these people running, running, running and shouting, 'They're coming! Hide!'"[5] Maria was convinced that she would be trampled by the onrushing mob. As the crowd parted around her, she heard a terrible noise and then she saw a descending ball of fire falling from the heavens. She was convinced that this flaming cometlike object would crush her but it passed by her. She heard a terrible crash and in the distance witnessed a huge explosion, much like that of a plane crash. As she approached the site, all she could see was a great burning hole in the ground. At this point she awakened Buddy.

As Buddy tried to comfort her, he related to Maria a dream he had just moments before in which he was flying in a small plane with his brother Larry and her. For some reason Larry convinced Buddy to leave Maria on the top of a building but reassured him that they would soon return to pick her up. The dream created so much guilt within Buddy that he broke into tears saying that he just couldn't understand why he left her and she wasn't with him. In a few short weeks both these dreams would come back to haunt Maria Elena: "We were both dreaming the same dream at the same time. And there was so much that came true if you put two and two together. Buddy leaving me [the day he left for the Dance Party Maria had her bags packed to go with him but he convinced her to stay due to her morning sickness] . . . an airplane crash . . . on a farm . . . it was like someone saying something to me but I didn't listen."[6]

Eerily, Buddy Holly had been fascinated with piloting small planes and had taken at least one flying lesson shortly before his death. His brother Larry was along with him. In this particular lesson the flight instructor cut the small plane's engine and put the plane into a nosedive. Holly recalled that the dive felt like it lasted a good forty minutes before the pilot calmly leveled the plane and continued the flight. Sadly, this saving motion would not occur on the night of February 3, 1959.

During his successful tour of England in 1958, Buddy was startled to find a note delivered to him personally by legendary British recording engineer and producer Joe Meek. Meek had become fascinated with the occult and had graduated from his Ouija board to tarot card readings. During a tarot session in January of 1958, vocalist Jimmy Miller of Jimmy Miller and the Barbecues joined Joe Meek. Miller had enjoyed using his Ouija board as a method to help pick up girls. He noticed it helped break the ice, and many of his dates found the spooky readings to be fascinating. It just seemed natural that Jimmy would graduate to higher forms of spiritualism with Joe Meek, especially since Joe was the band's producer.

According to Miller, on this particular night Joe Meek had invited Faud, an Arab friend and another dabbler in the occult sciences, to make up the third party, and the tarot cards were brought out into an appropriately darkened room. Miller recalled, "That was the first time I had handled tarot cards, and even now I am getting tingles down my spine."[7] These slight tingles would later turn to petrifying fear as the evening progressed. Meek told Jimmy to shuffle and cut the cards with his left hand. The right hand of each man securely gripped the left of the man sitting next to him. Joe placed himself in the middle and Faud's right hand was kept free to write down on a writing pad any spiritual messages that might make their way through the veil. Miller recalls that the cards felt strange and that he became nauseated.

Slowly, he turned each card with his left hand. Halfway through the deck, Jimmy grasped Joe's hand so tightly that the singer's fingernails dug deeply into the producer's knuckles, cutting into the flesh. Faud began slowly writing down individual letters that created the message now being obtained from the beyond.

When the cards were completely turned, Joe Meek screamed in pain and wrenched his hand free from the now equally terrified Miller. In horror the three men looked at the spiritual message that had been recorded by Faud. The message stated a date—"February the third." The date was followed by the name "Buddy Holly" and "Dies." "The whole affair was amazing because the message was written in what looked very much like my [Miller's] own handwriting," Miller said.

As Miller recalled it, Joe Meek was now a man filled with a terrible urgency. Not only was he a fan of Buddy Holly, but now he had only a few short weeks to get the message to Buddy to be extremely careful on February the third. Meek contacted record companies, music publishers, and any other inside sources that could carry the prophetic message of doom to the popular American singer.

When February 3, 1958, finally came and passed without incident, Miller said Joe felt relieved but still felt it was his responsibility to personally deliver the message to Holly when the singer and his backup group the Crickets arrived in Great Britain in mid-February to begin their UK tour. When Meek told Holly the incredible events of the tarot reading the singer very politely thanked Joe for his concern and promised that he would always be extremely careful in the future when February the third would come around.

In an interview with the BBC at the tour's end, Holly remarked that his tour of England had been very strange. First, a fan threw a brick with an autograph book attached through his dressing room window, almost hitting him, and then he received a message telling him that he was going to die. If only Buddy Holly had remembered Joe Meek's warning the next year when on February 3, 1959, Holly climbed into a small chartered airplane on a cold winter's night in Iowa. Fate would not present Buddy Holly with a second chance.

Fate had a different outcome in mind for the members of Holly's backing band. Drummer Carl Bunch was hospitalized due to his contracting severe frostbite on his feet. Providence would also play a major role in allowing both Waylon Jennings and Tommy Allsup to escape the one-way flight in the doomed Beechcraft Bonanza. The band was forced to honor a grueling schedule of performances. Sometimes they would be forced to travel over five hundred miles in one night following a performance.

To make matters even more unbearable, the musicians were forced to travel on reconditioned school buses that kept breaking down during the long road trips. Coupled with temperatures that reached twenty-five degrees below zero, the musicians' morale was quickly diminishing. After performing at the Surf Ballroom in Clear Lake, Iowa, Buddy Holly made arrangements to charter the small plane to help escape the misery of the school bus caravan. Gaining a few hours would allow him to have his clothes laundered.

When the Big Bopper discovered the plan to fly to the next show, he asked Waylon Jennings for his seat on the plane. The Bopper was sick with the flu and wanted to see a doctor. For Jennings, who enjoyed the camaraderie of the other performers, it was no great sacrifice to give up his seat. The final bargaining item was the Big Bopper's new sleeping bag. When Buddy found out that Jennings had given up his seat he admonished Jennings to have fun on the Arctic school bus and laughingly joked that he hoped the school bus would break down. Jennings quickly shot back a comment that haunts him forever when he remembers that night. Jennings quipped, "Yeah, and I hope your old plane crashes."

The most surprising test of fate occurred when Ritchie Valens kept asking Tommy Allsup for his seat. Finally, Allsup produced a half-dollar and told Ritchie to "call it." Valens called "heads" and watched intently as Allsup flipped the coin into the air. As the coin came tumbling down, Ritchie smiled as he saw that he had made the correct call. According to Alan Freed, Valens claimed this was the first time he had ever won at anything.

Allsup notified Buddy that Valens would take his seat on the plane. Tommy then gave his wallet to Buddy to pick up a registered letter that was waiting for him at the band's next stop. Shortly after the crash, for a few anxious hours, investigators believed that there were five victims in the wreckage and looked frantically for the missing body that had to be hidden somewhere in the frozen cornfield. Luckily, Allsup had called home informing his parents about the tragedy just minutes before the call came to notify Tommy's mother and father that their son's name was given as one of the victims of the accident. Tommy Allsup was given a second chance. To commemorate his good fortune he opened his own saloon when he returned to Austin, Texas. He called the bar the Head's Up Saloon. This would remind him in the future how a simple coin toss had saved his life.

A few days before the fatal crash, Buddy had called up fellow rocker and friend Eddie Cochran. Holly was afraid that he had lost his creative touch and that he would never again have a song at the top of the charts. Cochran assured him that he was still the top star in the rock galaxy and that it was only a matter of time before Buddy again topped the pop charts. Cochran was scheduled to be with his friends Buddy Holly and Ritchie Valens on the Winter Dance Party tour. He and Ritchie Valens had just finished the film *Go, Johnny, Go!* but Eddie had a performance scheduled for early February on *The Ed Sullivan Show* and Buddy reminded him that the show would be much more important for his career that slowly freezing to death in the reconditioned school buses plodding wearily through the midwestern winter. When Cochran heard of the crash and death of his friends he was shaken. He was supposed to have been there too. Had he cheated death?

At his next scheduled recording session Cochran had planned to record "Three Stars," a tribute written by DJ Tommy Dee of KFXM in San Bernardino, California, to honor Buddy Holly, the Big Bopper, and Ritchie Valens. Dee had written the song the day after the accident and Cochran recorded his version of "Three Stars" on February 5, 1959, just two days after the ominous crash. The original purpose was to split the song's royalties among the families of the three fallen stars.

The song contains three verses of spoken narrative, and Eddie describes each of his departed friends with heartfelt emotion. For Ritchie Valens, Cochran sang, "Everyone calls me a kid, but you were only seventeen." He describes the Big Bopper as wearing a big Stetson hat and added, "Don't forget those wonderful words 'you know what I like.'" Cochran's voice was completely wracked with emotion as he mentioned Buddy Holly. "Well you're singing for God now in his chorus in the sky, Buddy Holly, I'll always remember you with tears in my eyes." The session proved to be so moving for Cochran that he entered into the control room and told his producer that if that song was ever released he would never cut another record. The record remained unreleased until 1964 when Liberty Records issued the single four years after Cochran's own tragic death.

In early 1960, Eddie Cochran left for England to perform a series of tour dates with Gene Vincent. The English crowds loved Eddie. One teenager in particular, George Harrison, followed Cochran from city to city acutely studying where Eddie placed his fingers as he played the guitar. A few days before her twentieth birthday, Sharon Sheeley came to England to join Eddie on tour.

Sharon was a hit songwriter herself and was the youngest songwriter ever to score a number one hit with "Poor Little Fool," a song she had penned for teen idol Ricky Nelson. Sheeley had fallen in love at first sight with Eddie Cochran when Phil Everly introduced her to the singer. She imagined him as a blond Elvis and loved to watch him perform. Sheeley also had a tragic link to Ritchie Valens. She had met Ritchie through Eddie, and Valens recorded Sharon's "Hurry Up" as a cut for his Del-Fi album.

When Sharon arrived in England, she found Eddie to be severely depressed. He was taking tranquilizers to deal with clinical depression. He was convinced that he had cheated death by avoiding the Winter Dance Party and now he would be destined to die a violent death just like Buddy. On one occasion, he asked Sharon to buy as many of Buddy's records as she could find. He would then sit in his room playing the songs over and over again. When Sheeley asked, "Doesn't it upset you hearing Buddy this way?" Eddie answered her in a faraway voice with, "Oh, no, 'cause I'll be seeing him soon."[8] Eddie mentioned that he had a new guitar lick he wanted to show Buddy.

Following one performance, Cochran visited a fortune-teller to determine just how long he had before he would meet an untimely death. This preoccupation continued throughout the English tour, with Eddie awakening from a troubled sleep one night screaming out "My God! I'm going to die and there's nothing anyone can do to stop it!"

On Easter Sunday, April 17, 1960, Eddie Cochran, Sharon Sheeley, and Gene Vincent were headed to London's Heathrow

Airport for a return flight to California. Eddie had scheduled a new series of UK performances but wanted to return home for a short visit before continuing the tour. On the way to the airport, the chauffeur-driven Ford Consul suffered a blown tire, putting the car into a frenzied spin like a hellish Tilt-A-Whirl reeling completely out of control until it smashed into a light post, bringing the car to a complete and violent stop. Cochran was thrown from the car, as was Sharon Sheeley. Sheeley suffered a broken neck and a broken back. Gene Vincent reinjured his leg that had previously been maimed in a motorcycle accident. Vincent would carry the limp with him for the rest of his life.

When Sheeley regained consciousness, she asked, "Where is Eddie?" Vincent, trying to reassure her, replied, "He is in the car having a cigarette." Sharon knew something had to be seriously wrong. If Eddie wasn't seriously hurt he would be with her. He would be there to comfort her. He wouldn't leave her alone to bleed to death by the side of the road. When the ambulance arrived they found Cochran's orange Gretsch guitar lying next to him in the pasture. The guitar had been hurled from the wreckage but miraculously didn't receive a single scratch.

All three passengers where rushed by ambulance to St. Martin's Hospital in Bath. Ironically, the Crickets were in England finishing up an Everly Brothers tour. Immediately Sonny Curtis, who had rejoined the Crickets, and Jerry Allison rushed to the hospital to see Eddie. Joe B. Mauldin, fearing that there would be too many visitors in the way, decided to wait until the next day to see Cochran. Sadly, the next day Eddie Cochran would die from massive head injuries. In an eerie coincidence, Ritchie Valens's mother was the first to call Sharon Sheeley's parents notifying them of the accident in what must have been a tragic sense of rock and roll déjà vu. Ritchie's mother and the Sheeleys knew each other through Ritchie's recording of Sheeley's "Hurry Up."

In another sense of bitter irony, the last single released by Eddie Cochran was entitled "Three Steps to Heaven," and the Crickets served on the recording as his backup band. Eddie also proved to be prophetic when he told Buddy that another of Holly's compositions would soon top the charts. Holly's last single was aptly entitled "It Doesn't Matter Anymore." Though the song was released shortly before his death, it exploded onto the charts following the news of his death and reached number one in Great Britain. Buddy was making yet another point in rock and roll history, and that was that a dead rock star was very good business and a fortune could be made in the sale of rights and royalties.

When the Crickets returned to the United States they would find that they would be involved in a series of other rock and roll tragedies. For whatever reason, bad luck seemed to follow anyone associated with the band. The first victim of the Holly curse was singer Ronnie Smith. Smith, a fellow Texan, had performed with drummer Carl Bunch and Tommy Allsup in Ronnie Smith and the Poor Boys. In February 1959, he was hired to replace Buddy Holly for the remainder of the Winter Dance Party tour. He fronted the band now composed of Jennings, Bunch, and Allsup. When the tour ended the band continued to record as the Jitters due to an injunction concerning the rights to the name the Crickets. In 1962, Smith was committed to a Texas state hospital for drug abuse. On October 25, 1962, a despondent Ronnie Smith hanged himself in the bathroom of the state hospital.

The original Crickets, Jerry Allison, Joe B. Mauldin, and Sonny Curtis, continued as a group and brought in seventeen-year-old David Box to replace Buddy Holly. Box was born and raised in Sulphur Springs, Texas, and joined the Crickets in 1960. His first two recordings with the Crickets were "Peggy Sue Got Married" and "Don'tcha Know." Neither song was successful on the charts and in a few years Box left the Crickets to follow a solo career. David Box proved to be a regional success with one single, "Summer Girl," doing well in the local Texas markets.

On October 23, 1964, David Box hired a Cessna Skyhawk 172 to fly to a show in Harris County, Texas. He, drummer Bill Daniels, who was also the pilot, and guitarist Buddy Groves left immediately after the show to fly back to their homes in Houston. Shortly after takeoff, the Cessna nosedived into the ground, killing all three passengers in yet another case of terrifying rock-and-roll déjà vu. Sadly, Box was scheduled to be in Nashville, Tennessee, to cut his next single on October 24. He was upbeat about his career and it appeared that he was poised to make a name for himself on the national stage. Box's parents met with Buddy Holly's parents a few days after the crash. Buddy's father remarked, "People will tell you the pain eventually goes away, but I can tell you now that it never does."[9] Besides his perishing in a plane crash, there was one more similarity to Buddy Holly. David Box was twenty-two years of age when he died—the exact same age as Buddy Holly at the time of his own untimely death.

Fate continued to play its dark hand when Bobby Fuller and the Bobby Fuller Four emerged from Texas in the early 1960s. Fuller admired Holly's work and had modeled his sound after that of Buddy and the Crickets. Buddy's parents had received a demo from Fuller and sent the tape to Norman Petty in Clovis, New Mexico. Petty had worked as Buddy's producer and had gained songwriting credits for a number of Buddy Holly's songs.

At the time of Buddy's death, he and Petty had dissolved their business ties, but there were many accounts of Norman Petty hiding vast sums of Holly's money. Some of Buddy's friends go as far as accusing Petty of being responsible for Buddy's death. If Norman Petty had paid Buddy the money he owed him, then Buddy would not have been forced to go on the Winter Dance Party tour. Petty produced two tracks for Bobby Fuller, "Gently

My Love" and "My Heart Jumped." Both tracks were regional successes, but national attention did not come easy for the Bobby Fuller Four.

Fuller attempted to make his sound more up to date by writing songs about surfing and drag racing. If the Beach Boys and Jan and Dean could sell records by this set formula, then surely there would be some success in it for Fuller as well. All he needed was a hit song that would allow him to break into the pop charts. In 1963, Fuller moved his band to Hollywood, where Bob Keane of Del-Fi Records signed the band immediately after personally witnessing an intense performance in a local club.

In 1965, Crickets guitarist Sonny Curtis provided Fuller with the song that would change Bobby's luck and fortune, "I Fought the Law." The Crickets had tried a recording of the same song earlier but their performance was nothing compared to the fiery treatment that Bobby Fuller put on vinyl. The Hollyesque rocker conjured forth images of prime Buddy Holly in all his glory.

By returning to his roots, the rock of Eddie Cochran and Buddy Holly, Fuller at last had his hit song, and "I Fought the Law" made its way into the top ten. But his career was about to come crashing down around him in what has become one of rock's greatest unsolved mysteries. The tragic comparisons to Holly continued throughout his short-lived career. It took a song by the Crickets to break Fuller to the national stage. The last song Bobby Fuller recorded was "Love's Made a Fool of You," which ironically was written by Buddy Holly. Other haunting similarities to Holly included Fuller being contacted by Norman Petty to return to Clovis and continue his career under Petty's guidance, much in the same way as Buddy had been contacted by Petty to return and work out their differences. Bob Keane had also been Ritchie Valens's manager, and this helped form a connection to that terrible night in early February. Bobby Fuller, like Holly, had just broken with his backing band and was putting together a solo career. Another striking comparison was that Bobby Fuller would also die at the age of twenty-two—just like Buddy.

At 1:00 A.M., in the early morning hours of July 18, 1966, Fuller received a phone call at his Hollywood apartment that he shared with his mother. He left after receiving the call and told his mother that he would be right back. He had just purchased a new Corvette but on this night he drove his mother's white Oldsmobile.

When Fuller didn't return to the apartment by the next morning, his now worried mother asked the band's road manager to look for the car. At approximately 5:00 P.M. the car mysteriously appeared in the driveway. When she went to the car to check on her son she found his body lying across the seat. He had been badly beaten. Blood was caked on his shirt and there was a small pool of blood on the floor. His hair was matted and his body and clothes were soaked in gasoline. Gasoline was also found in his stomach. Bob Keane said that when he arrived on the scene he witnessed a police office take a gasoline can from the backseat of the Oldsmobile and throw it meaninglessly into a Dumpster. Incredibly, said Keane, no foul play was suspected. The car was not dusted for fingerprints nor was it impounded. Bob Keane was told that it was just another rocker who had OD'd. Bobby Fuller's death was listed as a suicide by the Hollywood police department.

Of course, as with Buddy Holly's death, many rumors have circulated about the death of Bobby Fuller. The predominant theory had Fuller as a victim of a gangland slaying. It seemed that Bobby had a romantic interest in a young lady who was also dating a major underworld figure. For this youthful indiscretion Bobby Fuller was said to have paid with his life, and his last recorded song hauntingly stated the double irony that indeed "Love's Made a Fool of You."

Throughout the years following Bobby Fuller's death, other artists have fallen victim to the so-called Buddy Holly Curse. In 1977, Hollywood finally brought the life and career of Buddy Holly to the motion picture screen. The film was entitled *The Buddy Holly Story* and starred a thirty-three-year-old Gary Busey as Buddy Holly, but it contained a great many distortions. First there was no mention at all of Norman Petty, nor of the original Crickets Jerry Allison and Joe B. Mauldin. In the movie Buddy's parents discouraged his desire to play rock and roll; however, in reality, nothing could have been further from the truth. Buddy's parents wholeheartedly endorsed his love of music and encouraged him to follow his dreams.

Other inaccuracies suggested that Buddy could read and write music charts, that his recordings took place in New York instead of Clovis, New Mexico, and that on the Winter Dance Party Buddy was backed by an orchestra. Sadly, the roles of Waylon Jennings and Tommy Allsup were left out of the film as well. In another surprise Gary Busey did his own singing in the film and refused to lip sync to the early Holly recordings. A soundtrack album was released following the film's debut. The soundtrack didn't sell well but Holly's original recordings gained new sales as a new audience discovered the West Texas rocker from Lubbock. But Busey's performance was captivating and the actor was nominated for an Oscar.

The film, however, was not exempt from the Holly tragedy. Gary Busey was almost fatally injured in a motorcycle accident following the completion of the film, and Robert Gittler, who wrote the screenplay, committed suicide shortly before the film's theatrical release.

Buddy Holly was still extremely popular in England in the late 1970s. In this case it would only seem natural that if a curse existed it would also find more victims across the Atlantic. The death of T. Rex founder Marc Bolan contained another Holly similarity. Bolan died in a terrible car crash on September 16, 1977. As investigators searched through the rubble, they noticed a peculiar pin. Its message was "Everyday is a Holly day."[10] Unfortunately Bolan, like Holly, achieved the bulk of his success posthumously.

Malicious fate struck a second time and claimed rock and roll's original madman, Keith Moon. Moon, the Who's drummer, had attended the London premiere of *The Buddy Holly Story* with Paul and Linda McCartney on the night of September 6, 1978. As he and his companion, Annette Walter-Lax, returned to Harry Nilsson's flat in Mayfair, Keith took a handful of sleeping pills along with a sedative called Heminevrin. The sedative had been prescribed for Moon for his bouts with alcoholism and mania.

When he awoke early the next morning at 7:30 A.M., he fixed himself something to eat, drank some champagne, and took a few more Heminevrin. In a few short hours Keith Moon was dead. He was pronounced dead on September 7, 1978. The strange Holly connection was that September 7 was Buddy Holly's birthday. Earlier that year, on February 3, 1978, the nineteenth anniversary of Holly's tragic death, the city of Lubbock, Texas, condemned for demolition Buddy Holly's birthplace. Many of Holly's die-hard fans demanded that the house be bought, restored, and made into a Buddy Holly museum. Buddy's mother, however, objected to the plan to restore the early family home and without her support the campaign to save the house was forgotten. What is strange is that the house was never demolished. The house was bought and moved from the foundation. I suppose the ultimate Holly mystery is where the Holly home is now, with its peculiar playing-card window shutters? The mystery continues.

There are two other tragic entries into the Buddy Holly curse. Both involve American musicians who gained their fame at the same time Buddy Holly was raving on. Ricky Nelson was the all-American boy who grew up on American television. He, along with his brother, David, and his mother and father, starred on *The Adventures of Ozzie & Harriet*. When Ricky brought out his guitar on the popular series the girls swooned, and Ricky Nelson was well on his way to becoming a teenage idol.

Ricky Nelson had met Buddy Holly only once but highly respected Holly's music. Sharon Sheeley wrote Nelson's number-one hit "Poor Little Fool" and completed a link between Nelson, Holly, Eddie Cochran, and Ritchie Valens. In 1979, Ricky Nelson recorded "Rave On" and "True Love Ways," both songs written by Buddy Holly, and both songs would be released the year after Nelson's tragic death. Ricky Nelson's last performance was in Guntersville, Alabama, on December 30, 1985.

Though Nelson had changed his musical style throughout the years, he still knew what to give his audience. They came for the oldies, and he didn't disappoint them as he generously sprinkled them in between his new recordings. For an encore Ricky chose to do Buddy Holly's "Rave On." It brought the house down, and the last line reverberated throughout the hall: "Rave on for me." After the show Nelson and his band flew off in a re-conditioned DC-3 and came to a fiery crash in De Kalb, Texas. Nelson and his band were killed while the pilot and copilot survived. Ironically, the plane had earlier been purchased from Jerry Lee Lewis, who had a premonition that he would perish in this plane in a terrible crash.

Del Shannon hit the rock charts in the early 1960s. His classic hit "Runaway" filled the radio airwaves in 1961 and introduced what sounded like a Moog synthesizer, but was most likely a Musitron, an organlike instrument. Other Shannon hits included "Hats Off to Larry" and "Little Town Flirt." Sadly, Del

Shannon was doomed to be yet another victim of the British invasion during the mid-1960s.

In the late 1980s, Del Shannon was attempting a comeback. Tom Petty had worked with him and included the line "Me and Del were singing 'Little Runaway'" in Petty's "Running Down a Dream." Even though Shannon's career was about to be rekindled, he suffered from severe bouts of depression. His last performance came at the Surf Ballroom on February 3, 1990, the thirty-first anniversary of the Holly plane crash. His backing band that night was the Crickets. Del returned home and on February 9, 1990, took out his shotgun and took his own life. Shannon was unaware that he had been just been selected to take the late Roy Orbison's place in the superstar band the Traveling Wilburys.[11] Some medical experts claimed that the antidepressants Del was taking might have contributed to his death, while others remembered another night just thirty-one years earlier when three young rock stars soared into the heavens to gain rock and roll immortality. The last performance for Buddy Holly, Ritchie Valens, the Big Bopper, and Del Shannon was at the Surf Ballroom in Clear Lake, Iowa.

In the middle 1960s a generation of American teenagers immersed themselves in the British invasion and the American rock stars of the 1950s were cast aside. I suppose it was with a sense of irony that the Beatles landed in New York City on February 7, 1964, to prepare for their first appearance on *The Ed Sullivan Show.* February 7 is significant because that was the day in 1959 that Buddy Holly was laid to rest in Lubbock, Texas. The Beatles were devoted fans of Holly and their name itself was a play on the Crickets.

Few people know that Holly first suggested the name the "Beetles" for his own group's name. Just think. Buddy Holly and the Beetles does have a certain ring to it, doesn't it? The Beatles recorded a faithful rendition of the Holly classic "Words of

Love." As a matter of fact, the first recording the Beatles completed, on a borrowed tape recorder, was Buddy Holly's "That'll Be the Day," with John Lennon taking the lead vocal. Today Paul McCartney owns the Buddy Holly song catalog and is able to combine business with the music he loves. When it comes to great rock and roll, truly some things just do not fade away.

3. "THE DEVIL WENT DOWN TO GEORGIA"

Crossroads, will you ever let him go?
— Allman Brothers Band, "Melissa"
The smell of death's around you.
— Lynyrd Skynyrd, "That Smell"

IN CHARLIE DANIELS'S "THE DEVIL WENT DOWN TO GEORGIA," Satan entices a fiddle player named Johnny to match his fiddle playing skill against his own. The wager, in the best Faustian tradition, is to be Johnny's soul against a shiny fiddle made of gold. In the fictional world, where good should always overcome evil, Johnny wins and proclaims that he is "the best that's ever been."

Rock and roll is not the first form of music to have been associated with the devil or evil. Niccolò Paganini, a nineteenth-century Italian composer and violin virtuoso, was accused of consorting with the devil, who enabled Paganini to astonish listeners with his playing. Paganini's physical appearance only encouraged this rumor. He has been described as being very pale and extremely thin, with long black hair that fell into his face as he performed. Women were said to have screamed and passed out as he produced musical passages that some listeners claimed were totally unworldly. In addition, rumors circulated that he was selfish and cruel, a gambler and a murderer. It was his musical ability, however, that caused the most speculation. Surely he had sold his soul to the devil. Many even claimed to have proof and watched as the devil pulled the violin bow while Paganini's fingers flew across the violin's neck. Ever the consummate showman, Paganini would saw halfway through three of his violin strings before a performance. As he frantically played the instrument, the strings would break one at a time until Paganini was doing incredible passages on the one remaining string. In an issue of the *Journal of the American Medical Association* (January 2, 1978), Dr. Myron Shoenfield suggests that Paganini's mysterious feats were due to Marfan's syndrome, a condition resulting in "hyper-extensible fingers" that would have allowed the violinist incredible reach and dexterity.

Once before a performance in France, Paganini was forced to bring a note from his mother claiming that the devil was not his father. Before he died in Nice in 1840, Paganini refused the last rites of the Church. Obviously, the master musician didn't accept the fact that he was dying. Unfortunately, when his impending death became a grim reality, it was too late to summon a priest. Paganini's body remained unburied for three years as the Church would not allow him to be buried in consecrated ground. His body was kept on display under glass to slow its decay. One businessman offered 30,000 francs to place the body on exhibit. Finally, in 1845, five years after his death, the courts ruled that Paganini could be given a proper burial. Despite a logical explanation for Paganini's unusual skills, the association between good and evil in his playing has continued. In Johann Wolfgang von Goethe's *Faust*, Mephistopheles first appears holding a violin. This possible tribute to Paganini may show that the devil's instrument of choice is the violin and not a beat-up Stella guitar. However, the tale of Paganini does have a strong correlation to that of Robert Johnson. Ironically, the Robert Johnson similarities have found a home in Macon, Georgia, and perhaps the story does not end as happily as in the Charlie Daniels ballad.

Macon has produced a long list of musicians who have made a significant impact in music history, including James Brown, Little Richard, Otis Redding, and the Allman Brothers Band. James Brown is perceived by some fans as being a bad boy of rock and roll. Though Brown is an icon of the music industry, in September of 1988, he led police on an interstate car chase that resulted in Brown being given a six-year prison sentence. He was paroled on February 27, 1991, after serving a little over two years. Both James Brown and Little Richard have been inducted into the Rock and Roll Hall of Fame and both have had struggles with the demons of rock and roll, but at least they have both survived. Otis Redding was not so fortunate. Redding was born in Dawson, Georgia, on September 9, 1941. He first hit the pop charts with the soul classic "These Arms of Mine" in 1963. His follow-up hits included "Respect" and "I've Been Loving You Too Long," accompanied by the legendary Stax recording house band Booker T. and the MG's. At the Monterey Pop Festival in 1967, Otis Redding stunned the crowd with an incredible, energetic performance. It appeared that Redding was on his way to even greater prominence. But on December 10, 1967, at the youthful age of twenty-six, Redding was killed when his plane crashed into Wisconsin's Lake Monona. Killed with him were four members of his backup band, the Bar-Kays—Jimmy King, Ronnie Caldwell, Carl Cunningham, and Phalin Jones. Ironically, "Sitting on the Dock of the Bay," was recorded three days before his death and released posthumously. This song spent four weeks at number one, and is considered his greatest hit. To Steve Cropper, legendary Stax Records guitarist and Otis's cowriter, the opening sounds of surf and sea birds are an ironic reminder of the terrible crash. Yet another example of irony is found in the name of the band that was to open Otis's last concert—the Grim Reapers (the Reapers were an early precursor of Cheap Trick). Of course, record companies have always been able to capitalize on posthumous releases by popular artists. For example, Buddy Holly, killed in a plane crash on February 3, 1959, at the age of twenty-two, recorded his last hit, "It Doesn't Matter Anymore," shortly before his fateful accident. Fans have noted the dramatic irony in the song's title.

Two years after the death of Otis Redding, a new presence had taken up residence in Macon, Georgia. Duane and Gregg Allman had assembled a group of musicians who would prove to be the genesis of the southern rock movement. The Allman Brothers Band relied upon the dual harmonies of Duane Allman and Richard Betts's guitars to help establish their presence in rock history. Duane Allman was a disciple of the blues, and the band would go into extended jams on blues classics by Robert Johnson, Sonny Boy Williamson, and T-Bone Walker, among others. Phil Walden, the young soon-to-be head of Capricorn Records, had earlier served as Otis Redding's manager. At Redding's funeral,

Walden felt determined never again to get as close to another artist, but that was before he had heard the incredible guitar work of Duane Allman! Allman was a session player whose backing guitar tracks had earned him international fame. His admirers included Eric Clapton, who invited Duane to record with Derek and the Dominos. It was Duane Allman who contributed the opening guitar riff to Clapton's immortal "Layla." The listener can hear Allman's passionate playing throughout the project as his soaring slide guitar lines added emphasis and served as a foil to motivate Clapton's playing to yet another level. The two guitar greats fed off each other's energy and formed a bond of friendship based upon mutual respect and admiration. Clapton was first introduced to Allman's playing when he heard Wilson Pickett's version of the Beatles' "Hey Jude." It was claimed that Allman suggested doing the number, and when Pickett hesitated the guitarist asked him, "What's the matter? You haven't got the balls?" Pickett answered by laying down a scorching rhythm-and-blues track in the best Muscle Shoals tradition. For his efforts, Wilson Pickett rewarded Duane Allman with the nickname "Sky Dog." This served as a reference to the hippie southern guitarist who had extremely long strawlike blond hair, dressed in bib overalls, and loved to get high. His guitar work, however, soared like a free bird in flight.[1]

Tradition and urban legend has it that the Allman Brothers Band would take their guitars into Rose Hill Cemetery and jam late into the night. Uncannily, much like Robert Johnson, this peaceful setting provided the inspiration for many of the Allman Brothers' classic recordings. The haunting "In Memory of Elizabeth Reed" was said to have been composed by Dickie Betts while he was making love to a girl in the cemetery. The melody was running through his head and when he looked at the tombstone above the grave he could make out the stone-cut name— Elizabeth Reed. It seems that Duane Allman was the source of this legend in a 1970s *Rolling Stone* interview. Dickie Betts now denies this myth, in the proper role of a southern gentleman. Duane Allman's beautiful instrumental "Little Martha" takes its name from yet another resident of Rose Hill Cemetery. Ironically, this song was to prove to be one of his last recordings.

The Allman Brothers' strange parallels to Robert Johnson contained much more than jamming to the blues great's songs in lonely graveyards at night. At the very peak of his career, tragedy claimed Duane Allman. A few days before Halloween, October 29, 1971, on his way to a birthday party, Duane Allman was killed in a fateful motorcycle accident. There was another passion in Allman's life aside from his guitar; that passion was a Harley-Davidson Sportster. Growing up in Daytona Beach, Florida, Allman developed a love for the motorcycles that made their yearly pilgrimage to the beachside city for Bike Week. It was also the time period for Peter Fonda's *Easy Rider,* and Duane Allman's bike was "chopped" accordingly to bring back memories of Captain America and Billy. The long fork legs, unfortunately, made the bike much harder to handle. Shortly after 5:30 P.M. Duane Allman shot through the intersection of Inverness Avenue. As he approached Bartlett Avenue, a large Chevy flatbed truck slowed down in front of the motorcyclist, blocking the intersection. Allman tried to miss the truck by swerving to the left but he collided with the corner of the truck's bumper, or perhaps a cable or a weight ball hanging from a crane in the truck's bed.

The bike's skid marks measured ninety feet. Allman's helmet was ripped from his head and the heavy chopper fell upon him, causing serious internal damage. Duane Allman was rushed to the hospital where it was determined by Dr. Charles Burton that the guitarist's internal injuries included a ruptured coronary artery as well as major liver damage. A little after three hours from the time of the accident, Duane "Sky Dog"Allman died at 8:40 P.M.[2] He was dead at the untimely age of twenty-four. The terrible news of

Duane's death shattered the other band members. Close friend and bassist Berry Oakley totaled his car on the way from the hospital after hearing of Allman's death. It would not be the last tragic irony associated with Oakley and Allman. Butch Trucks, one of the Allman Brothers' drummers, remembered a bizarre story that took place in Nashville, Tennessee, in 1970. It seemed that Duane Allman was rushed to a Nashville hospital suffering from a drug overdose. His vital signs were low and the doctors didn't give him much hope of survival. It was then that Berry Oakley entered into a personal bargain with God. Oakley pleaded with God to give Duane just one more year of life, one more year to play his music and live his dream. Amazingly, and seemingly against all medical odds, Duane Allman survived his OD that night in that Nashville hospital, but there is an old parable that states, "Be careful what you wish for. You may get it." The date of the accidental overdose in Nashville was October 29, 1970. Exactly one year later, and to the exact day, Duane Howard Allman was killed in the motorcycle accident in Macon, Georgia.[3]

Duane Allman's funeral was held a few days after his death in a proper good-bye to a talented musician. His band performed at the service, playing a final tribute to a fallen brother. The ceremony ended with a powerful rendition of "Will the Circle Be Unbroken" with the crowd of mourners joining in. But it would not be the last tragedy for the surviving brothers. One year and two weeks later, November 11, 1972, Berry Oakley was preparing for a jam session that night at a club he had booked in downtown Macon. He drove his 1967 blue Triumph motorcycle along Bartlett Avenue and crashed into the side of a city bus. The accident occurred at the intersection of Inverness Avenue as the bus driver tried to avoid the approaching motorcycle. After the impact Oakley was thrown from his bike and the heavy Triumph fell across him. The skid marks stretched fifty-eight feet from the scene of the accident. At first Berry Oakley walked around and surveyed the crash sight, giving everyone hope that the band had narrowly avoided a second tragedy. Oakley refused medical attention and went back to the Big House, the band's Macon headquarters. Onlookers noticed a thin trail of blood trickling from Berry's nostril and feared that he might have suffered a severe head injury. Unfortunately, this proved to be the case, and a few hours later Berry Oakley was rushed unconscious to the medical center where he died at 3:40 in the afternoon. The cause of death was listed as complications arising from hemorrhaging associated with a fractured skull.

Thirteen days after the death of Berry Oakley, ABC television broadcast an *In Concert* special featuring the Allman Brothers Band. It was Berry's last performance, recorded just a matter of weeks before his death. The show was dedicated to him, but the timing was eerie. The same uncanny timing was shown with the release of Duane Allman's final performances with the Allman Brothers Band. The album was called *Eat a Peach,* and the rumor circulated that the band had chosen the name of the LP in reference to Duane Allman's death by hitting a peach truck. Of course this wasn't true, but as we all know rumors can become undying folklore. The actual title reference was given by Duane when he was asked what he was doing to promote "the revolution." He replied that when he was home he played a lick and "we eat a peach for peace."

There are a number of other chilling coincidences in the deaths of Duane Allman and Berry Oakley. Both men were killed at the same crossroads. Allman had crossed Inverness Avenue and was killed at Bartlett, while Berry, traveling from the opposite direction, had just crossed Bartlett and was killed at Inverness; both men's accidents occurred within a thousand feet of each other. Inverness Avenue summons forth memories of the legendary castle of Macbeth, the Scottish king who had met with supernatural powers to claim the throne of Scotland. Shakespeare tells us that it was at Inverness that Macbeth murdered his king and cousin, Duncan, and fulfilled his bargain with the witches, thereby sealing his pact with hell. While the similarities of Inverness being a crossroads is in itself a form of dramatic irony, it becomes twofold as we remember the legendary pact made by a young Robert Johnson who, like Duane Allman, was without peer as a blues guitarist. One of Duane Allman's favorite songs was "Melissa," a beautiful ballad written and sung by his brother Gregg. The haunting lyric asks two questions: "Crossroads, will you ever let him go?" and "Who will hide the dead man's soul?" Of course this now provides a chilling irony in retrospect.

Duane Allman and Berry Oakley were both only twenty-four years of age when they died. The drivers of the truck and bus were also only twenty-four years of age at the time of the accidents. The first Allman Brothers LP features a photo of the band taken at Rose Hill Cemetery. In one photo, Berry Oakley stands in what appears to be a chapel window dressed as some Christ figure, in robes with his arms held wide open; standing in front of him is Duane Allman. The irony of the photo relates to the burial services of Duane Allman and Berry Oakley. An interesting legend suggested by Scott Freeman in his *Midnight Riders: The Story of the Allman Brothers* is that Duane Allman's body was kept in cold storage for a year. At the time of Oakley's death, it was determined by the families to bury both friends together side by side at Rose Hill Cemetery. Each member had a special grave marker. Freeman states in *Midnight Riders* that both tombstones were carved with mushrooms, the adopted symbol of the brotherhood that was tattooed upon each member's right calf. On Duane's headstone, "the dates of his birth and death are circled by the music to 'Little Martha'; a winged scarab, an ancient symbol held sacred by the Egyptians (a symbol of the afterlife), is engraved above his name. Duane's gravestone has a Les Paul guitar (Duane's favorite instrument) carved in rich detail, and there is an inscription that comes from a quotation Duane had written in his diary: 'I love being alive and I will be the best man I possibly can. I will take love wherever I find and offer it to everyone who will take it . . . seek knowledge from those wiser . . . and teach those who want to learn from me.' At the base of his grave are two small angels (representing his daughters Galadriel and Brittany) kneeling in prayer.[4]

"The inscription on Berry's headstone reads: 'Our brother B.O. . . . Raymond Berry Oakley III . . . And The Road Goes On Forever . . . Born In Chicago Apr. 4, 1948 . . . Set Free Nov. 11, 1972.' Above the name is a ram's head, symbolizing his astrological sign. A Fender bass is carved into the gravestone, along with an inscription that everyone thought best summed up Berry's philosophy of life: 'Help thy brother's boat across and, lo! thine own has reached the shore.'"[5]

The Allman Brothers Band has survived member changes, internal feuds, and the constant battles with their own excesses. Strangely enough, the coincidences of tragedy did not end with the deaths of Duane and Berry. Longtime friend and road manager Twiggs Lyndon continued on as a road manager for the Dixie Dregs. While the band was in New York, Lyndon went skydiving. He jumped from a plane and fell over 8,000 feet to his death. Some intimate friends hinted that Twiggs Lyndon had never made peace with the deaths of Duane Allman and Berry Oakley, and that his accidental death may have actually been a suicide. The evidence to this was found in Lyndon's still unopened chute. His death occurred on November 16, 1979, in a small town called Duanesburg. The irony of Twiggs Lyndon's death being in a small town that reminded him of Duane and taking place in the same month as Berry Oakley's death is yet another disturbing coincidence.

After Berry Oakley's death the band chose Lamar Williams to be their new bassist. Williams later left the band with keyboardist Chuck Leavell to form Sea Level, an obvious pun upon C. Leavell. In the early eighties, Williams had fallen upon hard times following the eventual breakup of Sea Level. He was diagnosed with lung cancer, thought to be brought on by his exposure to Agent Orange during the Vietnam War. The date of his exploratory surgery was October 29, 1981, exactly ten years to the day from the date of Duane Allman's death. Over one-third of his lung was removed but this proved to be of no avail. Lamar Williams died on January 21, 1983, at the age of thirty-six. In August 2000, bassist Allen Woody of the Allman Brothers and Government Mule passed away and became the latest fatality in a tragic road that seems to go on forever.

The other surviving members of the Allman Brothers Band struggled with an assortment of personal demons, including substance abuse, divorce, the threat of prison terms, and in some cases living near poverty. The latest gathering of the band recalls the creative brilliance of the original. With Warren Haynes on guitar, the band invokes the fire that was captured in the early performances and recordings of Duane Allman. Strangely, their debut album *Seven Turns* has the band standing in a deserted country crossroads. It would appear that the band had returned full circle. The seven turns would allow the members to return to where they had once started. In this case, Robert Johnson would have certainly been very proud.

While the Allman Brothers defined the genre of southern rock and roll, other bands followed the carefully constructed formula of blues lyrics backed by the melodic phrasing of twin guitars in perfect harmony. It didn't take long for another bar band from Jacksonville, Florida, to burst from the endless drudgery of the club circuit to stake a claim to the throne of southern rock and roll. In 1973, Lynyrd Skynyrd released their debut album, *Pronounced Leh-Nerd Skin-Nerd,* and the results would help redefine the future of rock and roll. The band traced its origins back to 1964 when the British invasion served as an early introduction of basic American rhythm and blues. By 1969, each member had dropped out of high school to follow the course of his musical dreams. In a parting shot at their former gym teacher, who had constantly harassed them about their long hair, the band jokingly referred to themselves as Leonard Skinner. With a phonetic re-spelling of their name, Lynyrd Skynyrd swept through the South with the urgency of a cyclone, laying down a revamped southern boogie that was beyond simple imitation. They had taken the roots of the Allman Brothers' sound, twisted it from the earth, and replanted it complete with a triple guitar attack, and above all, a new anthem of rock and roll—"Free Bird"!

Undoubtedly, it was a great compliment to be the anointed saviors of southern rock; however, Ronnie Van Zant and the other members turned down a recording contract with Capricorn Records only because they felt that they would be compared too closely with the Allman sound. It was obvious that the members believed in themselves, and they waited for the right moment to unleash their music to sold-out concert audiences. This was accomplished when Lynyrd Skynyrd opened for the Who on the English group's 1973 American tour. Word quickly spread throughout the United States praising Skynyrd's electrifying stage show. It was also at this time that American FM stations launched "Free Bird" to their radio audiences, and Lynyrd Skynyrd soared to the top of the rock charts. To this day "Free Bird" is second only to Led Zeppelin's "Stairway to Heaven" as the most requested song in radio airplay.

As with many bands at the pinnacle of their fame, there had to be replacement members for those tired road warriors who had had their fill of the self-proclaimed torture tour. Original drummer Bob Burns was replaced by Artimus Pyle, a hard-hitting session drummer, and original guitarist Ed King was later replaced by Steve Gaines. Gaines's sister Cassie was a backup singer for the band as a new member of the Honkettes. This would later prove to be a double tragedy for Lynyrd Skynyrd's many fans.

With the addition of Steve Gaines, Skynyrd returned to its jolting three-guitar attack. It appeared that Gaines brought out the best in each member's performance. This blistering onslaught of a southern rock guitar arsenal is demonstrated in the 1976 release of *One More From the Road*. Ronnie Van Zant liked to go on stage barefoot, because "he liked to feel the stage burn" under his feet. Lynyrd Skynyrd pumped out its greatest live hits to thunderous applause from Atlanta's Fox Theater. The band also contributed a faithful version of Cream's salute to Robert Johnson's "Cross-roads." At this point the dramatic irony begins. The title "One More From the Road" suggested one last drink before going home from a hard day's work. It also suggested a live recording that would finally do justice to Lynyrd Skynyrd's incredible live show. What it didn't suggest was the true meaning behind the invention of the phrase. In England it was customary for a condemned nobleman, on the day of his execution, to meet his friends outside the Tower of London, drink one final toast to their friendship, and then be escorted to Tower Hill where he would be put to death on the scaffold. In this case, one for the road signaled the cataclysmic beginning of the end.

After the release of *One More From the Road*, band insiders noticed that the group had turned the corner and was now ready to go on to even greater fame. This became evident with the release of *Street Survivors* in October of 1977. Steve Gaines had contributed "I Know a Little" and "Ain't No Good Life," and had cowrittten "You Got That Right" and "I Never Dreamed" with Ronnie Van Zant. Gaines was maturing as a songwriting equal to both Van Zant and guitarist Allen Collins, and of course this could only make the band that much stronger. Within three days of the *Street Survivors* release, the rock world would yet again relive the terrible news of a plane crash and the death of three promising stars.

The strange coincidences concerning the fateful crash were numerous. The band's plane, a rented Convair 240, had been named *Freebird* in honor of Skynyrd's hard-rocking anthem. The band had composed the song as a musical tribute to guitarist Duane Allman. This became evident due to the melodic slide guitar phrasings and the scorching guitar solos that pushed the track to its conclusion. It was ironic that the plane crash was on October 20, 1977, since strangely, Duane Allman's death had also occurred in October (October 29, 1971). The macabre Robert Johnson link, which now seemed to form a shocking bond of fate between the bands, was due to the plane crashing in the Mississippi swamp. Killed in the crash were Ronnie Van Zant, Steve Gaines, Cassie Gaines, and road manager Dean Kilpatrick. The remaining band members and crew were seriously injured; it would take several years for them to recover. In an Associated Press release the week of the accident it was reported that several of the group's members had had terrible misgivings about taking the aging plane after performing what was to be their last concert in Greenville, South Carolina. The band's stage manager, Clayton Johnson, remarked from his hospital bed, "There had been a lot of mistrust of that airplane since we chartered it." Johnson said he and four friends met shortly before boarding the piston-type, twin-engine Convair on Thursday and discussed the possibility of refusing to fly it any longer. He said Cassie Gaines, the singer who died in the crash, also had talked with him about possibly riding from concert to concert in the equipment truck instead of in the plane. Ronnie Van Zant convinced Cassie to make the flight, saying that if your time was up it was up. Van Zant had made comments both to fellow band members and to family that he would not live to see thirty. He was right. Honkette backup singer Jo

Billingsley made a phone call to guitarist Allen Collins describing a terrifying dream in which she saw the plane crash. She asked Collins to tell the other band members and not to get on the plane.[6] The plane crashed while attempting an emergency landing about eight miles short of the McComb (Mississippi) airport. They were on their way to a Friday-night concert at Louisiana State University in Baton Rouge.

The morbid happenstance between the *Street Survivors* album art and the fate of Ronnie Van Zant, Steve Gaines, and Cassie Gaines was so great that MCA pulled the albums from the stores and replaced the album art with the band standing in front of a somber black background. But the original David Alexander cover concept was much more interesting. The prototype cover showed the members of Lynyrd Skynyrd superimposed in front of a burning city prop. Menacing flames swirled around the members and engulfed guitarist Steve Gaines. Immediately to his right stood singer Ronnie Van Zant, who was to be yet another victim of the horrible disaster. Gaines's eyes are tightly closed as he stands almost corpselike in the flames that now very well suggest a blazing funeral pyre.

The fans were deeply shocked as they discovered irony after irony. This tour was to be called the Survivors tour. There was also an order form enclosed, advertising a Lynyrd Skynyrd survival kit consisting of a T-shirt, pendant, and booklet. Strangest of all, perhaps, was the song penned by Allen Collins and Ronnie Van Zant concerning the self-destructive lifestyle of band guitarist Gary Rossington. The song was titled "That Smell," and its lyrics stated that "the smell of death's around you." Steve Gaines, Ronnie Van Zant, and Cassie Gaines of the Honkettes shared in the performance. It was the only song on that album in which all three had been involved in the production.

"That Smell" was to become a prophecy. Each time song lyricist Van Zant sang "the smell of death's around you," listeners could feel the creeping tinges of dramatic irony as now his voice spoke from beyond the grave. Ronnie Van Zant was buried in Orange Park, Florida, wearing his trademark Texas Hatter's black hat. His favorite fishing pole was also buried with him. The funeral music consisted of Merle Haggard's "I Take a Lot of Pride in What I Am" and David Allen Coe's "Another Pretty Country Song." Charlie Daniels led the mourners in a moving version of "Amazing Grace" and composed a simple elegy for the fallen singer. The last line of the poem stated, "Fly on, proud bird, you're free at last."

Tragedy seemed to follow individuals associated with the band as well. Shortly before the crash, the band fired both guitar tech Chuck Flowers and drum tech Raymond Watkins over what was said to be a dispute over a hotel bill. Chuck Flowers was decimated by the loss of his friends in the crash and took his own life with a rifle that Ronnie Van Zant had given him as a gift. A year later, Raymond Watkins was killed in a domestic dispute.[7]

Like the mythical phoenix, the survivors of Lynyrd Skynyrd arose from the slow-burning ashes of "Free Bird" and formed a new band that would help maintain the legacy of southern rock and roll. The new lineup included former Skynyrd members Gary Rossington, Allen Collins, Leon Wilkeson, and Billy Powell. Drummer Artimus Pyle had been injured in a motorcycle accident and was unable to take part in the project. This new alliance took the name Rossington-Collins Band in honor of its two-guitar attack. The glaring difference between the old Lynyrd Skynyrd and the new version was in the selection of the lead vocalist. The members chose Dale Krantz, the former female backup singer for .38 Special, to be their singer. Perhaps this choice was made to honor the memory of Ronnie Van Zant and stop any of the very likely comparisons that fans would cast upon a new male singer trying to take the place of a legend. The debut album of the Rossington-Collins Band was entitled *Anytime, Anyplace, Anywhere*. The band chemistry was right, and at times volatile, but if the band had been resurrected so had the curse. Tragedy again stalked the members but seemed to pay special attention to guitarist Allen Collins. After the release of *Anytime, Anyplace, Anywhere*, the group was preparing to hit the road and support their album, which had already sold in excess of one million copies. Before the tour was firmly in place, Collins's wife, Kathy, died tragically from complications during a devastating miscarriage (very similar to the death of Robert Johnson's wife). Kathy Collins had taken her two daughters to the theater when she suffered the miscarriage. Ironically, Judy Van Zant (wife of Ronnie Van Zant) was in the same theater at the time.[8] Allen and Kathy were married in 1970 and had two daughters, Amie and Allison. A short while after the funeral, Gary Rossington broke his foot and the tour was set back another six months. There was a release of a second album, but further tensions gripped the band when Gary and vocalist Dale Krantz fell in love. The couple left the band, and married, and Allen Collins continued on alone with the Allen Collins Band.

In 1986, ten years after the recording of "That Smell," the final irony began. Allen Collins crashed his car in a terrible accident, killing his girlfriend and receiving injuries that would permanently paralyze him from the waist down. His upper body was also affected, making it impossible for him to continue with the music he so dearly loved. During his court case, Collins pleaded no contest to the DUI manslaughter charges that were filed against him in Jacksonville, Florida. The haunting first line of "That Smell" stated, "Whiskey bottles, and brand-new cars, oak tree you're in my way." Other references refer to "one more drink, fool, would drown you," and "tomorrow might not be here for you." It is true that in 1976, Gary Rossington smashed his new car into an oak tree while he was drinking. This, in turn, served as the inspiration for the lyrics to "That Smell." However, ten years later the irony had come full circle; Ronnie Van Zant was dead and now Allen Collins had fulfilled the haunting prophecy of the song he had cowritten with Van Zant. In 1987, Lynyrd Skynyrd had re-formed for their ten-year tribute. Allen Collins was brought along to serve as musical director. He was able to choose his replacement in the band, and as an integral part of his sentence lectured the crowd on the dangers of driving while drinking and other forms of substance abuse. In 1989, Allen Collins developed pneumonia as a result of his paralysis. He died on January 23, 1990.

In another bizarre twist, the graves of Ronnie Van Zant and Steve Gaines were disturbed on June 29, 2000. It seems that Ronnie Van Zant's coffin had been removed from his tomb and was placed on the ground. Steve Gaines's urn had been opened and was found lying on the ground as well. The Van Zant and Gaines families moved the bodies but have left the monuments for the fans to visit and pay their respect. Today, Ronnie Van Zant's body lies beneath a slab of concrete to make sure that this terrible feat is never reenacted.

The Skynyrd curse struck again on July 27, 2001, when bassist Leon Wilkeson's body was discovered in his hotel room in Ponte Vedra, Florida. The cause of death was determined to be complications from emphysema. During the autopsy, the medications oxycodone and diazepam were found in his system as well as evidence of cirrhosis of the liver. The doctors suggested that the combination of these medications could have slowed Leon's breathing to the point that he suffocated as he lay face down in his pillow.[9] Another terrible debt had been paid at the crossroads.

4. "MR. CROWLEY"

Mr. Crowley, what went on in your head?
Mr. Crowley, did you talk with the dead?
—Ozzy Osbourne, "Mr. Crowley," *Blizzard of Ozz*

Do what thou wilt shall be the whole of the law.
—Aleister Crowley, *The Book of the Law*

His reputation had been that of a man who worshiped Satan, but it was more accurately said that he worshiped no one except himself.
—Martin Gardner, *On the Wild Side*

SURPRISINGLY, FEW PEOPLE RECOG-
NIZE THE PORTRAIT of the man with the clean-
shaven head gazing ominously from the crowd of onlookers on
the cover of the Beatles' *Sgt. Pepper's Lonely Hearts Club Band*
album. Perhaps some onlookers may be shocked when they learn
that the likeness belongs to none other than Edward Alexander
(Aleister) Crowley, whom the English press proclaimed "the
wickedest man alive," and whom his mother sweetly referred to as
"The Great Beast" from the book of Revelation in the Bible.
Crowley lovingly returned the favor by referring to his mother,
Emily, as "a brainless bigot of the most narrow, logical and in-
human type."[1] The many theories and adventures of Crowley
helped shape the very mythology of drugs, sex, and rock and roll.

Aleister Crowley's early life was far from that of a man
destined to "worship" Satan and the "dark side." It is documented
that at Crowley's birth "on the infant's body were, unknown to his
mother or his evangelist father, the three most important dis-
tinguishing marks of a Buddha. He was tongue-tied, until the
fraenum linguage was cut; he had the characteristic membrane
which 'necessitated an operation for phimosis some three lustres
[fifteen years] later.' Lastly, he had upon the centre of his heart four
hairs curling from left to right in the exact form of a Swastika."[2]
His parents raised him as a strict fundamentalist Christian within
the Plymouth Brethren sect. As Crowley grew older he became rebellious against the teachings of the order and was eventually expelled from school for "corrupting" another boy. At the age of
eleven, Crowley was said to have predicted his father's death from
cancer of the tongue, and at twelve years of age was dabbling with
the butchery of cats and other animals (only in the name of science, of course): "His first victim was the family cat. He was eager
to discover whether it had nine lives and administered a large dose
of arsenic then chloroformed it, hanged it above the gas jet,
stabbed it, cut its throat, smashed its skull and, after it had been

thoroughly burnt, drowned it and threw it out of the window so that the fall would remove its ninth life. He added, 'I was genuinely sorry for the animal; I simply forced myself to carry out the experiment in the interest of pure science.'"[3] Following the death of his father, Crowley received a large inheritance. This allowed him to indulge in a life of excess and constant debauchery.

Ironically, Crowley attended Trinity College in Cambridge, and there he immersed himself in the study of the occult. It was at this time that Crowley took the name Aleister and became convinced that he was the reincarnation of an earlier magician, Alphonse-Louis Constant, who later took the magical name Eliphas Levi, based upon the Hebrew kabbalah. Through his studies Crowley found that he was born in the year that Levi had died, 1875. He also noticed that his life contained several parallels with Levi. Levi had been raised in a devout Catholic family and had studied for the priesthood. It was his love of magic and the occult that led to his expulsion from his order. Levi's greatest work was *Le Dogme et Rituel de la Haute Magie* (*Dogma and Ritual of High Magic*). From this work Eliphas Levi stated that "to attain the sanctum regnum, in other words, the knowledge and the power of the magi, there are four indispensable conditions— an intelligence illuminated by study, an intrepidity which nothing can check, a will nothing can break, and a discretion which nothing can corrupt and nothing intoxicate. To know, to dare, to will, to keep silence—such are the four words of the magus."[4] The teachings of Levi helped influence not only a young Aleister Crowley, but also many teachings of the Rosicrucians and the Order of the Golden Dawn. It was said that Albert Pike borrowed many of Levi's beliefs in the 1867 constitution of the Ku Klux Klan.[5] Other influences can be found in the teachings of Gerald Gardner and Anton LaVey. Levi's symbol of Baphomet, a satanic figure of a woman with a goat's head, with an inverted pentagram on her forehead, was said to influence David Berkowitz in his ghastly Son of Sam murders and is the adopted symbol of the modern-day Church of Satan.

Confronted with a better understanding of his destiny (Crowley also believed that he had lived other lives as Cagliostro and Pope Alexander VI), Crowley began his practice of the "black arts." He was reported to have placed a curse on one of his professors by making a wax figure of the teacher. In the presence of several classmates, Crowley invoked a curse upon his hapless victim. Was he successful? Crowley didn't seem too surprised to find that his prey had fallen down a flight of stairs and had broken his leg—the same leg that Crowley had cursed (or so he claimed). Crowley's diabolic reputation continued to grow. As a young man he enjoyed mountain climbing. It was whispered that some of his climbing companions had met with sudden death and that in 1905 Crowley had left two partners to die in a terrible avalanche. His notorious reputation began to grow and he began to attract many followers with his newly found magic.

In 1898, Aleister Crowley met George Cecil Jones, a member in good standing of the Order of the Golden Dawn. The order was a secret society that studied magic, alchemy, astrology, tarot, the kabbalah, and other occult practices. Its leader was S. L. MacGregor Mathers, who secured membership for himself by translating a mysterious coded manuscript concerning instructions of the kabbalah and the tarot. It seemed that Mathers's wife was clairvoyant, and it was through her powers that the work was deciphered. According to Mrs. Mathers, the Golden Dawn studied "the intelligent forces behind Nature, the Constitution of man and his relation to God, the main objective being man's ultimately regaining union with the Divine Man latent in himself."[6] Members of the Order of the Golden Dawn included such literary figures as Algernon Blackwood, Bram Stoker, and William Butler Yeats. Each of these men had a keen interest in the supernatural and would attend meetings with the Matherses. These meetings would include spirit writings and a peculiar game of four-player chess. Yeats and Mrs. Mathers would play against MacGregor Mathers and a summoned spirit. Yeats's magical name within the society was Daemon est Inversus (the devil is God reversed). It would later be Yeats who became instrumental in barring Crowley from advancement within the order. Yeats would claim, "We do not think that a mystical society was intended to be a reformatory."[7]

The appeal of secret occult societies has existed throughout history. In Great Britain, the Hellfire Clubs flourished in the eighteenth century. The most infamous was a sect started by Sir Francis Dashwood, whose membership included the Earl of Sandwich, Charles Churchill, and John Wilkes (members of Parliament), Lord Bute (Prime Minister of England), and Thomas Potter, the son of the Archbishop of Canterbury (the highest churchman in England). Francis Dashwood would himself be appointed Chancellor of the Exchequer. Dashwood referred to his followers as the "Unholy Twelve," and it was said that one very important guest at the festivities was Benjamin Franklin of the United States. Though black masses and incantations were used in an almost theatrical manner, it was sexual debauchery and the use of drugs and alcohol that served as the main rituals. The Hellfire Clubs were outlawed in the later part of the eighteenth century following the downfall of Lord Bute's government. Of course this was due to the revelation of the scandalous behavior of the "Unholy Twelve." A precept that Crowley would borrow from the Hellfire Club was its very motto, "Do What Thou Wilt." This phrase can first be found in Rabelais's Abbey of Thelema from his *Gargantua and Pantagruel.* The Abbey represented the continued, everlasting pursuit of a life of excess. Crowley was so taken with this mystical place that he established his own pleasure palace he called "The Sacred Abbey of the Thelemic Mysteries" in Sicily. (After hearing of the strange rituals and the one death that occurred behind its walls, Mussolini had Crowley expelled from the country in 1923.)

After meeting George Cecil Jones, Crowley became an initiate of the Order of the Golden Dawn. He took as his magical name Brother Perdurabo, which translates as "I shall endure to the end." Perhaps this should have served as a warning to Mathers. Crowley obviously enjoyed the ritualistic ceremonies but became dissatisfied with the order's avoidance of drugs and sex. Crowley and Mathers argued violently and used magic against each other in the forms of conjured spirits and other spells. Obviously, this helped split the order. In 1900, Aleister Crowley left England in search of Eastern mysticism. He also purchased Boleskine House in Inverness, Scotland, oddly enough in the same vicinity that Shakespeare's Macbeth had met with witches and sealed his own fate. This estate would later be purchased by Led Zeppelin guitarist Jimmy Page in 1968. In 1903, Crowley married Rose Kelley; unknowingly, she was to help lay the foundation of Crowley's greatest work.

Throughout her life Rose Kelley had no hint of her developing powers of clairvoyance. It was during her honeymoon with Crowley that she mentioned to him that the Egyptian God Horus was trying to contact him. Since Rose had no early interest in the occult, an investigation into her sudden psychic powers became necessary. Crowley took his new wife to the Boulak Museum in Cairo and asked her to point out the god Horus. Incredibly, Rose Kelley led her husband to a painted funeral stela from the twenty-sixth dynasty. The god Horus was depicted receiving a sacrifice from a deceased priest who was named Ank-f-n-khonus. What really impressed Crowley was the number given to the exhibit—number 666. This had to be a sign that Rose would help Crowley usher in a new age of Horus. For three consecutive days (April 8, 9, and 10, 1904), Crowley sat in a darkened room while he claimed a shadowy presence recited to him what was to become

The Book of the Law. Rumors spread that one of Crowley's assistants went mad trying to help in the translation. Of course, this helped generate more publicity for Crowley and his sect. The shadowy presence was said to be Aiwass, a lesser god who served as Horus's narrator to his newly found scribe and prophet. The law was called Thelema, a Greek word meaning "will," and the precept of Thelema became "do as thou wilt." An interpretation by some ardent Satanists utilizes this law to justify any means they may choose to obtain their will. Crowley meant that the phrase was to be interpreted simply as "live in harmony with your destiny." It was not a license to do what you like. It may be interesting to note that Crowley never considered himself a Satanist, because he never chose to believe in God or the devil. Without a belief in one there cannot be a belief in the other. In Crowley's "Hymn to Pan" he states that "I rave; and I rape and I rip and I rend." Evidently, this was to become the harmony of his own personal destiny.

Upon returning home from Egypt, Crowley adopted the Egyptian title "Prince Chioa Khan" and chose a title for his wife. Everyone was to address them only by their new titles. It was also at this time that Crowley referred to himself as "the great beast 666" and justified his new indulgences through this verse from *The Book of the Law*:

> *Be strong, O man! Lust, enjoy all things of sense in nature:*
> *fear not that any god shall deny thee for this.*
> *Now ye shall know that the chosen priest and apostle of*
> *infinite space is prince-priest the Beast.*

In 1906, Crowley and Rose lost their young firstborn daughter. By 1909, a son was born, MacAleister, but by this time Crowley was granted a divorce and Rose died a tortured alcoholic in a mental asylum. Lady Caroline Lamb once claimed that the poet Byron was "mad, bad, and dangerous to know," but perhaps Aleister Crowley deserves this appellation to a greater extent. Think of this: Crowley's wife went insane, five mistresses committed suicide, and "scores of his concubines ended in the gutter as alcoholics, drug addicts, or in mental institutions."[8]

The personal feud between Mathers and Crowley ended with Mathers's death in 1918. Of course, Crowley was quick to take credit by stating that he had placed a death curse upon the old enemy who had denied him the reign of the Brotherhood of the Golden Dawn. Crowley began his own secret society as an outlet for spreading his Thelemic doctrines. He was invited to join Ordo Templi Orientis (O.T.O.), a German magic society that is still in existence. It was said that this society had discovered the true secrets of magic and was descended from the Knights Templars who had also established the rights of Freemasonry. By this time Crowley had run out of his inheritance. He had always been a prolific writer who reveled in each accusation cast his way. His bizarre sense of humor sickened readers who considered what Crowley meant as the "perfect sacrifice": "For the highest spiritual working one must accordingly choose that victim which contains the greatest and purest force. A male child of perfect innocence and high intelligence is the most satisfactory and suitable victim." Crowley also stated that he had performed this ritual 150 times a year between 1912 and 1928.[9] This would suggest over 2,500 victims, but this grim humor was only meant to shock his audience. Strangely enough, legend has it that Crowley summoned some unnamed elemental spirit in some mystic rite and that his only son MacAleister died from a heart attack within the confines of the locked room.[10]

In Crowley's last years he became a hopeless drug addict, often injecting ten grains of heroin a day. In many cases one grain can be fatal. He discussed his lifestyle in his *Diary of a Drug Fiend*: "I am myself a physical coward, but I have exposed myself to every form of disease, accident, and violence." (Crowley's addiction to heroin began when he was a child. It seems that before the enforcement of drug laws, heroin was a prescription for chronic asthma, of which Crowley suffered throughout his life. Of course, he also experimented with many other drugs.) Due to his bizarre behavior, Crowley was removed from membership in many of his mystical orders, and he left for Sicily to find new followers. Those followers often turned out to already be alcoholics, drug addicts, or the emotionally disturbed. After the death of one of his disciples—sources claimed that the hapless victim "drank the blood of a distempered cat"—Crowley was deported from Sicily. With his return to London more accolades followed him. He was said to wear "a Perfume of Immortality made from one part ambergris, two parts musk, and three parts civet, which gave him a peculiar odor, but which he said attracted women and also horses, which always whinnied after him in the streets." [11] His behavior grew more and more erratic: "He had two of his teeth filed into a point, so he could give women the 'Serpent's Kiss' when introduced. One woman, bitten on the arm, contracted blood poisoning; another had her left nipple bitten off and almost died from the resultant infection. He was prone to the most unsocial of habits, evacuating his bowels on drawing-room carpets, and when his hosts protested, he claimed his excreta was sacred. . . . He believed he could make himself invisible at will. Diners at the Café Royal in London were astonished when Crowley appeared one evening, dressed in a wizard's robes and wearing a conical hat. He strode around the tables and left without saying a word. 'There you are,' he said afterward, 'that proves I can make myself invisible! Nobody spoke to me, therefore they couldn't have seen me.'" [12]

On April 14, 1934, Crowley brought a libel suit against Constable and Co. Publishers and former friend Nan Hammett, author of *Laughing Torso*. In her book, Hammett stated that "Crowley had a temple in Cefalu in Sicily. He was supposed to practice Black Magic there, and one day a baby was said to have disappeared mysteriously. There was also a goat there. This all pointed to Black Magic, so people said, and the inhabitants of the village were frightened of him." [13] For some strange reason Crowley thought that he could force through a quick settlement to help soothe his damaged character. When the defense attorneys got him on the stand he was barraged with epithets in which he was portrayed as "The monster of wickedness," "a dirty degenerate cannibal," and "the Great Beast 666." Then an article from the *Sunday Dispatch,* written by Crowley himself, was read aloud: "They have called me the worst man in the world. They have accused me of murdering women and throwing their bodies in the Seine and to drug peddling." [14] The jury made their decision in the courtroom without deliberation and found unanimously against Crowley. He was in shock at the verdict. The results of the verdict made Aleister Crowley a complete outcast and led him to financial ruin. Ironically, his fall had to do with Eliphas Levi's advice to the magus: to know, to dare, to will, and to keep silent. Unfortunately for Crowley, he didn't heed Levi's advice. It was impossible for Crowley to keep silent.

Aleister Crowley died on December 1, 1947, at Hastings, England. It was said that true to his reputation, he cursed his physician for not giving him a last injection of morphine. The unfortunate doctor died within eighteen hours of Crowley's death. (Ironically, Crowley's alter ego, Eliphas Levi, had come back to his Christian faith and perished safely in the last rites of the Church.) Crowley's other writings included *Magick in Theory and Practice, The Book of Thoth, 777 and Other Qabalistic Writings,* and *The Holy Books of Thelema.* Thelemic holidays were established in the following manner: The Equinox of the Gods (March 20) marked the Thelemic New Year and began the Aeon of Horus in 1904; Three Days of the Writing of *The Book of the Law* (April 8, 9, 10) was the translation period of the book and each chapter was to be read on the day it was created; First Night of the Prophet and Bride (August 12) celebrated the first night of the marriage between Aleister Crowley and his wife Rose Kelley, who would play a great role in *The Book of the Law*'s translation; Crowleymas (October 12) was the anniversary of Crowley's birth; and Crowley's Greater Feast (December 1) was a celebration that marked the death of Aleister Crowley. Of course followers also attended the standard meetings at equinoxes in March and September, and solstices in June and December.

Crowley's influence in rock and roll is perhaps due to his life of excess. Some individuals have admired the way in which he lived such a life of depravity. Earlier in English history the poets Byron and Shelley pursued the same goals. They embraced the many pleasures of life and turned a deaf ear to the demands of a puritan society. Each new adventure provided a thrill that thrust each man further along in the pursuit of still greater pleasure. Samuel Taylor Coleridge, like Crowley, became addicted to a prescribed medication, laudanum (opium dissolved in alcohol), in childhood, and his excessive use of the medication cost him his wife and family as well as his friendship with Wordsworth. His poem "Kubla Khan" was written under a hallucinatory dream state. Just so, newly crowned rock stars have admired the constant pursuit of the senses and tragically been consumed by their own passions into untimely death. The apostle of LSD, Timothy Leary, was a follower of Crowley's "Do What Thou Wilt" and interpreted the meaning as to "do your own thing." In this case, Leary was convinced that to do your own thing actually meant to expand your consciousness with drugs. With this point Crowley would readily agree.

Rock star Daryl Hall, who owns a signed and numbered copy of Aleister Crowley's *The Book of Thoth* (Thoth was the Egyptian god of writing, wisdom, and magic), reveals that "Around 1974, I graduated into the occult, and spent a solid six or seven years immersed in the cabala and the Chaldean, Celtic, and druidic traditions, [and] ancient techniques for focusing the inner flame, the will that can create unimagined things and truly transform your individual universe. I became fascinated with Aleister Crowley, the nineteenth-century British magician who shared those beliefs. . . . I was fascinated by him because his personality was the late-nineteenth-century equivalent of mine—a person brought up in a conventionally religious family who did everything he could to outrage the people around him as well as himself."[15] Hall went on to say, "I don't believe in the dictionary concept of the occult because there's no reason to make anything secret. Secrets were for oppressive societies where people had to go underground to literally keep their heads—which unfortunately may not be that far away from recurring. But at least in this point in time we can say whatever we want and share it and feel it . . . I've got a cousin who's a pro-Sandinista Methodist minister, and, of course, he's got me. We're a rare bunch, but then, my great-great-grandfather had to be unique to be a witch, and dedicated, too."[16] (Ironically, Hall's birth date is October 11. Crowley's birth date [Crowleymas] is October 12.)

Ozzy Osbourne is one performer who constantly seems to bear the brunt of criticism for each crime said to be committed in the devil's name. Album imagery, Gothic stage sets, and the illusion of the supernatural world are fixed symbols of an Ozzy Osbourne performance. The release of *Blizzard of Ozz* (1980) united Ozzy Osbourne and a young Randy Rhoads. Rhoads was to become not only the driving force behind Osbourne's music, but one of the singer's greatest friends. The *Blizzard of Ozz* LP contained not only the heavy-metal anthem "Crazy Train," but also "Mr. Crowley," a song dedicated to Aleister Crowley himself. Osbourne sings: "You fooled all the people with magic, you waited on Satan's call." Rhoads contributed the music, complete with a blazing guitar riff. With the release of *Diary of a Madman* (1981), the band was on the way to greater heights. The album jacket of

Diary of a Madman contained many symbols that listeners took to be satanic, when actually they were just used as an "artistic" quality, for the standard Gothic heavy-metal effect.

During the tour for *Diary of a Madman,* on March 19, 1982, Randy Rhoads went for a short flight in Osbourne's private plane. The pilot had made one previous flight and had convinced Rhoads and Ozzy's female hairdresser to go up with him for a second adventure. It appeared that everything was going well when all at once the plane soared lower toward the band's bus as if it were going to crash into the side. Some of the crew believed this to be a practical joke, others mention that the pilot had just ended a painful romantic relationship and had dipped the plane in the direction of his former lover. For whatever the reason, the tip of one of the plane's wings hit the tour bus, forcing the plane to crash into a nearby house. All the plane's passengers were killed. Strangely, the date of the plane crash fell upon March 19, the very eve of Aleister Crowley's Equinox of the Gods and the start of a Thelemic New Year. In this case Rhoads's death paralleled the lyric in "Mr. Crowley": "Your lifestyle seemed so tragic with the thrill of it all."

5. "SYMPATHY FOR THE DEVIL"

Pleased to meet you. I hope you guess my name.
—The Rolling Stones, "Sympathy for the Devil"

Rape, murder . . . It's just a shot away, it's just a shot away!
—The Rolling Stones, "Gimme Shelter"

They look like boys whom any self-respecting mum would lock in the bathroom! But the Rolling Stones—five tough young London-based music makers with doorstep mouths, pallid cheeks, and unkempt hair—are not worried what mums think!
—The *Daily Mail*[1]

WHAT A CHANGE FROM THE BEATLES!

When the British invasion began, the Beatles represented the boys next door. They were well groomed and polite, and their songs merely hinted at holding your daughter's hand. The Stones, however, represented the rebellious side of rock. Not only did they not want to hold your daughter's hand, they brazenly suggested that they should spend the night together! Most audiences were in complete shock as this seeming antithesis of the Beatles made their way across the pop charts and the flickering television screens of the America public. The irony in all of this was the fact that the Beatles were every bit as working class as the Stones. Their early performances came complete with black leather jackets and trousers. They were even promoted as "The Savage Young Beatles." The smooth transformation into tailor-made suits was due to the public-relations genius of Brian Epstein. Though their outward appearance changed radically, the Beatles saw themselves as very much in the same mold as the Rolling Stones.

The Rolling Stones rank as one of rock and roll's greatest and most prolific bands, with their music spanning four decades. Perhaps the longevity of the band is due in part to their ability to adapt to the changing styles of music and their experimentation with different instruments as well as varying themes in their songs. While they have consistently portrayed an image of bad-boy rock and rollers, there is a period in their music that is chilling in retrospect. The Rolling Stones were the creation of Brian Jones, a shag-haired blond guitarist with an angelic face. Jones was born in Cheltenham. His father was an aeronautical engineer and his mother was a piano teacher. In his early youth Brian Jones was a good student who participated in school sports, cricket and swimming. But his real love, even then, was music, as he excelled at the piano, clarinet, and saxophone. His parents became convinced that he would pursue a career in classical music. When Jones reached the age of thirteen he became rebellious. His school grades suffered and at this young age he stood at his own cross-roads and sold his soul for American blues. He became a disciple of Muddy Waters, Robert Johnson, and Howlin' Wolf, and became one of the first British guitarists to take up the slide guitar. After he was forced from his home by his parents (Brian's father claimed that his son's music gave him a migraine), Jones often hosted jam sessions in his small flat. His fellow musicians comprised a who's who of devotees of American rhythm and blues, and the small voluntary contributions of his sparse audiences helped pay his rent until his music finally allowed him to support himself.

In 1960, Brian Jones was to meet the two essential musicians who would complete his musical dreams. Mick Jagger and Keith Richards were performing together in Little Boy Blue and the Blue Boys. Their overpowering love of the blues led them to listen to Alexis Korner's Blues Incorporated, and they became enthralled by Jones's slide guitar work in the group. When Brian placed an ad in the *Jazz News* for musicians to put together a new group, Jagger and Richards decided that they would schedule an audition. The resulting chemistry, with a few personnel changes, would give birth to what would later become one of the most prodigious groups in rock and roll history. Brian Jones took the group's name from an old Muddy Waters song, "Rolling Stone." They managed an early appearance at the Crawdaddy Club and altogether split the grand total of £24. Little did the crowd of sixty-six people realize that they had witnessed the birth of a legend.

It wasn't easy for the Stones to duplicate the success of the Beatles. They were not able to immediately sweep into America and win the hearts and loyalty of American fans. Decca Records released the Stones' versions of Chuck Berry's "Come On" and Willie Dixon's "I Want to Be Loved." Both tracks were lackluster, but Decca was now infamous as the label that had rejected the

Beatles. They did not want to make the same mistake with another band that could help feed the public's insatiable appetite for new rock and roll groups in the Beatles' image.

The American tour became even more frustrating when their "Little Red Rooster" single was actually banned from certain U.S. stations as being obscene. Even the group's first performance on *The Ed Sullivan Show* in 1964 was such a failure that Sullivan himself remarked, "I promise you they'll never be back on our show."[2] The Stones admired the great American black blues artists and managed to record at Chicago's Chess Studios on their first American tour. To the young Englishmen this was rock and roll mecca. Keith Richards remembers the group's first meeting with the artist who had supplied their inspiration. When the Stones arrived at Chess Studios they saw Muddy Waters for the first time. The blues guitarist was dressed in white overalls on top of a stepladder, painting. Someone said, "'Well, meet Muddy Waters,' and we look up and he's standing on a stepladder painting the ceiling. And we're all toppling over ourselves, bewildered, thinking, 'What's this? Is this a hobby of his?' Can you imagine? And we're recording in the same studio where he made his records! After that, you start to realize how tough the business can be. Here's one of your gods painting the ceiling, and you're making a record of some of his songs."[3]

Of course, things changed drastically after the release of their first big hit singles, "The Last Time" and "(I Can't Get No) Satisfaction." It was now 1965, and the winter of the Stones' discontent was now well over. Finally, America surrendered, and the Stones established themselves as the heirs apparent to Beatlemania. Hit singles one after another helped entrench the Rolling Stones at the same level as the Fab Four. The public was now split into two camps, each constantly arguing over which group was the best. Which of these groups would break from the mold and lead the listening audience into new unexplored dimensions of sound? The competition seemed to bring out the very best in both bands. New instruments like the sitar and the dulcimer found their way into Beatles and Stones recordings. Brian Jones had a special knack for picking up a new instrument and immediately mastering it in only a matter of minutes. With this the Stones more than matched the Beatles' creative output. That was of course until 1967, the year that the Beatles unleashed *Sgt. Pepper's Lonely Hearts Club Band.*

It was now the "Summer of Love" and the strains of psychedelic music permeated the airwaves, much like the pungent smell of bittersweet incense. It was a new age and the Beatles had once again led the way with an innovative collection of songs that differed greatly from anything previously heard at this time. The Stones would have to venture into the unknown waters of psychedelia and away from their firmly planted blues roots, which had always supplied their musical foundation. Surely, the Stones would have to meet the Beatles' challenge head on and produce an album equal to *Sgt. Pepper's.* Newfound fame soon brought new relationships to the band. These new associates would provide novel avenues of escape for the frequently bored musicians who had now tasted the many pleasures of life. This is where the Rolling Stones began a flirtation with the dark side, and a fascination with witchcraft and magic. One of these newfound confederates was none other than American filmmaker Kenneth Anger.

Kenneth Anger was born in Hollywood, California, in 1930. He made his first film appearance when he was but four years old in Max Reinhardt's *A Midsummer Night's Dream.* Later in his career he danced with Shirley Temple and in 1947, at the age of seventeen, he completed his first, critically acclaimed film, *Fireworks.* This he accomplished using only his parents' home movie camera. It was during his teenage years that Anger developed his interest in Aleister Crowley. He has stated that he intended for his films "to cast a spell, to be a magical invocation of his fusion of dreams, desire, myth, and vision." This would be a way for the filmmaker to transform his mystical views to his audiences.

In 1960, Kenneth Anger published his best-selling book *Hollywood Babylon,* which reveled in the scandalous behavior of the beautiful people in the film capital of the world. Anger's grandmother had once served as a studio wardrobe mistress and repeated to him all the sordid details of the scandals and gossip encompassing Hollywood royalty. This proved to be Kenneth Anger's inspiration for his book. (Alternative rock group the Gin Blossoms took their name from a caption in *Hollywood Babylon II* for a photo of W. C. Fields's bulbous red nose, his skin described as having a bad case of "gin blossoms" from his years of drinking heavily. Tragedy later followed the band. Founding member, lead guitarist, and main songwriter Doug Hopkins had recurring problems with alcohol abuse and depression—not the best of partnerships—and was fired by the band after the recording of *New Miserable Experience.* After the release, the band enjoyed its greatest success, but Hopkins committed suicide in December of 1993, when he became yet one more victim of his own personal demons.)

It was also during the late sixties that Anger, now the renegade avant-garde filmmaker, took up residence in Great Britain and became a social fixture in the many gatherings attended by rock's superstars. Anger first met Mick Jagger at gallery owner Robert Fraser's home in Mayfair. It seemed that Kenneth Anger was very enamored with the almost supernatural power that the Stones held over their audiences. He was also most impressed with Mick Jagger's personal charisma. After this meeting, Anger provided lectures concerning the occult powers of Aleister Crowley and the concept of "Do what thou wilt." Led Zeppelin's guitarist Jimmy Page was so impressed by the Crowley legend that he actually purchased Crowley's mansion at Boleskine, Scotland.

With their newfound interest in the occult to serve as a guide, the Stones were determined to match the Beatles' success with *Sgt. Pepper's Lonely Hearts Club Band.* This became more of a compulsion with Jagger and also served as a major power play to cast Brian Jones from the band. Jones was a rhythm and blues purist. He was convinced that an uncharted journey into psychedelic sounds would only serve as a terrible mistake. The Stones would simply be Beatle imitators and could go so far as to alienate their fans. As Jones told friend Tony Sanchez, "If he [Jagger] insists on recording this kind of crap, the Stones are dead." Jagger replied, "It's psychedelic, man, pretty soon everything is going to be psychedelic, and if we aren't in there on our next album, we will be left behind. No one is going to want to listen to rhythm and blues anymore." Mick Jagger easily won Keith Richards over and work began on *Their Satanic Majesties Request.* During the recording Brian Jones did little to contribute to the swirling psychedelic cacophony. At times cruel jokes were played upon him such as having him attempt the overdubbing of guitar lines with the tape recorders off. The mantle of leadership had now fallen from Brian Jones's shoulders and he had lost control of his very creation. The *Satanic Majesties Request* album cover was designed by Michael Cooper (who had also photographed the *Sgt. Pepper's* cover). The cover art portrayed the Stones dressed as wizards and magicians complete with a pointed wizard hat: "Jagger purchased books at the Indica Shop. Among his favorite references were *The Secret of the Golden Flower, The Golden Bough,* and *Morning of the Magicians*—each was filled with cryptic allusions—green suns and celestial travelers."[4] A special camera had been flown in from Japan to shoot a 3-D image for the cover. If you look closely you can see the images of the four Beatles in the shrubbery. This was done by the Rolling Stones to repay the plug the Beatles had given them on the *Sgt. Pepper's Lonely Hearts Club Band* cover (on the *Sgt. Pepper's* front cover there is a stuffed doll wearing a "Welcome the

Rolling Stones" sweatshirt). The *Satanic Majesties Request* album title was given as a sarcastic parody of the Queen. Unfortunately, the Stones managed only to parody themselves.

Their Satanic Majesties Request became a critical failure for the band. Brian Jones was right. Critics claimed that this album was merely released to cash in on the success of the Beatles' *Sgt. Pepper's Lonely Hearts Club Band.* The Stones would return to their musical roots but for now it seemed as if the die had been cast. Brian Jones would not be a Stone much longer and he was being stalked by the shadowy essence of death. When production began on *Beggars Banquet,* the Rolling Stones were now much deeper into their studies of black magic. Kenneth Anger continued his influence and was said to have suggested the creating of a rock anthem to Satan, "Sympathy for the Devil." In 1970 Mick Jagger starred in the lead role of the cult film *Performance,* in which he played the role of Turner, a rock star who dressed in makeup and feminine clothing. Jagger's character also studied the occult and was obsessed with black magic. This role obviously shaped Mick Jagger's persona in the years that followed, as if he had assimilated the fictional character into his own being. In this case, life did imitate art! The occult props from the movie set constantly disappeared. It seemed that Anita Pallenberg had them taken so that she could become the high priestess in the Stones' newfound beliefs. Pallenberg was a beautiful blonde who was originally Brian Jones's lover. At this time she had left Jones and was now living with Keith Richards.

The concept for the "Sympathy for the Devil" was based on Mikhail Bulgakov's *The Master and Margarita,* a book that dealt with satanic fantasy. During this time period Kenneth Anger developed a concept for his salute to Satan. He intended to create a film that he would entitle *Lucifer Rising.* Anger was later to state, "I was going to film a version of *Lucifer Rising* with the Stones. All the roles were to be carefully cast, with Mick being Lucifer and

Keith as Beelzebub. Beelzebub is really the Lord of the Flies and is like the crown prince next to the king in the complicated hierarchy of demons. Beelzebub is like a henchman for Lucifer. . . ." Mick Jagger had agreed to compose a musical score to be used as the sound track for Anger's *Lucifer Rising*. After Jagger dropped out of the film role, Anger used Chris Jagger, Mick's brother, as Lucifer and Marianne Faithfull as Lilith. Anger dropped Chris Jagger after one day of filming, and his search for Lucifer was to continue. Mick Jagger helped with the production of the film, which was shot in exotic places, using Egypt as the main focal point (perhaps since it was here that Aleister Crowley received the inspiration for *The Book of the Law*). In Marianne Faithfull's book *Faithfull: An Autobiography*, she recalls the creation of *Lucifer Rising*: "One day, into my cheerless routine came a flamboyant figure out of my past. Kenneth Anger, underground filmmaker and *soi-disant* magician. Having misread Mick's pantomime Satanism, he must have assumed that I believed in black magic (and was ripe to be his apprentice)." Anger wanted Faithfull to portray the role of Lilith in *Lucifer Rising*. She didn't believe that Anger possessed psychic or magical powers, but she did believe in his powers as a filmmaker: "Lilith is obviously one of the great female archetypes, another form of the Great Mother like Ishtar and Astarte, Diana, Aphrodite and Demeter. From the point of view of the patriarchy, of course, she is the pure incantation of evil. Lilith did not eat from the Tree of Knowledge of Good and Evil, so she never knew right from wrong."

One of Marianne Faithfull's scenes took place in Giza, with the Sphinx as a backdrop. It was here that she sensed that Anger's creative powers of "magus or a director" were overrated: "Even as inept as Kenneth was, I knew he was dangerous in a way. I knew that simply by being in the film I was involving myself in a magic act far more potent than Kenneth's hocus-pocus Satanism." After smearing herself with stage blood, Marianne filmed a sequence where she crawled around an Arab cemetery shortly before dawn as the sun slowly rose over the pyramids. Thinking back on this particular scene, Faithfull claimed, "If I'd been my normal self I would have just laughed, but by then I was a hopeless junkie. I used to feel a lot of the bad luck in my life came from that film."

For the next film sequence the setting changed to Star Mountain, an ancient neolithic place of worship in Germany. According to Faithfull, "There are two hundred stone steps cut into the mountain. When the sun rises on the solstice, the rays go through an aperture and hit a sacred spot." To achieve the mystical effect the filming began on the morning of the winter solstice. Marianne Faithfull began climbing the mountain in what she calls a "dope sick" condition until she reached the top. As the sun was shining through the aperture and illuminating the rock, she passed out: "What had happened, of course, was that I had run out of smack and had a slight dope fit. I think I lost consciousness for a second time and when I came to I realized I was falling off the mountain. I came to as I was tumbling through the air and remembered in midfall that I had to do some somersaults and land on my feet. Which I did. They rushed me to hospital. They thought I must at least have a concussion. But nothing. So there, Kenneth Anger. My magic was bigger than yours! (Kenneth would have liked me to fall off the mountain and die. It would have been a magnificent climax for his film.)"[5]

As she thought about her performance in *Lucifer Rising*, Marianne Faithfull also remembered the aftereffects of her role: "Doing the film was bad enough, but there were further consequences. Pictures came out in the papers with me looking like death in gray makeup and a nun's habit, with pyramids in the background. All contributing to creating a quite fiendish, devil-worshiping image of me. Even old photographs of me outside Yew Tree cottage now took on a sinister aspect! That sweet little cottage began to look like a witch house. After *Lucifer Rising* I ended up on the wall and became a junkie. I felt unclean and dangerous to the people I loved."[6]

If Kenneth Anger had misread Mick Jagger's "Satanic pantomime," he was convinced that within the group there lurked other kindred spirits: "The occult unit within the Stones was Keith and Anita and Brian. I believe that Anita is, for want of a better word, a witch. You see, Brian was a witch, too. I'm convinced. He showed me his witch's tit. He had a supernumerary tit in a very sexy place on his inner thigh. He stated, 'In another time they would have burned me.' He was very happy about that. Mick backed away from being identified with Lucifer. He thought that it was too heavy."[7]

In seventeenth-century witchcraft, "the witch's tit" was also referred to as the Devil's Mark. This mark was made when the witch pricked his or her finger with a silver pin in order to sign the Devil's Black Book. Of course, the signature had to be in his or her own blood. When this was accomplished, Satan would provide the newly initiated witch with a familiar spirit, a demon in the form of some animal, that would enable the witch to cast spells against her enemies and do the will of her unholy master. The mark would then move to some other location upon the body (perhaps on the inner thigh?) and the familiar would use this mark to feed on the sorcerer's soul. Remember, in the Salem Witch trials the visionary girls claimed to see a yellow bird that would appear around the accused witch. Since no one in the crowd could see the creature, it was taken as evidence of the accused being in league with Satan. This so-called "spectral evidence" led to the hanging of many innocent victims in Salem, Massachusetts.

Early witch finders also believed that this "witch's tit" could take the shape of a mole, freckle, or a third nipple. In this case victims were rather easy to find. The legend also goes that this mark would emit no sensation. The witch finders would often plunge

needles into suspicious blemishes to determine the guilt or innocence of the accused witch. If the victim was found guilty, she
could be hanged or burned alive. Of course, the ultimate test was
throwing the defendant into a body of water to see if he or she
would float. The reasoning behind this is that water is a purity
symbol of baptism and would cast up a servant of Satan. If the
victim sank, and could be freed before drowning, that person was
innocent. Isn't it rather strange that Brian Jones drowned in his
pool on July 3, 1969?

One of the great ironies associated with the Rolling Stones'
interest in black magic was guitarist Keith Richards being a former choirboy at Westminister Abbey: "I was once a choirboy—
Westminister Abbey, soloist. To me it was a way of getting out of
Physics and Chemistry, because if you gave me a Bunsen burner
back then I'd set the school on fire . . . There was a certain part of
the 'Hallelujah Chorus,' a section for three sopranos, and it was
me, a guy called Spike, and another named Terry. We were the
reprobates of the school, definitely, but at the time we sang like
angels."[8]

When it became obvious that Keith Richards was falling
in love with Anita Pallenberg the tension mounted between
Richards and Brian Jones, Pallenberg's first lover within the
Stones. Marianne Faithfull was living with Mick Jagger and remembers, "Anita was certainly into black magic. And although I
can't really say whether she was a witch or not, there's no denying
the fact that Anita was sort of a black queen, a dark person, despite her blond looks. . . . It's very hard to define wickedness, but
when Anita looked at you sometimes with that incredible smile
on her face, it was not a smile you had ever seen before, it was a
smile that seemed to be a camouflage for some dark secret that
she was hoarding. . . . The best way I can describe Anita is that she
was like a snake to a bird and that she could transfix you and hold
you in place until she wanted to make her move."[9]

Anita Pallenberg, when told of Marianne Faithfull's description of her powers, answered, "Oh, she's probably referring to that spell I put on Brian. She knew about that." Brian and Anita had a terrible fight and Pallenberg was forcibly thrown from the house. She picked herself up all "scraped and bloody" and went to a friend's house. The longer she sat there the angrier she became, and since revenge is a great motivator, she explained, "I was sitting there, in tears, angry, getting my wounds treated, feeling terrible, and I decided to make a wax figure of Brian and poke him with a needle. I molded some candle wax into an effigy and said whatever words I said and closed my eyes and jabbed the needle into the wax figure. It pierced the stomach."

The following morning Anita returned to Jones's house and found him very ill and suffering from severe stomach pains: "He'd been up all night, and was in agony, bottles of Milk of Magnesia and other medications all around him. It took him a day or so to get over it." Anita also commented that "Yes, I did have an interest in witchcraft, Buddhism, in the black magicians that my friend, Kenneth Anger, the filmmaker, introduced me to. The world of the occult fascinated me, but after what happened to Brian, I never cast another spell." Pallenberg has also claimed that "I have a very old soul from another time that entered my body and lives in me. I feel younger now than when I was eight years old. When the soul entered my body I felt very oppressed, very heavy, that something was bearing down on me. But now I am young and released with this new soul in my body." [10] But according to Rolling Stones insider Tony Sanchez, this would not be the last time she would cast a spell!

Sanchez recalled one episode in which there was an old man dying in a roadway outside Marrakesh. It appeared that the man's simple cart had been struck by a truck. As the crowd gathered around the overturned cart, Anita Pallenberg made her way through the crowd and dipped a handkerchief in the old man's blood: "Later Anita was to attempt to use the same handkerchief to put a curse on a young man who had angered her. Subsequently, he died."[11] Of course, Kenneth Anger had taught Anita the power of a dying man's blood. Throughout history onlookers at public executions would attempt to dip handkerchiefs in the blood of the condemned. It was believed that the shed blood of kings would contain even more magical properties. At the execution of Louis XVI onlookers dipped handkerchiefs in his blood and pulled hairs from his powdered wig as his decapitated body quivered upon the scaffold. The same held true at the execution of King Charles I of England and for other members of the unfortunate English nobility. One legend mentioned a Puritan doctor whose family obtained the very cervical vertebra split by the executioner's ax in the execution of King Charles I. This talisman stayed in the family until Queen Victoria determined it should be reburied with her unfortunate ancestor. It also seemed that instead of using this grisly object for the purpose of magic, it had been used instead as a salt and pepper holder for the good doctor's family's dinner table.

It has been rumored that Anita Pallenberg also placed a curse upon Joe Monk, a former friend of Keith Richards. After a drug bust had occurred in the summer of 1973, Pallenberg had become convinced that Monk had served as an informant for the police. She claimed that she would get her revenge upon the supposed double-crosser by placing a curse upon him: "A short while later Joe Monk was driving along a lonely cliff-top road in Majorca when his car crashed and he was killed. Nobody saw it; no other vehicle was involved. The police said it was the strangest accident that they had ever heard of. One can only assume it was a *coincidence* of course."[12]

The influence of Kenneth Anger continued to grow, and with this the Stones began to fear the powers of their new guru. Anger claimed to be a magus, a magician of the highest order, and an equal to that of Aleister Crowley. Mick Jagger's musical compositions for *Lucifer Rising* were used as the sound track for Kenneth Anger's *Invocation of My Demon Brother*. This short film included scenes of magic, the Stones in concert, and American soldiers fighting in the Vietnam War. The staring role of Lucifer went to Bobby Beausoleil. Beausoleil was a former guitarist with the California rock group Love and was Anger's first choice for the starring role in *Lucifer Rising*. Beausoleil was cast as Lucifer but after a few months of filming he became involved in a terrible argument with Anger. It has been suggested that Beausoleil stole the film negatives and tried to extort money from Anger. Kenneth Anger responded with a "ritualistic curse." Strangely enough, shortly after this argument, Beausoleil became a member of the Manson family. He reportedly tortured and killed Gary Hinman, a musician who had sold the family some bad drugs. After the murder Bobby Beausoleil scribbled "political piggy" in his victim's own blood. Some sources now claim that the Manson family committed the Sharon Tate murders as a sort of copycat killing in order to convince the police that they had arrested the wrong man, and to force them to free Bobby Beausoleil.

One chilling photograph taken at this time portrays Beausoleil dressed in nineteenth-century apparel in front of a church with Crowley's slogan "Do What Thou Wilt" painted upon the wall. Of course Manson and his family were close to the Satanic movement in San Francisco. Convicted killer Susan Atkins had once been a topless dancer for one of Anton LaVay's early sideshows while he was founding the Church of Satan. It has also been rumored that Sharon Tate, shortly before her death, had developed a strong interest in witchcraft. In one of her later films, *Eye of the Devil,* she played the role of a character involved with the occult. There is some suspicion to this day that the murders of Tate and her friends were due to a drug deal that went bad rather than an unprovoked ritual killing. It was also ironic that Tate's husband, Roman Polanski, had completed the occult classic *Rose-*

mary's Baby at the time of the killings. Chilling coincidences exist, with Sharon Tate's unborn baby being killed by Satanists, and the film character Rosemary being led to believe by Satanists that her baby had died. The terrifying scenes of a very pregnant Mia Farrow carrying a long, sharp butcher's knife were also very disturbing, knowing the outcome of the Tate murders. It was also during this time that Sharon Tate had become well acquainted with Alex and Maxine Sanders. The Sanderses were leaders of an occult society called the Alexandrians and billed themselves as the king and queen of witches. While doing a series of lectures on magic, the Sanderses came into contact with another occult society whose members gave up all material possessions to become members. One follower asked to borrow several rare books dealing with ritual magic. When the books were returned Maxine Sanders noticed that one passage in one of the books dealing with blood rituals had been underlined. The highlighted passage stated "kill the pig . . ." Some investigators took this as an early involvement wih California cults that may very well have included the Manson family.

The Stones' break with Kenneth Anger came after a series of strange happenstances. Tony Sanchez remembers, "We were all just a little afraid of Kenneth. Again and again inexplicable things involving him would happen." Once, for example, Stones and Beatles insider Robert Fraser sponsored an opening party for some sculptures created by John and Yoko Lennon. Since the sculptures were white, all the guests were to follow suit and dress in white as well. According to Sanchez, "We were even forced to drink a white mineral water." Then Sanchez noticed Kenneth Anger at the party. As Sanchez moved toward the filmmaker, Anger seemed to have vanished into thin air. Strangely, says Sanchez, Anita Pallenberg, Marianne Faithfull, Keith Richards, and Mick Jagger all had the same experience. Each noticed Anger moving through the crowd and as each sought him out for conversation, Kenneth Anger seemed to just disappear. "Anyway," said Anita, "it's very strange because Kenneth told me he wouldn't be able to come to the exhibition because he was going to be away on business in Germany."

Kenneth didn't return for two weeks, and by then numerous other people who had been at the party—John, Yoko, Robert, artist Jim Dine—all remarked on having seen Kenneth across the crowded room, but having been unable to speak to him: "Eventually we asked almost everyone who had been there if he or she had spoken to him—and none of them had. 'Were you there?' I asked him one day. And he only laughed." [13] When Keith Richards and Anita Pallenberg suggested that they would like to marry, but didn't want the legal paperwork hassle of a marriage between an English citizen and a German-Italian, it was Anger who suggested a pagan service. He said that the door to their house was to be painted gold with a special paint enriched with magical herbs. This newly painted door would then represent the sun, and the marriage service would then be blessed. Early the next morning Anita's screams awakened both Richards and Sanchez. The heavy three-inch mahogany door had been flawlessly painted during the night. To do such a masterful job, the door would almost certainly have had to have been removed from the hinges. This would have been impossible due to the heavy lock. Sanchez says that he, Richards, and Anita Pallenberg, then trembling, came to the belief that Kenneth Anger somehow could enter their home by his mere will alone. Anita began carrying strings of garlic after she was convinced by Anger that her enemies would send a vampire to destroy her. He repeated the tale of Aleister Crowley's struggle with a vampire sent by MacGregor Mathers to kill him until Crowley "smote the sorceress with her own current of evil."

Pallenberg's interest in the occult continued to grow, and she was to later tell Sanchez never to disturb her while she was casting a spell. He claims he noticed a strange chest that she kept in her room: "The drawers were filled with scraps of bone, wrinkled skin and fur from strange animals. I slammed the door shut in disgust and ran from the room." Keith Richards was impressed with being considered as another of the great rebels of English literature to dabble with the occult. Obviously, Anger made it very flattering for Keith Richards to consider himself alongside great English writers like Byron, Blake, Wilde, and Yeats. In an interview with Robert Greenfield in *Rolling Stone*, Richards stated: "Kenneth Anger told me I was his right-hand man. It's just what you feel. Whether you've got that good and evil thing together. Left-hand path, right-hand path, how far do you want to go down? Once you start there's no going back. Where they lead to is another thing. It is something everybody ought to explore. Why do people practice voodoo? All these things are bunched under the name of superstition and old wives' tales . . . before, when we were innocent kids out for a good time, they were saying, 'They're evil, they're evil.' Oh, I'm evil, really? So that makes you start thinking about evil. What is evil? Half of it, I don't know how much people think of Mick as the devil or as just a good rock performer or what? There are black magicians who think we are acting as unknown agents of Lucifer and others who think we are Lucifer. Everybody's Lucifer." [14]

The Rolling Stones' newfound interest in voodoo would provide inspiration for both *Get Yer Ya-Yas Out* and later *Goat's Head Soup*. The phrase "Ya-Yas" was said to be an often repeated phrase found in African voodoo. Brian Jones had earlier flown to North Africa, where he recorded the pipes and drums of the Joujouka tribe. After staying in Africa for nearly a month he returned with his creative juices flowing and a new mission for the Stones. This is what he said about his experience in Africa: "Their [the Joujouka tribe] music is going to cause a sensation . . . People are becoming bored with rhythm and blues, and they are looking for something new. I really reckon this could be it. The music has got this incredible, pulsing excitement and I've got it all down on tape. It's going to make the most amazing album."[15] But Jones would also become frightened that a curse had been placed upon him as he did the ceremonial recordings. Ironically, the strange rhythms that introduced the Rolling Stones' "Sympathy for the Devil" would represent the last performance that Brian Jones would undertake with the Rolling Stones. During the production of *The Rolling Stones Rock and Roll Circus,* the Stones invited a who's who of rock royalty to attend and star in what Mick Jagger hoped would be a rock film to end all rock films. Rock greats included John Lennon and Yoko Ono, Eric Clapton, the Who, and Jethro Tull. Many of the performers were dressed in costumes: Bill Wyman and Charlie Watts of the Stones were dressed as clowns, Yoko Ono as a witch, Mick Jagger and Keith Richards as ringmasters, and Brian Jones in a silver top hat complete with horns. He would represent the devil, complete with his pants legs tucked nicely into his boots to give the appearance of cloven hoofs. The Stones closed the show with "Route 66," "Jumpin' Jack Flash," and finally "Sympathy for the Devil." Brian Jones performed dressed in his appropriate costume. As the song reached a fever pitch, Jagger tore off his red shirt to reveal a "temporary" tattoo of the Prince of Darkness. This was Jones's last performance with the Stones. On July 3, 1969, a few short weeks after Jagger and Richards had replaced him with Mick Taylor, Brian Jones would be found drowned at the bottom of his swimming pool. Many insiders felt that his death was not accidental.

To many of the Stones' followers it seemed odd that the group would perform a large free concert at Hyde Park two days after Brian's death. Of course, Mick Jagger claimed this to be in tribute to their fallen friend and band mate. Many fans had never guessed the extent of the hatred and rivalry between the three band members, Jones, Jagger, and Richards. Marianne Faithfull, however, realized the importance of her loss and took an overdose of sleeping pills. She would be in a coma for days before fully physically recovering, but would be dropped from the cast of the film *Ned Kelly,* in which she and Jagger were to star. During her coma, Faithfull was convinced that the spirit of Brian Jones visited her. He was smiling and happy, but told Marianne she would have to return and could not stay with him. Shortly after this vision, she was awakened from her deep coma.

The concert at Hyde Park went on as scheduled and the English Hell's Angels served as the band's security. Hundreds of thousands of fans listened intently with tears in their eyes as Mick Jagger read from Percy Bysshe Shelley's "Adonais." Shelley had written the poem as an elegy for the poet John Keats. Strangely, there were a number of parallels between the life of Shelley and that of Brian Jones. The poem "Adonais" contains several references to drowning. Both men died before the age of thirty, both drowned, both men were considered to be outcasts from society due to their creative forces, both men were cast out by their fathers, both had radical political views concerning anarchy ("Street Fighting Man"), both experimented with drugs, and both were fascinated with the occult. The passages from Shelley were more than appropriate! After the reading, thousands of white butterflies were released from cages positioned upon the stage. Perhaps this was a token to metaphorically represent the freeing of Brian Jones's soul as it soared ever closer to heaven. Sadly, the heat had been too much for the delicate creatures and many fell into the crowd like gossamer snowflakes, perishing as yet another sacrifice at the altar of the Rolling Stones. The concert was a great success and served as an introduction for Brian Jones's replacement, Mick Taylor.

The Rolling Stones prepared for their 1969 American tour with the desire to upstage the Woodstock festival. It was the Age of Aquarius and the dawning of a new epoch of peace and enlightenment. But it would turn out to be anything but that! Mick

Jagger's costume designer Ossie Clark recalled the preparations for his stage costume in A. E. Hotchner's brilliant *Blown Away: The Rolling Stones and the Death of the Sixties:* "One night I was at Mick's house in London—I was designing the costumes for this 1969 tour. The principal costume I made for him was dominated by a black and red shirt with streamers—half black and half red with one black streamer and one red streamer, set off by a red white and blue Uncle Sam top hat . . . He'd put on a tape of the music that would be played on the tour and he'd dance around and say, 'I'd like to do this and that,' and we kind of evolved our costume ideas together. But for this trip, our costume night was different. Mick danced around with great intensity and he was telling me in a stream of what seemed subconscious feelings, somewhat incoherent, what he wanted to convey. It was more than just describing costumes or anything like that, it was as if he had became Satan and was announcing his evil intentions. He was reveling in this role. Frightening, truly frightening. I always knew that Mick had several clearly defined personas—talk about a split personality! But this was a side of Mick never revealed before. He was rejoicing in being Lucifer." [16]

Clark also remembered a Stones performance in Los Angeles, November 7, 1969: "We went out and took our seats, the Stones appeared, the first note was played and the whole place erupted like a tiger roaring. I almost blacked out. This was not the wave of adulation I was accustomed to hearing, no, this was like a mob being exhorted by a dictator. And then when Mick went into his Lucifer routine with the black and red streamers flying, the audience seemed to spit out its defiance.

"He introduced himself as 'a man of wealth and taste' who had been around a long time, had taken men's souls, and achieved a catalogue of Satanic triumphs. I was trembling I was so frightened. And the more the audience's reaction intensified, the more Mick baited them. I expected a riot, an explosion. I escaped before the concert ended, went back to the house, packed my bag, and immediately left for New York. Even when I got to New York I couldn't shake off the scary, ominous feelings of that night. It stayed with me. For a week or more after that, I'd wake in the night with a heavy sweat."[17]

If Woodstock served as the birth of the Age of Aquarius, then what was to happen at Altamont Speedway a few weeks later would serve as the death knell. The Stones, perhaps arrogantly, decided that this tour would be filmed as a testament to rock and roll. If they were to give a free concert in San Francisco they could smash the attendance figure set at Woodstock, and the Stones could live up to their reputation as the world's greatest rock and roll band. But the entire venture was a tribute to ineptitude. There was just no way in which the needs of that large of a crowd could be met. Everything was in short supply. Few doctors, food vendors, or bathrooms; however, the greatest concern was the show's security. The Grateful Dead had suggested that the Stones use the California branches of the Hell's Angels. Some sources claim that the Rolling Stones paid the Angels a truckload of beer valued at $500 to provide the security at the concert. Everything was rushed into place so that the concert and documentary could soon be under way.

At Woodstock, the promoters had consulted astrologers to determine the perfect day for their event. Not so with the Stones. California astrologers warned before the show was under way, "It's going to be a very heavy day. The Sun, Venus, and Mercury are all in Sagittarius, and the moon's on the Libra-Scorpio cusp . . . Anyone can see that, with the moon in Scorpio, it's going to be an awful day to do this concert. There is a strong possibility for violence and chaos, and any astrologer could have told them. Oh, well, maybe the Stones know something I don't."[18] The Stones pushed on because to postpone the concert meant to postpone the movie. One thing that disturbed Mick Jagger was the report of an underground college play in which a famous rock performer is stabbed to death in a concert at the conclusion. There was no doubt as to who the character represented as the players screamed, "He's killed Mick!" (In the early seventies, during the making of *Goats Head Soup*, Mick Jagger would once again receive a warning concerning an appointment with an early death. Surprisingly, the letter came from a student of the occult in California: "At great length and obvious sincerity the writer set out all the reasons why Jagger was doomed to be the next rock star to die. Though ridiculous, his reasoning was eerie enough to be unnerving; all the rock stars who were doomed to die in the sixties and seventies had the letters *I* and *J* in their names—like Brian Jones, Janis Joplin, Jimi Hendrix, and Jim Morrison. Moreover, the order of deaths fitted in with a formula which indicated that the next to die would have *I* as the second letter of the first name and *J* as the first letter of the second name. Additionally, the seventeenth-century Dutch artist Franz Hals, who was a celebrated warlock, had painted a picture called 'The Merry Lute Player'—the central character of which was Jagger's double." [19] To make matters worse, Mick had received the letter the day before his destined death. According to Tony Sanchez, the next day Jagger stayed in his room all day with a security force in order not to tempt fate.)

Jagger knew of the existence of a lunatic fringe element in California, but felt safe in a city of peace and love where gentle people lived "with flowers in their hair." Little did the group know that that night all hell would break loose! The Rolling Stones arrived at the Altamont Raceway in a helicopter. Everything seemed to be quite normal, so the Stones retired to their tents.

The Stones absolutely refused to take the stage until nightfall. Jagger was sure that the lighting was one of the most important aspects of the show and that it was imperative to the creation of the film. What would be filmed, however, was violent murder. Meredith Hunter, a black man, had dared come to the concert with a white girl, and for this he was singled out. The Angels started to beat him while the Stones started the hypnotic beat to "Sympathy for the Devil." Tony Sanchez recalled naked audience members trying to crawl onto the stage only to be pummeled with crushing blows from heavy pool cues. This he referred to as offerings to some Satanic altar. Marty Balin of the Jefferson Airplane was knocked senseless by one of the Angels as he tried to rescue an onlooker. The bad vibes were everywhere, but now the bitter smell of blood was in the air. The frenzy had begun. Don McLean in his "American Pie" chronicled the tragedy at Altamont. The reference to "Jack Flash" would refer to the Stones' opening song at the concert. McLean also sang, "As the flames climbed high into the night/To light the sacrificial rite,/I saw Satan laughing with delight/The day the music died." These fires represented the bonfires lit by the audience and what was to be the terrible death of Meredith Hunter. While performing, Jagger saw a black man in a green suit point what appeared to be a gun at him from the crowd. Obviously, Jagger remembered the death scene from the underground play and retreated to the back of the stage. The eighteen-year-old Meredith Hunter disappeared under an avalanche of Hell's Angels. The Angels stabbed him. They beat him. They kicked him. One Angel ground a steel bucket into Hunter's eyes and they left him to die in the midst of the crowd. Blood was spurting everywhere and when some of the onlookers tried to aid the dying man, one Angel said, "Leave him alone. He's going to die anyway." The cameras kept rolling and captured the carnage firsthand. The documentary to the Stones was now a tribute to unnecessary death. A film to glorify rock had now become a legitimate snuff film to showcase a sacrifice to the dark forces that contolled the fate of those present. When the festival had ended the price had been high: "four dead—one murdered, two run over (some of the Angels drove their bikes into the crowd), one drowned in a drainage ditch—and hundreds injured, some seriously." [20]

One audience member wrote a letter to *Rolling Stone* magazine: "To those that know, it's been obvious that the Stones, or at least some of them, have been involved in the practice of magick ever since the *Satanic Majesties Request* album. But there at least the colour was more white than black. Since then the hue has gone steadily darker and darker. At Altamont He appeared in his full majesty with his consort of demons, the Hell's Angels. It was just a few days before the Winter Solstice when the forces of darkness are at their most powerful. The moon was in Scorpio, which is the time of the month when the Universal vibration is at its most unstable. It was held in a place dedicated to destruction through motion. Then Mick comes on only after it is dark enough for the red lights to work their magick. I don't know if they are sadder and wiser from the experience. But an agonizing price was paid for the lesson. And we were all guilty because we have eaten of the cake the Stones baked." [21]

The resulting movie was entitled *Gimme Shelter*, taken from a song the Stones played during the beatings. The lyrics ran like a prophecy: "Rape, murder, it's just a shot away, it's just a shot away." After their return to England a black cloud seemed to follow the Stones. Keith Richards and Anita Pallenberg's young son died tragically. Sanchez says that their addictions to drugs, especially heroin, became so extensive that Richards underwent a radical treatment. According to Sanchez, Richards had a complete blood transfusion to temporarily rid him of his heroin addiction. (Of course today this is considered one of rock's greatest urban legends.) Following this, Anita and Keith split up, and Richards finally decided that his music was much more important than his drugs. He married model Patti Hansen and says that he is now finally straight. Anita Pallenberg was connected with another tragedy. It seems that a young boy died from a gunshot wound to the head while he was in her bed. At the inquest it was determined to be a suicide, although Sanchez reports that many neighbors testified to hearing strange chants and seeing dark cloaked figures on the night of the tragedy. Mick Jagger followed the advice of Doctor Faustus. He burned his books on magic, and stopped taking calls from Kenneth Anger. Anger even mentioned that in Mick Jagger's wedding to Bianca that "he wore a rather prominent cross about his neck."

The tragedy of Altamont ended the sixties in a blazing funeral pyre. A generation dedicated to peace and love melted into the sure realities of the Vietnam War, civil injustice, and senseless death. The magic was gone. It would never be rekindled.

6. THE SORCERER'S APPRENTICE

Walking side by side with death, the devil mocks their every step.
—Led Zeppelin, "No Quarter"

THOUGH THE LATE 1960S PRODUCED A NUMBER OF STELLAR ROCK GROUPS, none came close to unleashing the tumult of musical sound and fury that was Led Zeppelin. Zeppelin's sound appeared to be conjured forth from the seething rural blues of the American South and then combined with the omnipotent force of John Bonham's thunderous drums. If Steppenwolf was the first band to use the term heavy metal, Led Zeppelin became the epitome of the very genre. As the group grew in legend, fantastic rumors surfaced, tales of Celtic mythology and a hint of something dark that beckoned ever so softly from the electrifying rhythms of the band's music. The music became the master and Zeppelin, like Icarus, soared to incredible heights only to plummet to a horrifying and premature death. The Led Zeppelin mystique involved whispered innuendos of undisclosed blood pacts and mortal curses, and as in most classical legends, this echoed the all too familiar fate of those who dared to fly too high by seeking unobtainable, forbidden knowledge. In the beginning, however, there was innocence.

In 1957, on a British television variety show, two young boys performed "Mama Don't Wanna Play No Skiffle No More." One of the guitarists was twelve-year-old James Patrick Page, who had just received his first guitar: "When I was at school, I had my guitar confiscated every day. They would hand it back to me each afternoon at four o'clock. I always thought the good thing about guitar was that they didn't teach it at school. Teaching myself to play was the first and most important part of my education."[1] Page, as well as many other British guitarists, had been inspired by Elvis Presley's "Baby, Let's Play House," but for the young musician who grew up with memories of his great uncle's pastoral manor farm combined with the family moving into the suburban shadows of London's Heathrow Airport, a musical career was not the foremost goal of his young dreams. According to the PBS *History of Rock and Roll* series, when the television host asked what

Jimmy Page's future would hold, the young guitarist answered shyly that he would like to become "a biotechnologist and work with germs." Page actually applied for the position of a lab technician, but his love of music would eventually lead him to the path of rock superstardom.

Jimmy Page first went on the road with Neil Christian and the Crusaders in the early 1960s. Even though he was still in school, Page talked his parents into giving him the opportunity to fully explore his musical dreams. However, after becoming ill and suffering from glandular fever from the hardships of the never-ending cycle of night clubs, Jimmy Page decided that he should return to school. He chose a major in art and put his guitar down for two years while he wielded an artist's paintbrush instead. But Page's reputation as a first-rate guitarist grew and it would not be long before he would pursue his vocation as a studio guitarist. Some critics have claimed that from 1963 until 1965, Jimmy Page performed on 50 percent to 90 percent of all recordings released in Britain in those years.[2] This was obviously an exaggeration, since the top session guitarist was Big Jim Sullivan. The number of sessions credited to Page is legendary. Was it Page who played on Van Morrison and Them's "Baby, Please Don't Go"? Did he perform on Donovan's "Sunshine Superman" and "Hurdy Gurdy Man"? Page remembers playing rhythm guitar on the Who's "I Can't Explain," but for some rock stars, crediting Jimmy Page with their recordings became a monumental clash of egos. The best case in point involves Ray Davies and the Kinks. It has long been rumored that Page had played the rhythm and lead guitar parts to "You Really Got Me" and "All Day and All of the Night." Davies contradicts this assumption, saying that Page only contributed a tambourine section to "You Really Got Me," and that Dave Davies, Ray's brother, performed the lead guitar solo while a disheartened Page frowned and squirmed throughout the playback. Professional jealousies helped add to the résumé of the budding superstar guitarist.

Jimmy Page's first real break came when he joined the Yardbirds. The Yardbirds were known for their incredible guitarists. Legendary alumni of the group include both Eric Clapton and Jeff Beck. At first, Page was a replacement for bassist Paul Samwell-Smith, but for a short time he shared some of the guitar duties with Beck. When the Yardbirds became victims of their own excesses, Page was left with the name but none of the original members. It was then that he recruited the musicians who would form Led Zeppelin and pave the way for the future of heavy metal. The New Yardbirds included Robert Plant on vocals, John "Bonzo" Bonham on drums, Page on guitar, and master musician and arranger John Paul Jones on bass and keyboards. It was during the fulfillment of the Yardbirds' final concert contracts that the Who's drummer, Keith Moon, informed Page that his new band would go over like a "fucking lead balloon." This inspired happenstance resulted in giving the band a fresh name that would undoubtedly reflect their creative energies. John Entwistle has always argued that he was the first to come up with the name Led Zeppelin, and that Keith Moon and Richard Cole, Zeppelin's future road manager, had taken his idea. He has also suggested that he formulated the concept of a blazing, crashing zeppelin for the album's cover design. Entwistle exclaimed that his band name was a takeoff on a British band joke. When one band asked another how they went over, the other band would state, "Cor, we went down like a lead zeppelin!"[3] The only seriously negative reaction to the name came from the Zeppelin family in Germany, the descendants of the creator of the zeppelin airship. It was touchy playing in Germany under the constant threat of a lawsuit.

The first Led Zeppelin album was released on January 12, 1968, three days before Page's twenty-fifth birthday. The Beatles owned the number-one spot with *The Beatles* ("The White Album"), but the *Led Zeppelin* LP, bolstered with 50,000 advance sales, started on *Billboard*'s charts at number ninety-nine and soared as high as number ten by May 17, 1968. The album would stay on the charts for an incredible seventy-three straight weeks.[4] The first American tour was remarkable. At times Zeppelin was only billed as "supporting act," but they blew more-established rock bands off the stage. No one wanted to follow the powerful aftermath of Led Zeppelin! The thunderous sounds of heavy British blues enthralled their audiences and helped establish Zeppelin as the future heirs to the mythical throne of rock and roll.

Following that, on October 22, 1969, Led Zeppelin struck gold again with the release of *Led Zeppelin II*. This album was certified gold on the day of its release, and probably more amazing, the first *Led Zeppelin* LP was still on the charts at number eighteen. Both albums were now certified million sellers, and with *Led Zeppelin II,* the band managed to replace the Beatles' *Abbey Road* as *Billboard*'s number-one bestselling LP. Surprisingly, Zeppelin fought against a single release of "Whole Lotta Love" due to the exclusion of the middle section for more conservative radio airplay. The band remained loyal to their music and fought against radio and market exploitation. Led Zeppelin had now arrived, and rock and roll would never be the same. Many rock superstars really didn't know how to explain the Zeppelin sound. Eric Clapton once stated, "I don't know about them. I've heard their records and I saw them play in Milwaukee—we were on the same bill. They were very loud—I thought it was unnecessarily loud. I liked some of it; I really did like some of it. But a lot of it was just too much. They overemphasized whatever point they were making, I thought."[5] This "overemphasis" would lead Zeppelin to experiment with different textured sounds, and on their third album they would depart from their established thunder to explore a light acoustic feel. For this many rock critics hammered

the band for leaving their established roots. Led Zeppelin, however, was a constantly changing entity, filled with creative power.

Surprisingly, to some onlookers, Led Zeppelin's meteoric
rise in prominence defied popular convention. Jimmy Page and
John Paul Jones were both highly respected session musicians.
Robert Plant and John Bonham, however, were relatively unknown performers. When Zeppelin went on tour, their offstage
escapades became legendary. The many groupies flocked to the
band as if some supernatural force drew them. There were tales of
television sets being cast from hotel windows, drinking binges,
fights, and strangely enough, sexual assault with a shark (though
Richard Cole in his *Stairway to Heaven: Led Zeppelin Uncensored*
denies that a shark was used—he claimed it was only a red snap-
per!). The seemingly magical power of fast success and adoring
women seemed to emulate the very legend of Robert Johnson.
Robert Plant and Jimmy Page were devoted to Johnson's music.
Some of the blues great's lyrics were actually "borrowed" and
placed in Zeppelin's songs. For example, the lyric "squeeze my
lemon till the juice runs down my leg" found in "The Lemon
Song" is drawn from Robert Johnson's "Traveling Riverside
Blues." Plant eerily tries to imitate Johnson's voice on "Bring It
On Home." In at least one interview there has been a suggestion
that Robert Plant has a glass container filled with the dirt from
the very crossroads where Robert Johnson sold his soul to the
devil. This mojo vial was said to have been given to Plant by an
American Led Zeppelin fan.

This juxtaposition of seasoned professional musicians mixed
with the pure, raw energy of youthful enthusiasm gave birth to the
Zeppelin sound. Hearsay spread throughout certain groups that
this newfound fame may have had as its origin the peculiar fascination and hobby of the band's founder, Jimmy Page. Some fans
who dabbled with the occult noticed Led Zeppelin's uncanny rise
in popularity and hinted that the band members, perhaps follow-

ing in the prominent footsteps of Robert Johnson, might have well
struck their own bargain with Lucifer. In some ways, this theory
may have been very close to the truth. One of the greatest legends
concerning Led Zeppelin has to do with a mythical pact with the
devil. This contract was said to have been drawn up in early 1968;
in it, the band members pledged to follow the left-hand path in exchange for musical success. Three of the members readily signed;
however, one refused. John Paul Jones was said to be the member
who declined the invitation. For that reason, he seemed to be un-
touched by the so-called Zeppelin curse that seemed to follow the
band in the mid-seventies. As one strange coincidence, when I
asked a friend to name the members of Led Zeppelin, he replied,
"Page, Plant, Bonham, and the other guy." Of course his take on
this after hearing about the legend was to rationalize that he
couldn't remember Jones's name because he hadn't signed the pact
and therefore fame had eluded him! Whatever!! In this case, superstitious fans, like my friend, could understand how Zeppelin exploded onto the music scene, very much like the reemergence of a
young Robert Johnson, filled with sinking despair, and spinning
haunting pentatonic riffs that hypnotically transfixed their audiences. Richard Cole recalled: "The most ominous rumor was ele-
vated to mythological status. It proclaimed that in their earliest
days, the band members—except for John Paul, who refused to
participate—had made a secret pact among themselves, selling
their souls to the devil in exchange for the band's enormous success. It was a blood ritual, so the story went, that placed a demonic
curse upon the band that would ultimately lead to the deflating of
the Zeppelin. And perhaps the death of the band members themselves. To my knowledge, no such pact ever existed. Jimmy was a
great one for spinning yarns, especially with young ladies who
were fascinated with the 'dark' side of the band, so maybe that's
how the story got started. But despite Jimmy's preoccupation with
the supernatural, he rarely discussed his dabbling in the occult

with the rest of the band. One of the roadies once said to me, 'I tried to broach the subject once, and Jimmy went into a rage. I'd never raise the issue again.'"[6]

The seventeenth-century concept of a pact with Satan followed guidelines much like these agreed to by Louis Gaufridi and the devil:

"I, Louis, a priest, renounce each and every one of the spiritual and corporal gifts which may accrue to me from God, from the Virgin, and from all the saints, and especially from my patron John the Baptist, and the apostles Peter and Paul and St. Francis. And to you, Lucifer, now before me, I give myself and all the good I may accomplish, except the returns from the sacrament in the cases where I may administer it; all of which I sign and attest."

On his side, Lucifer made the following agreement with Louis Gaufridi:

"I, Lucifer, bind myself to give you, Louis Gaufridi, priest, the faculty and power of bewitching by blowing with the mouth, all and any of the women and girls you may desire; in proof of all which I sign myself Lucifer."[7] This contract alludes to the fact that Lucifer actually appeared before the priest and signed the covenant. In the twentieth century any agreement would be symbolic and perhaps used only as a parlor trick, but the image of conjuring up the devil was very dark and frightening.

Jimmy Page was a serious collector of Aleister Crowley artifacts, and through his hobby he developed a deep appreciation for the practice of magic. Page once owned an occult bookstore, The Equinox, that dealt in Crowley memorabilia (the name was taken from Crowley's magazine that detailed his teachings, which was first published in 1909). It was also rumored that Page had financed the reprintings of Crowley's works. Richard Cole remembers driving Page from place to place on his Crowley shopping sprees: "'Richard, I'm in the mood to go shopping for some Crowley artifacts.' We'd drive from auction house to rare-book showrooms, where Jimmy would buy Crowley manuscripts or other belongings (hats, paintings, clothes). 'What is it about this chap Crowley that fascinates you?' I asked Jimmy on one of our outings. 'This guy was really quite remarkable,' Jimmy said. 'Someday we'll talk about it, Richard.' But we never did."[8] Pamela Des Barres, a former Page groupie, had once purchased an annotated Crowley manuscript for Page in Gilbert's Bookstore on Hollywood Boulevard in California. She remembers, "He was really into that stuff. I believe Jimmy was very into black magic and probably did a lot of rituals, candles, bat's blood, the whole thing. I believe he did that stuff. And of course the rumor that I've heard forever is that they all made a pact with the devil, Satan, the black powers, whatever, so that Zeppelin would be such a huge success. And the only one who didn't do it was John Paul Jones. He wouldn't do it. Who knows where the rumor came from? But that was the rumor."[9]

Pamela Des Barres's future husband, Michael Des Barres, also recounted his impressions of Jimmy Page's occult collection: "Jimmy was incredible because he was the classic rock star with the moated castle, the velvet clothes, the fabulous cars that he couldn't drive (Page never bothered to get a driver's license) and the eighty thousand rare guitars. And, like an idiot, I was dabbling with the Aleister Crowley thing at the time. I used to go down and see Jimmy at Plumpton Place and he'd pull out Crowley's robes, Crowley's tarot deck, all the Crowley gear that he'd collected. I thought, 'This is great!' It was so twisted and debauched, their whole thing. That's what Jimmy represented to me. I don't know what I represented to Jimmy. I always thought that Jimmy liked me because I happened to say 'Rimbaud' at the right time."[10]

During the late sixties, Jimmy Page met Kenneth Anger and listened intently as Anger told tales about the magical prowess of Aleister Crowley. Kenneth Anger first became aware of Jimmy Page when the guitarist outbid him for an original Crowley manuscript, *The Scented Garden,* at Sotheby's. When Anger first met with Page in Sussex, Page was delighted to bring out his Crowley memorabilia: the books, the canes, and especially the ceremonial robes of the black magician. Though Page was the consummate collector, there was one important piece missing from his collection—Aleister Crowley's manor at Boleskine, Scotland, on the dark shores of Loch Ness. (Anger had actually lived at Boleskine for a summer before Jimmy Page had acquired the residence.) The frightening legends that surrounded the estate scared off many would-be buyers, but Jimmy Page thought that the estate was perfect for his needs. Kenneth Anger told of a heavy painting that seemed to just float from one of the walls and sit silently on the floor. Anger turned to the other visitors in the house and asked if they had all witnessed this strange event. The spirits were now very restless.

Publicly, Jimmy Page prefers to keep quiet about what he rightfully considers his very private life, but one time Page spoke of his strange fascination with Aleister Crowley and his most unusual home. In a January 1975 interview with *Rolling Stone* magazine the interviewer asked, "You live in Aleister Crowley's home. Crowley was a poet and magician at the turn of the century and was notorious for his black magic rites." Page had this to say about his dark abode: "Yes, it was owned by Aleister Crowley. But there were two or three owners before Crowley moved into it. It was also a church that was burned to the ground with the congregation in it. And that's the site of the house. Strange things have happened in that house that had nothing to do with Crowley. The bad vibes were already there. A man was beheaded there and sometimes you can hear his head rolling down. I haven't actually heard it, but a friend of mine, who is extremely straight and doesn't know anything about anything like that at all, heard it. He thought it was the cats bungling about. I wasn't there at the time, but he told the help, 'Why don't you let the cats out at night?

They make a terrible racket, rolling about in the halls.' And they said, 'The cats are locked in a room every night.' Then they told him the story of the house. So that sort of thing was there before Crowley got there. Of course, after Crowley there have been suicides, people carted off to mental hospitals. . . ."

When *Rolling Stone* asked Page whether he had any contact with spirits, he simply stated, "I didn't say that. I just said I didn't hear the head roll." Curiously, the magazine asked about what Page's attraction would be to this house. Page answered that he loved the unknown and that he took the necessary precautions so that he wouldn't walk into things blind and unaware. Then the interviewer asked Page if he felt "safe in the house?" To that question Page replied, "Yeah. Well, all my houses are isolated. Many is the time I just stay home alone. I spend a lot of time near water. Crowley's house is in Loch Ness, Scotland. I have another house in Sussex, where I spend most of my time. It's quite near London. It's moated and terraces off into lakes. I mean, I could tell you things, but it might give people ideas. A few things have happened that would freak some people out, but I was surprised actually at how composed I was. I don't really want to go on about my personal beliefs or my involvement in magic. I'm not trying to do a Harrison or a Townshend. I'm not interested in turning anybody on to anybody that I'm turned on to . . . if people find things, they find them themselves. I'm a firm believer in that."

After purchasing Boleskine, Page had Satanist Charles Pierce redecorate the home with mystical symbols in the proper manner for the new Laird of Boleskine. The house obviously held many secrets. It was claimed that Crowley had misplaced his *Book of the Law* and that the work lay hidden for years in one of the darkened rooms. In the residence Crowley was said to have summoned forth demons such as Thoth and Horus. The house was constantly engulfed in dark shadowy shapes. Crowley once mentioned that the rooms became so dark in Boleskine House during the middle of a sunny day that he had to use artificial light to aid him in the drawing of his magical symbols. At this time, according to legend, the lodge keeper went insane and tried to murder his family. Of course today this would sound like the scene in the film adaptation of Stephen King's *The Shining* when Jack Torrance tries to kill his family when he becomes the overseer of the Overlook Hotel, only to find it to be a lodging filled with ghastly apparitions and the secret sins of excess and murder (or should I say *redrum*?). One of Boleskine's caretakers mentioned that Page would never spend the night in the dark house. On one occasion while the caretaker was sleeping in one of the rooms he heard a sound at his door. The heavy breathing on the other side of his bedroom door sounded like a large dog that wanted into the room. First, there was a sound like claws scraping at the door and then a thunderous impact rocked the door and reverberated throughout the house. The terrified caretaker stayed in bed and eagerly awaited the morning sunlight and the quietness that signaled the end of the supernatural attack. One thing was for sure. This was not the sound of cats playing in the antiquated hallway.

Obviously, Jimmy Page was well aware of the exploits of the past master of Boleskine. The shadows reflected along the walls may have represented the dark forces conjured up from the protection of the magic circle. In his journals, Crowley mentioned summoning demons to do his bidding. In one episode a powerful demon was invoked in the desert. When summoned the demon took control of Crowley's body and changed shape into that of a beautiful girl. When the demon started to speak of mystical secrets, Crowley's disciple, protected by the magic circle, took his eyes off the demon and started to write down the information. At this the demon threw sand across the circle and attacked the disciple with fangs and claws. It was only with the aid of a magic knife that the follower was able to drive back the entity and restore the circle." [11] When Crowley became conscious he claimed that his powers had been strengthened a thousand-fold. This was to be yet another of the continuing legends of Boleskine. When *Led Zeppelin III* was released, the first hint of Jimmy Page's eccentric pastime became known.

Led Zeppelin III was released on the Atlantic label on October 5, 1970. Over 70,000 advance orders were placed in the United States alone. Demonstrating the staying power of Zeppelin, *Led Zeppelin II* was still at number eighty-nine after fifty-two weeks on the charts. Other new releases that week included the Stones' *Get Yer Ya Ya's Out* and the second offering of the Allman Brothers Band, *Idlewild South.*[12] Strangely enough, the new creative vision of Zeppelin was condemned by most of the critics. Some critics accused the band of copying the Crosby, Stills, and Nash style of sweetly produced acoustic numbers. The Beatles had been praised for their innovative ideas with *Sgt. Pepper's,* but Page and Plant were criticized for breaking away from the heavy strains of heavy-metal anthems. Apparently, *Led Zeppelin III* became a statement focusing upon the duality of light and heavy, in many ways representing the very paradox of rock and roll itself.

The presence of Aleister Crowley can also be seen with the early pressings of *Led Zeppelin III*. If you look closely in the run-out grooves of the pressings, a very distinct "Do What Thou Wilt" can be seen. Some editions have the phrase on both sides, while later pressings have the slogan only on side two. Some early pressings contain the phrase "So Be It Mote." This slogan has been described as the binding spell upon the magician's incantation. But if the spell was to guarantee the financial success of the album, it was a failure.

Zeppelin album art had progressed from the burning Hindenburg dirigible to that of the "brown bomber" of *Led Zeppelin II*. Of course, the cover art of the second LP contained photos of the group superimposed upon the faces of a German zeppelin crew. If you look closely you can see Peter Grant's (Zeppelin manager) and Richard Cole's faces along with actress Glynis Johns and legendary bluesman Blind Willie Johnson.

Led Zeppelin III, however, required special treatment. The album cover was a tribute to psychedelia, complete with cutouts and spinning wheels. Unfortunately, there was a disconnect between the concept of the artist, whose name is given only as Zacron, and Jimmy Page's original concept: "It was intended to be something like one of those gardening calendars or the zoo-wheel things that tell you when to plant cauliflower or how long whales are pregnant. But there was a misunderstanding with the artist—who is very good in fact but hadn't been correctly briefed—and we ended up on top of a deadline with a teeny-bopperish cover which I think was a compromise." [13] Though the album contained brilliant music, the critics slammed it, and *Led Zeppelin III* left the charts after only thirty-one weeks. This would be the shortest time on the charts of any of the first five Zeppelin albums. If there was to be a hidden meaning in any of the song selections on the third album, perhaps it would be found in "Gallows Pole." This new musical treatment for the medieval ballad "The Maid Freed from the Gallows" suggests "The Hanged Man" from the tarot cards. "The Hanged Man" represents change and new direction. However, if this were the case, then the next album should have blazed itself into rock legendry.

For the recording environment needed for the production of the fourth Led Zeppelin album, a mobile unit was brought to Headly Grange, a two-hundred-year-old mansion. The mansion had served for some time as a Victorian workhouse. When the band members first arrived there was a chilling presence felt throughout the house. On one particular evening, Jimmy Page glimpsed a gray, ghostly figure at the top of the stairs. He was now convinced that the mansion was haunted, due in part to its terrible past filled with the stories of the suffering, neglected poor. Page also noticed that in his bedroom the sheets upon his bed always seemed to be wet. As far as Plant and Bonham were concerned, they felt very uneasy in the dark sequestered halls. After the recordings were made, however, Page commented that the place developed a lighter feel, as if the music helped purge away the darkness. Jimmy Page, Robert Plant, John Paul Jones, and John Bonham were convinced that their music should be allowed to stand alone. Obviously, there was little concern for the critics' views. For this reason, the fourth album was released untitled on November 8, 1971. Some fans refer to the album as *The Four Symbols* or simply enough, *Led Zeppelin IV.* Page exclaimed, "The music is what matters. Let people buy it because they like the music. I don't want anything on the cover! Period!" [14] Atlantic Records finally agreed to the band's terms. Jimmy Page had suggested that each member of the band create a specific symbol for the album art. Some critics claimed that these occult symbols were Icelandic runes and contained cryptic metaphysical meanings. Page said, "Robert's symbol is his own design—the feather, a symbol on which all sorts of philosophies have been based, and which has a very interesting heritage. For instance, it represents courage to many red Indian tribes." Plant himself finally elaborated, "My symbol was drawn from sacred symbols of the Mu civilization, which existed about 15,000 years ago as part of a lost continent somewhere in the Pacific Ocean between China and Mexico. All sorts of things can be tied in with the Mu civilization, even the Easter Island effigies. These Mu people left stone tablets with their symbols inscribed on them all over the place—in Mexico, Egypt, Ethiopia, India, China and other places. And they all date from the same period. The Chinese say that these people came from the East, and the Mexicans say they came from the West—obviously it was something in between. My particular symbol does have a further meaning, and all I can do is suggest that people look it up in a suitable reference book." [15]

Jimmy Page continued with a discussion of John Paul

Jones's symbol: "John Paul Jones's symbol, the second from the left, was found in a book about runes and was said to represent a person who is both confident and competent, because it was difficult to draw it properly." [16] Other individuals swear that the runic symbol is taken from a symbol found on a book detailing the beliefs of the Rosicrucians, another secret society that has been said to exist since the Middle Ages.

John "Bonzo" Bonham's locking three circles were described by Plant as being representative of the Trilogy—man, woman, and child: "I suspect it had something to do with the mainstay of all people's belief. At one point, though—in Pittsburgh, I think—we observed that it was also the emblem for Ballantine beer." [17] One of the band's acquaintances suggested that Bonham's symbol was actually the wet circular rings left on a bar by placing his beer bottles down in a pattern. After all, Jimmy Page had once claimed that John Bonham was the champion beer drinker in all of England.

The mysterious symbol of Jimmy Page has yet to be deciphered. Plant once claimed that Page told him the meaning, but now he has forgotten. The symbol became so dominant that many fans refer to the fourth album as *Zoso*. At one time or another fans have suggested that the symbol is in the shape of three sixes (666), the Bible and Crowley's infamous Mark of the Beast. This is unlikely. At least some fans have suggested that the name is from *Curious George,* the Monkey, also known as Zoso, from a popular children's book series. Other suggestions state that the symbol is taken from Cerberus, the guardian of the gates of hell, or that the Zoso symbol bears a striking resemblance to the alchemical symbol for mercury.

The most likely meaning is a symbol that crosses into the mystical world of metaphysics between the living and the dead. The term *Zoso* sounds very much like the name of the first pharaoh of Egypt, Zoser, in Egyptian lore. Zoser established the first dynasty and built the first step-pyramid. (In ancient Sumer the ziggurats, step pyramids, were used by priests to determine the will of the gods.) Early civilizations believed that the steps on these structures resembled a ladder where the gods could visit man from the heavens—in this case, the original "Stairway to Heaven." Page, however, claims that the symbol is not a pronounceable word, so perhaps the talisman is an enigma of man's search for ultimate knowledge. Perhaps that is why some individuals see a smiling face in the symbol, a friendly reminder of just how far we have yet to come. Some followers believe that the four symbols are placed in a magical order, with Page and Plant's outer symbols protecting the weaker inner emblems. This has been taken to suggest the creative powers within the band, as well as Plant's and Page's fascination with the occult and ancient Celtic mythology.

Page and Plant designed the cover for the fourth album. The old man carrying the sticks upon his back is said to represent complete harmony with the natural world. This is a nineteenth-century Romantic characteristic very representative of William Wordsworth's leech gatherer in "Resolution and Independence." Page explains, "The old man carrying the wood is in harmony with nature. He takes from nature but he gives back to the land. It's a natural cycle and it's right. His old cabin gets pulled down and they move him to those horrible urban slums, which are terrible places."[18] When the album jacket is opened the old man's picture is found to be hanging on a wall that may suggest the cycle of past, present, and future, or Shelley's theme of mutability in which "everything ripens and rots." The old man, like Wordsworth's leech gather, completes a cycle of unity with nature. They both take from the land, but through their respective deaths, they in turn decay slowly back into nature, becoming one again with the Universal Spirit. Curiously, to some onlookers the "old man" appeared to be somewhat hunchbacked. In Ida Grehan's *Irish Family Names,* the author presents a genesis of the family name Crowley. Crowley is derived from O Cruadhlaoich, which is translated as "hunched back." Perhaps this includes yet another reference to "the wickedest man alive."

Jimmy Page's friend artist Barrington Colby completed the album's inner drawing. This artwork was produced in pencil and gold paint and the work's original title is *View in Half or Varying Light*. Page had this to say about the symbolism of the work: "The Hermit is holding out the truth of and enlightenment to a young man at the foot of the hill. If you know the tarot cards, you'll know what the Hermit means. (The divinatory meaning of the Hermit is usually interpreted as a warning against proceeding on a given course without retirement and contemplation)." [19] In Romantic literature, especially in Wordsworth and Coleridge's works, the Hermit is seen as Rousseau's "noble savage," a being who is one with nature in a pantheistic relationship. For those of us who delight in hidden images, there is a belief that if you should hold a mirror perpendicular to the mountain the Hermit is standing upon in the Colby drawing, the mountain, through its reflection, becomes a black dog or dragon. And as far as another hidden cryptic message in the vinyl run-offs, you will notice two hidden encryptions: on side one in the run-off band you can see "porky" and side two, the term "pecko duck" can be seen—not exactly Crowley's *Book of the Law*!

The ultimate Crowley reference, however, lies not in the artwork but in the recording of the number-one rock song of all time—"Stairway to Heaven." "Stairway to Heaven" has been voted the all-time rock favorite of FM rock. It was revolutionary in that the song lasted almost eight minutes and commanded great devotion from rock radio. One station in Florida was so enamored with the song that it played it continuously over and over at least fifty times. But this promotion didn't work and the station was soon off the air. The structure of the song demonstrated the depth of Led Zeppelin's creativity. The first section is very light and melodic, building to a thunderous climax of searing guitar and crashing pounding drums. There has been no other song before or since that has managed to capture both the texture and raw energy of this rock masterpiece.

In the United States during the late 1970s and early 1980s, a movement was formed to question whether hidden messages existed in popular recordings. The number-one target of this investigation was Led Zeppelin's "Stairway to Heaven." Knowing Page's fascination with Aleister Crowley, some fans felt that "Black Dog" was actually an introduction to the dark side. John Paul Jones commented that the song received its name from a black dog that kept entering the studio during the recording session, so the song was then named in its honor. But rock fans who had been raised on conspiracy theory, from the Kennedy and King assassinations to the "Paul is dead" rumors, would not accept such a simple answer. Books on the occult suggested that religious prayers and hymns were often recited backward as a tribute to Satan and an affront to Christianity. With these as a guide, the word "Dog" can be seen as a reversal of "God." With this logic the song could serve as a salute to a "Black God," who would then be identified as Satan. Obviously, this had to be quite a stretch. The lyrics suggest more of Robert Plant's feelings about large, "big-legged" women than his devotion to a dark lord. But there may be something to the hidden message in "Stairway to Heaven."

The lyrics mention that there are "two paths you can go by" and that "there's still time to change the road you're on." To followers of the occult, this suggested "the left-hand and right-hand paths" of Satan and God, of evil and good. There is also mention of a piper that "leads us to reason." The piper, to some listeners, could be viewed as a symbol of Pan, the mythological god complete with horns and cloven hoofs. Was this another reference to Lucifer and Crowley? It was also common knowledge that Crowley had instructed that his own poem "Song to Pan" be read during his burial service as a final tribute to his pagan views. The

Crowley contribution may well be suggested by a reading of his *Magick in Theory and Practice.* Crowley states that if a magician wants to truly practice magic that "he must train himself to think backward by external means, as set forth here following, let him learn to write backward, let him learn to walk backward, let him constantly watch, if convenient, films and listen to records reversed."[20] This declaration may finally explain the true purpose of the infamous hidden message in "Stairway to Heaven" along with the Zeppelin lyric that reminds us that "sometimes words have two meanings." In this case, the meaning can be determined by listening to the vocal lyric forward and then backward, much in the way that Aleister Crowley may have intended.

The hidden message occurs in the verse that states, "If there's a bustle in your hedgerow, don't be alarmed now. It's just a spring clean for the May Queen." Many listeners have pondered what a "bustle in a hedgerow" means. The answer may lie in two explanations. First, the track is not a true backward mask. In a backward mask a recording is simply played backward. This is the case in many of the celebrated recordings said to contain hidden messages, which will be discussed later. The "Stairway to Heaven" track is actually created with a phonetic reversal. The "hidden" message could be recorded and then turned over. As the tape is heard backward, new lyrics could be composed with the same basic phonemes creating what may be considered as strange word play. The Beatles were able to experiment with this method in "Revolution 9." The phrase "number 9, number 9" when reversed sounded suspiciously like "turn me on, dead man." This was one of many "clues" that created the "Paul is dead" hysteria that swept the Western world. Starting with the verse that begins with "If there's a bustle in your hedgerow . . ." and carrying on until "and it makes me wonder," a hidden Satanic prayer is said to be heard. Personally, I have no problem picking up key phrases. The first phrase begins with "Here's to my sweet Satan. The one will be the sad one who makes me sad whose power is in Satan." This is very clear, except for with "Here's to . . ." some listeners instead hear a phrase that sounds more like "The Lord is my sweet Satan." There is little doubt that the lyric, when reversed, does sound like "my sweet Satan" and "the one will be the sad one who makes me sad whose power is in Satan." The next line is said to be either, "He'll be with you, Satan, Satan, Satan," or "He will give you 666." This section is not as clear to me. The last line sounds like "So follow him with worship, bring me yourself, my sad Satan." The "my sad Satan" is extremely clear, whereas the simple phrase before it may be open to interpretation. The chorus section "and it makes me wonder," which follows this verse, plainly says "I will sing because I live with Satan." The last vocal phrase states, "And she's buying a stairway to Heaven." As the phrase is reversed some listeners claim that a backward phrase states, "Play music backward, hear words sung." When you experiment listening to this section backward try not to do it late at night. But if you do—just remember, I warned you!

The second explanation for the "bustle in your hedgerow" was rumored to be a sexual innuendo for the female genitalia. The "spring clean for the May Queen" was said to be a reference to a young girl's coming of age with the start of her first menstrual cycle. Perhaps the listener should decide which explanation is the oddest.

The strange use of Led Zeppelin's occult references continued with the release of *Houses of the Holy* in March of 1973. The album art design depicted two fair-skinned, blond, naked children climbing the rocks to the top of some mysterious mountain. The cover photograph was taken by Aubrey Powell and is hinted to be based upon the science-fiction novel *Childhood's End*. The color separation had first made the children purple, but when corrected the color was transformed into an orange glow. When the album jacket is opened, an image of a man is seen. He is holding one of the children above his head in an almost sacrificial rite directly in front of a ruined citadel. The two children eerily bear a strange resemblance to Robert Plant's two children, Karac and Carmen. The strange irony in this photograph lies in the fact that Karac would die mysteriously within four years of the album's release. He was not quite one year of age when this album was produced.

The song lyrics also contained many occult allusions and were printed on the album's inner sleeve. "Walking side by side with death, the devil mocks their every step" from "No Quarter" would effectively serve as a chilling premonition of the terrible tragedies yet to befall the band. In "The Ocean" Plant supposedly sings, "Got a hellhound on my trail 'cause it's hell I'm headed for." Strangely enough, by invoking the Robert Johnson lyric, Robert Plant would be the first member of the band to be devastated by tragedy. Unfortunately, this is a misheard lyric and an urban legend. It plays very nicely with the Robert Johnson connection; however, the actual lyric is said to be, "Got a date, I can't be late, for the high hopes hailla ball."

A major turning point in Jimmy Page's studies in the occult came the next year in 1974, when he decided that he would produce the sound track for Kenneth Anger's *Lucifer Rising*. Page felt it an honor to work with someone who had such a great understanding of Crowley's works and concepts. Though Jimmy Page had taken the responsibility to write the sound track, he was very up-front with Anger about his time restrictions. Page allowed Anger to use the cellar of Boleskine for filming and his Tower House residence for an editing facility to develop his cinematic tribute to Lucifer. Page even provided a very expensive film-editing table and tried to convince Peter Grant to finance the venture. Since Mick Jagger had left the project, Kenneth Anger was greatly impressed with Page's creative energies using the violin bow and reverse echo to help capture the proper mood for his film. But as time passed, Anger became angry that Page had not spent more time in finishing the sound track. In all Page had written and recorded a twenty-eight-minute composition of strange sounds and chants. Anger, however, wanted more. When Page was unable to meet Anger's schedule, the filmmaker went to the press to shred the guitarist's reputation: "The selfishness and inconsideration were appalling. . . . It was like rapping on inch-thick glass. Jimmy had more or less turned into an undisciplined, rich dilettante, at least as far as magic and any serious belief in Aleister Crowley's work was concerned. Page has only composed twenty-eight minutes of music in three years' work on the project. The way he has been behaving is totally contradictory to the teachings of Crowley and the ethos of film." [21] Anger mentioned Crowley's use of cocaine and heroin and how his strong physical condition allowed him to use these in excess to increase his powers, commenting that Page "couldn't handle it." He then accused Jimmy Page of having an affair with "the white lady." This was a reference to what Anger suggested was an addiction to heroin. Anger was then said to have placed a curse upon Jimmy Page and the other members of Led Zeppelin.

Jimmy Page was forced to fight back. He told the *New Musical Express,* "I must start by saying that I've lost a hell of a lot of respect for Anger. This whole thing about 'Anger's curse'—it was just those silly letters [to Page's friends and associates]. . . . He's implying that he received nothing from me, which is totally untrue. I gave him everything in plenty of time. . . . Then one day this whole thing just blew up and that's all I know about it. . . . All I can say is: Anger's time was all that was needed to finish that film. Nothing else! I had a lot of respect for him. As an occultist he was definitely in the vanguard. I just don't know what he's playing at. I'm totally bemused and really disgusted. It's truly pathetic. He is powerless—totally. The only damage he can do is with his tongue." [22]

The traumatic break with Anger did little to change Page's

interest in the occult. He was once asked what famous historic figure he would most like to meet. His answer was Machiavelli, the author of *The Prince*. "He was a master of evil," Page stated. "But you can't ignore evil if you study the supernatural as I do. I have many books on the subject and I've also attended a number of séances. I want to go on studying it. Magic is very important if people can go through it. I think Aleister Crowley's completely relevant today. We're all still seeking for truth—the search goes on."[23] When asked his opinion of women, Page answered, "Crowley didn't have a very high opinion of women and I don't think he was wrong." He mentioned that his "creative direction is now and that at times when I hit it, it's just like I'm a vehicle for some greater force." Page also mentioned that he never thought he would live to the age of thirty and that time may well be running out. When he contemplated the band's future he predicted, "We'll be together until one of us punts out."[24] How little did he know that the first punt would come on September 25, 1980.

Eventually, Kenneth Anger went on to complete his epic film *Lucifer Rising* in 1980. The total production time was ten years (1970–1980), and the finished product was twenty-eight minutes in length. It was strange that the film should be the exact same length as Page's soundtrack, however, the musical score was contributed by Bobby Beausoleil and the Freedom Orchestra. The sound-track recordings were made behind the walls of Tracy Prison, where Beausoleil is serving a sentence of life imprisonment for his role in the Manson murders. The role of Lucifer was played by Leslie Huggins, Marianne Faithfull's role as Lilith was maintained, and Kenneth Anger played the role of the Magus. Anger claimed in a promotional release for his film, "I'm showing actual ceremonies in the film, not reenactments, and the purpose is to make Lucifer rise. Lucifer is the light god, not the devil—the Rebel Angel behind what is happening today. His message is that the key to joy is disobedience." Anger goes on to compare the dawning of the Age of Aquarius to the ritual incantations that bring about the summoning of Lucifer.

Incredible success, and not Anger's curse, seemed to follow Led Zeppelin as their next album, *Physical Graffiti,* was released in February of 1975. This album was a double set with a new collection of musical sounds. Standard rockers such as "Custard Pie" blazed along in traditional Zeppelin style, while "Kashmir" reflected the influences of the mysterious East. The album cover photo of a building on 97 St. Mark's Place in New York City, complete with open window cutouts, brought back memories of *Led Zeppelin III.* Through the windows the viewer can see a number of figures, including individual band members, Marilyn Monroe getting undressed, King Kong, Charles Atlas, Elizabeth Taylor, the Queen, Jerry Lee Lewis, Neil Armstrong, and of course, a zeppelin. Today, there is a used clothing store in the basement of this building entitled, appropriately enough, Physical Graffiti. At the time of the release of *Physical Graffiti,* Led Zeppelin had managed what no other band could accomplish in rock history—six albums on the charts at the same time!

Some listeners can identify occult references in the lyrics to "Houses of the Holy." Robert Plant sings, "Let the music be your master, won't you heed the master's call? Oh, Satan and man!" "In My Time of Dying" was a Zeppelin cover of an old spiritual that had also previously been redone by Bob Dylan. In the song, Robert Plant cries out "Oh, my Jesus" several times. This lyric line would haunt him a few years later. For music fans who enjoy diving into album symbolism, as Beatle fans did with *Abbey Road* in 1969, there is a strange coincidence on the cover that should be noted. The male figure sitting on the steps resembles John Bonham. He sits in front of two doors that to some fans with vivid imaginations represent the "two paths you can go by" from "Stairway to Heaven." The back of the album has the two doors presented again. One door is closed but radiating a bright light, while the other door is opened to a darkened hallway. Does this represent the contradicting choices of light and shadow? Of good and evil? It would appear that Bonham is the one to make the choice. Strangely, he was to be the first to enter into one of the metaphysical paths.

The release of *Physical Graffiti* also launched the Led Zeppelin label, Swan Song. The concept of having their own label came up when their contract with Atlantic Records expired. Early names for the label included Slut, Slag, Superhype, and Eclipse. Finally the name Swan Song was agreed upon. First, however, some insiders objected to the name because it sounded so grim. After all, a swan song concerns the last beautiful sound a swan makes shortly before its death. Page thought that if Zeppelin were to die then they should go out still producing incredible music. The artwork for the Swan Song label is based on a canvas painting by William Rimmer entitled *Evening Fall of Day.* The beautiful winged male is the Greek sun god Apollo. Rumors have persisted that the figure is Icarus, the son of Daedalus, creator of the Minoan labyrinth. According to legend, Icarus disobeys his father and flies too close to the sun. The sun's heat melts the wax that holds his wings together and Icarus tragically plummets to his untimely death. Crowley-like, this figure may represent the concept that "the key of joy is disobedience." Others may feel that this angelic figure is representative of Lucifer being cast from Heaven. Led Zeppelin signed acts such as Bad Company and the Pretty Things to their new label and would throw lavish parties to celebrate each new release. Band manager Richard Cole stated, "Upon the release of Swan Song's first album in the U.K.—the Pretty Things' *Silk Torpedo*—Zeppelin hosted a Halloween party at Castlehurst Caves. There was enough food and booze (mostly wine) to meet the needs of the entire British army. . . . Much more eye-catching were the topless and, in some cases, fully naked women who mingled among the guests and rolled around in vats of Cherry Jell-O. Other nude women played the parts of virgins being sacrificed at makeshift altars. Strippers arrived dressed as nuns and peeled off their habits in an act that, if the Vatican were making the decisions, would have doomed us to an eternity in hell."[25] The Halloween party described by Cole seemed to be taken out of a chapter of the Hellfire Club's ritual meetings of the Unholy Thirteen.

After the Montreux Jazz Festival in July of 1975, the group went their separate ways on vacation. It was also at this time that Zeppelin's incredible luck seemed to begin to run out and it was finally time to pay the piper his terrible due. On August 4, Robert Plant, his wife, Maureen, their two children and Jimmy Page's daughter, Scarlet, were in Rhodes for vacation when Maureen lost control of a rental car and had a horrible accident. At first Plant was convinced his wife was dead. Fortunately, this was not the case, but she was badly injured. Robert Plant also received serious injuries. His ankle and elbow were broken. His children were also injured seriously, but Scarlet Page was uninjured. (Plant once said that while the accident was occurring that all he could hear was the chant from "In My Time of Dying" in which he sang, "Jesus, oh my Jesus.") Road manager Richard Cole immediately flew to Rhodes in a private plane, loaded the family into a rented car, and personally flew them to Rome. Cole had managed to bring fresh blood for Maureen and made sure that she was given a transfusion en route to the airport. Robert Plant is convinced that this particular action saved Maureen Plant's life. Some followers of "the Zeppelin Curse" maintain that the safety of Scarlet Page was due to the close relationship between Jimmy Page and the devil. Another rumor suggested that Page had named his daughter in honor of Crowley's scarlet women. Of course this was utterly ridiculous, but it seemed to start a pattern of strange coincidences. One such coincidence concerned Page's absence the day of the auto accident. He had gone to Sicily to check on some property that had once belonged to Aleister Crowley. The Crowley fascination continued to lead Page in search of more memorabilia, and to visit exotic locations that were of particular interest to Crowley. One location included Egypt, where Crowley had been inspired to write *The Book of the Law.* During a three-week break following an earlier U.S. tour, Page made one of his pilgrimages to Egypt. On a return flight to England, John Bonham asked Richard Cole, "Do you know the reason Jimmy is taking Mick [one of the crew] and not you to Egypt? He knows that if he decides to sacrifice someone, he'd find it a lot harder to do away with you than Mick!" [26]

After the accident, Robert Plant was confined to a wheelchair. It was also during this time that the writing and recording of *Presence* took place. The album was released on March 31, 1976. The album's cover contains a strange monolith that seems to fit in extremely well in several scenes taken from modern twentieth-century culture. The album opens with "Achilles' Last Stand." The tightly multitracked guitar lines and hard-driving rhythms showcased Zeppelin at its best. Plant sang the lyrics from his wheelchair, and with his broken ankle he resembled the Greek mythological hero Achilles. With the completion of this album, and time for Plant to fully heal from his injuries, Led Zeppelin was ready to turn their full attention to producing their own concert documentary on film. It would be called *The Song Remains the Same.*

The film's concept was more like the Beatles' *A Hard Day's Night* and *Help* than a rock documentary along the lines of *Woodstock.* At times the filmed sequences drift into a mystical stream of consciousness. The concert sequences were shot at New York's Madison Square Garden in July of 1973.

As the film opens, the audience sees Peter Grant and Richard Cole dressed in early 1930s gangster attire. This scene is straight out of *Little Caesar,* when the two confederates machine-gun a house in a drive-by shooting. There is one scene in which a faceless man is machine-gunned over a table filled with money and other valuable items. Perhaps this was a reference to the many critics who predicted that Zeppelin would have a very short flight. In the next section of the film, Led Zeppelin band members would each make their appearances: Robert Plant, his wife, Maureen, and children Carmen and Karac make their film appearance by a running stream. As the naked children innocently play in the cool water their images bring to mind the fair-haired children from *Houses of the Holy.* Ironically, that album image, showing one child being held aloft, perhaps in some strange sacrificial offering, foreshadowed the terrible tragedy that would await an unknowing Robert Plant. Also in the film, John Paul Jones is first seen reading "Jack and the Beanstalk" to his children. Their eyes are wide in wonder as Jones emulates the deep voice of the Giant. John Bonham appears serenely driving a farm tractor in his role as a gentleman farmer. Jimmy Page makes the last appearance, sitting in a garden at Boleskine House on a bright sunny day. His acoustic guitar is lying near him and he plays the hurdy-gurdy. Strangely, he sits with his back to the camera. When he turns, his eyes seem to reflect a demonic presence of the very fires of hell itself. In a strange way, I can hear Mia Farrow's voice from *Rosemary's Baby* when she sees her newborn baby for the first time and says over and over again, "What have you done to his eyes?" The head Satanist replies, "He has his father's [Satan's] eyes!" Also, a line from Edgar Allan Poe's "The Raven" has a certain relevance: "And the bird has all the seeming of a demon that is dreaming." The sight of Page's blazing red eyes combined with the strange sounds of the hurdy-gurdy provides a chilling cinematic memory.

The Song Remains the Same also contains a series of dream-like sequences that involve each band member. In John Paul Jones's segment, a group of masked men rides through what appears to be an eighteenth-century countryside. The scene invokes terror due to the reaction of the people to the dark riders. The scene is filmed at night and one major scene involves a graveyard. When one of the masked men, Jones, returns home, he removes his mask and his family greets him as if he is only returning from a busy day at the office. This portion of the film is reminiscent of the British Hellfire Clubs in which upstanding leaders of the community by day secretly met at night and indulged their many lusts. Perhaps this is Jones's answer to his double life as bassist for Led Zeppelin. Film director Joe Massot recalls the scene: "John Paul Jones decided to do an allegorical and symbolic horror tale about how one man and a bunch of masked riders terrify villagers, rape women, and act horribly. Eventually the man returns home on his horse expecting the continuation of the violence. But when he gets there, he takes off his mask and settles down peacefully with his wife and family—completely the opposite of what you've anticipated." [27] Interestingly, Jones had tried to gain permission from Disney Films to include the night rider scenes from *Doctor Sin,* but Disney had refused and Jones was forced to shoot his own scene.

Robert Plant's film sequence occurs during the band's performance of "The Song Remains the Same." In his dreamlike sequence, Plant becomes a medieval hero in search of a quest. He is filmed sailing in a ship with medieval banners and threshing oars to an unknown shoreline, perhaps to the very fabled shores of Albion. When he reaches the end of his journey he is met by a lady, his wife, Maureen, who presents him with a sword to right all wrong. After he prepares himself for battle, he attacks a castle ruin and frees a damsel in distress, only to have her vanish as in a dreamlike idyll. This short section pays homage to Robert Plant's insatiable love of mythology, and strongly resembles an Arthurian legend. Director Joe Massot's explanation of the sequence is that "Robert Plant decided to do a Welsh legend with a character perhaps similar to King Arthur. He overcomes all of his adversaries with the sword given him by a fair young lady. The deed done, he returns to the lady, who rewards him with gold. Then he leaves her and he's on his own again. Robert felt it was really him, and that he is on his own and alone. Robert wrote the story himself and there is dueling, horses, castles, green glades, the whole works." [28]

The strangest film segment deals with Jimmy Page's re-creation of the *Led Zeppelin IV* cover art, Barrington Colby's *View in Half or Varying Light*. Page becomes the young seeker of wisdom who climbs the mountain to find the unknown secrets held by the hermit of the tarot cards. When Page reaches the top, he finds that the hermit is actually himself and watches his regression from an ancient man into a fetus in his mother's womb, and back yet again to the aged hermit. The filming for this piece began on December 10, 1973. Page had the sequence filmed at Loch Ness, close to his home at Boleskine in Scotland. Of course, he had to wait for a full moon to complete the imagery, but the finished portion conveys an uneasy mood in light and shadow. Curiously, the filming occurred shortly between Crowley's Greater Feast (the date of Crowley's death, December 1) and the beginning of the winter solstice (December 21 or 22). "Jimmy's film was rather strange," says Mosset, in an avalanche of understatement. "Jimmy felt that he wanted to say something about time and the passage thereof. There's a mountain out the back of his place, Boleskine House, on the shores of Loch Ness in Scotland. So Jimmy decided that he would climb it and act out a symbolic tale about a young man fighting his way to the top to meet with the old man of the mountain at the summit, Father Time in symbolism. Jimmy plays both parts in the film. He insisted that his segment be shot on the night of a full moon. It was quite difficult lighting the mountain at night—we actually had to build special scaffolds on the side of it to put cameras on and mount arc lamps. It was a weekend and overtime for the crew but Jimmy wanted it to be right."[29]

In John Bonham's segment, the drummer skips the occult references and drag races in his hot rod around town. "John Bonham chose to be real, simply himself," says Massot. "He's sort of a teddy boy—playing snooker, riding hot rods, a whole exercise in energy and power. He drives a nitrogen-fueled dragster at 240 mph on a quarter-mile track [Bonzo was filmed at Santa Pod Raceway at the controls of an AA Fueler]. The sequence ties in nicely with his drum solo which is pure power and energy."[30] There is also a scene in which he practices his drums next to his young son, Jason, who has a matching scaled-down drum set just like his father. The interacting of all three film sequences helps create an atmosphere of illusion that drifts back and forth to the crashing sounds of Led Zeppelin in concert. At times it becomes difficult to determine the difference between reality and filmed fantasy. In a tragic foreshadowing, this tender scene between a father and son reinforces the terrible tragedy that will soon shake Led Zeppelin to its very core.

The Song Remains the Same was released on September 28, 1976. Within the next year tragedy would once again strike Robert Plant. During the American tour of 1977, Plant received an emergency phone call at his hotel in New Orleans. The call was placed by his wife and the news was almost beyond belief. When Plant returned to join his friends after a two-hour phone conversation, he announced that his young son, Karac, had just died. Karac was five years old at the time and can be seen innocently playing in a mountain stream in *The Song Remains the Same*. Plant had named his son after a great Celtic warrior, Caractacus. Caractacus waged a fierce war against the Roman invasion of Britannica in A.D. 43. When Caractacus was finally captured by the Roman legions and returned to Rome, the emperor Clau-

dius was so impressed with the hero's bravery that the captive warrior's life was spared. However, Robert Plant later stated that he
and his wife also referred to their infant son as "Baby Austin, after
that Bionic Man. He knows no fear, has no anticipation of danger. I envy him."[31] It seemed that Karac Plant had contracted a
respiratory infection the morning of July 26, 1977. His condition
worsened and an ambulance was called to take the child to the
hospital, but Karac died on the way. Doctors called the infection
"strange" and "extremely rare." Plant was devastated, as any father
would be. He stated, "All this success and fame, what's it worth?
It doesn't mean very much when you compare it to love of a
family."[32]

Plant immediately flew home and the remainder of the tour
was canceled. The funeral was held one week later, but Richard
Cole says that he and John Bonham were the only two Zeppelin
insiders in attendance. When Plant asked where Page, Jones, and
Grant were, Cole answered that maybe they were uneasy about
death and funerals. Plant replied, "Maybe they don't have as
much respect for me as I have for them. . . . Maybe they are not
the friends that I thought they were."[33] Plant then asked, "Why
do these terrible things keep happening? What the hell is going
on?" The press also seemed to have the same questions, and in the
tabloids the Zeppelin Curse made front-page news. Early fans recalled the rumors of a secret pact with Satan. Was this the pay-
back? Had Kenneth Anger's curse finally caught up with the
band? Critics blamed the misfortune on bad karma, and Jimmy
Page was forced to answer: "It's [karma] just the wrong term to
ever use, and how somebody could write that down, knowing the
full facts about what has happened, I don't know. It shocks me.
The whole concept of the band is entertainment. I don't see any
link between that and karma, and yet I've seen it written a few
times about us, like 'yet another incident in Zeppelin's karma—
John Paul Jones has a broken hand.' It's nonsense—that was years

back. It's all crap. This thing about karma really bothers me. Where's the clue? Why are they using that term? It's a horrible, tasteless thing to say." [34] A disc jockey from Detroit claimed that "If Jimmy Page would just lay off all that mystical, hocus-pocus occult stuff, and stop unleashing all those evil forces, Led Zeppelin could just concentrate on making music." [35] The press recalled Page's infamous sorcerer's suit that he wore in *The Song Remains the Same* and how he immediately flew to Egypt after interpreting a zeppelin flying over the pyramids as some mystic sign. Robert Plant was rumored to have blamed his son's death on Page's fascination with the occult. Only it was Plant who paid the demon's monstrous debt. If Plant had his doubts, he never acknowledged them publicly. Page again answered angrily: "The people who say things like that don't know what in the hell they are talking about. And Robert sure doesn't need to hear that kind of crap. A lot of negative things have occurred recently, but tragedies happen. Why do they have to have to make it worse by talking that way? Why don't they let Robert mourn in peace?" [36]

The death of Karac served only as a tragic prologue to the bizarre events that would follow. The following month, August 16, 1977, Elvis Presley died. Led Zeppelin had always considered Presley one of their main inspirations. (Presley and Zeppelin had actually met once, and Elvis wanted to know everything about the wild rumors connected with Led Zeppelin on the road.) The next month, September, while returning home from a pub, John Bonham suffered two broken ribs in a car accident. For the next year things became quiet while Plant mourned in seclusion with his family, but in September of 1978, Zeppelin friend Keith Moon of the Who died from an overdose of a medication prescribed to help him stop drinking. So within a year, an influence on the group (Presley) and the individual who was claimed to name the group (Moon) were both dead.

It was two years before Zeppelin began recording *In*

Through the Out Door. The album was released on August 15, 1979, ironically one day before the second anniversary of Elvis Presley's death as well as the sixty-first anniversary of Robert Johnson's death. The album's artwork was designed in a series of six shots. The bar scene resembles a Caribbean bar, and to some onlookers the man in the white suit burning a small slip of paper bears an uncanny resemblance to Jimmy Page. Each album was placed in a shrink-wrapped paper bag so that the buyer could not tell which artwork it contained. The albums are numbered on their spines with the letters *A* to *F.* (Some of the original vinyl recordings contain the term "strawberry" inscribed into the run-off grooves.) Each of the six photos reveals a different perspective of the bar as seen by a different onlooker. As a final touch, if the album jacket came into contact with warm water, it supposedly changed colors. The recording contained some brilliant work, such as the beautifully moving "All of My Love" composed by John Paul Jones and Robert Plant. Side one, however, begins with the haunting, discordant sounds of "In the Evening." Some of these musical passages were inspired by musical themes left over from Page's *Lucifer Rising* sound track. The release of the new album brought the group members attention on the promotional tour. It had now been over two years since the band had toured America in concert. A few concert dates in England seemed to rekindle the creative spark within the band. They all felt as if they had been reborn. Rehearsals were scheduled, and for yet another time, the possibility of the Led Zeppelin jinx would once again make headlines throughout the world.

On September 24, 1980, drummer John Bonham was chauffeured down to Jimmy Page's new Windsor mansion, the Mill House. He had purchased the estate from British actor Michael Caine for £1 million. On the way to the rehearsals, Bonham stopped in a pub and drank an estimated four quadruple vodkas. When he arrived at Page's new home he continued to drink, downing two or three large drinks. He then attended a reunion party hosted by Page and continued to drink at least a couple of larger drinks each hour. He passed out on a couch at midnight, and Zeppelin associate Rick Hobbs helped a very intoxicated Bonham to a bedroom. Hobbs placed Bonham on his side and left him alone to sleep it off. When Bonham had not made an appearance by midafternoon, Robert Plant's assistant Benji LeFevre went in to wake him. After shaking Bonham, LeFevre noticed the body was blue and cold. An ambulance was called and the ambulance crew worked diligently to resuscitate John Bonham, but it was to no avail, and John "Bonzo" Bonham was dead at the age of thirty-one.

With the announcement of Bonham's death the rumors of the Zeppelin Curse again took precedence at the newsstands. One fan claimed to have seen thick black smoke coming from Page's home the night Bonham died. Other fans swore that Page had spoken in strange, unknown languages. Another rumor made the rounds concerning the existence of a Zeppelin "Black Album." This mysterious recording was said to contain death chants translated by a German writer from Old Swabian. Also, "The *London Evening News* headlined 'Zeppelin "Black Magic" Mystery.' An unnamed source close to the group commented, 'It sounds crazy, but Robert Plant and everyone around the band is convinced that Jimmy's dabbling in black magic is responsible in some way for Bonzo's death and for all those other tragedies . . . I think the three remaining members of Zeppelin are now a little afraid of what is going to happen next.'" [37]

John Bonham's death was declared an accident after the coroner had determined that the drummer had consumed forty measures of vodka in a twelve-hour period. The body was cremated within a few days of his death and a memorial service was held for him on October 10, at Rushock parish church. Ironically, the funeral service was only two days before Crowleymas, the occult celebration of the birth of Aleister Crowley! All the surviving band members attended Bonham's funeral. Within a few weeks it was determined by a unanimous decision that Led Zeppelin would be no more. In 1982, a few outtakes and some unreleased recordings were made available. The album title was *Coda.* This was to prove appropriate, since in musical compositions a coda is the closing section of a song or movement. The black discs on the cover are said to represent records. Others believe that the circular objects are actually mystical crop circles. (If this is the case, then it would foreshadow the release of the four-CD box set with its crop circles theme.)

Plant, Page, and Jones went their separate ways and recorded their own solo projects. Page joined the Firm and later teamed with former Whitesnake vocalist David Coverdale. Plant recorded a number of successful solo albums, and if you look at the album jacket credits, on certain cuts you can see the Zoso symbol representing a Jimmy Page contribution. John Paul Jones retired to the studios and became a very successful writer and producer. Of course there were to be continued rumors of Zeppelin reunions throughout the years that followed. Some reports suggested that Jason Bonham would take his father's place within the band. When Led Zeppelin performed at the Atlantic Records anniversary shows, Jason Bonham took his father's place as the band ran through several of their classic hits. Yet, that year also ended with the cold realization that Zeppelin would fly no more.

The next few years saw the release of the *Led Zeppelin* box set in 1990. A large number of Zeppelin hits had been digitally remastered. The cover art portrayed a zeppelin flying over a field marked with crop circles. There is a series of numbers included in the corners of the album jacket. The numbers are: 54 (which happens to be the exact number of tracks contained in the set); 69 (the year of the first Zeppelin release); 79 (the year that the last studio album was recorded; and ∞ (the mathematical symbol of infinity, representing how long the music will last).

Since everyone had thought that the collaboration between Page and Plant was over, and that Plant was still upset over the rumors of Page's occult dealings, the music world was suitably stunned when Jimmy Page and Robert Plant announced that they would re-form a new group and continue onward. (Curiously, John Paul Jones was left out, and Jones made it known publicly when Led Zeppelin was inducted into the Rock and Roll Hall of Fame.) The new Zeppelin project was simply called *Unledded*. This recording had a number of Zeppelin songs that were performed with acoustic instruments. It was now perceived that the jinx was over, and that Plant and Page had made up and would continue to write new material. It was also believed that Page had ended his interest in the occult. However, when the date for a live broadcast was announced, viewers couldn't help but notice its significance. Ironically, it occurred on the night of October 12, 1994, the date of Crowleymas and the 119th anniversary of the birth of Aleister Crowley!

In 1998, Plant and Page released *Walking into Clarksdale*. While in concert in Memphis, Tennessee, Plant told the audience, "It all began just over one hundred miles from here." Of course he was referring to Clarksdale, Mississippi, one of the birthplaces of the blues. Page and Plant also made their way to a private collector who was said to have a film lasting only a minute or so showing Robert Johnson performing. The filmed musician was not Robert Johnson, however.

Today, four years later, many fans wonder if the title *Walking into Clarksdale* was a celebration of Page and Plant's blues background and a reference to the influence of Robert Johnson, or a subtle reminder of musicians in two different times who made a pact for fame and fortune. To those onlookers, it would appear that indeed, "The Song Remains the Same"!

7. "WELCOME TO THE HOTEL CALIFORNIA"

You can check out anytime you like, but you can never leave.
  —The Eagles, "Hotel California"

Satan has been the best friend the Church has ever had, as he has kept it in business!
  —Anton LaVey, *The Satanic Bible*

Rock has always been the Devil's music. You can't convince me that it isn't.
  —David Bowie, *Rolling Stone*, February 12, 1996, p. 83

IN THE LATE 1970S, MANY PARENTS GROUPS BEGAN TO COMPLAIN about "backward maskings" and occult references in rock recordings. Rock groups of the late 1960s and 1970s performed Gothic sets of music included with album art that seemed to come out of Hammer Films. When did pretense end and reality begin? One of the first groups who created headlines by using occult references was Black Sabbath, fronted by Ozzy Osbourne. Many followers at first believed that the group took its name from a witches' gathering, when in reality they took their name from the 1963 horror film that starred Boris Karloff. The song lyrics hinted at occult references, and at some shows the band performed in front of a cross that was turned upside down and exploded into yet another Satanic symbol. Throughout his career, charges of following the dark side have haunted Osbourne. To his credit Ozzy Osbourne has appeared on many talk shows explaining that he is far from a Satanist and that his shows include only elements of the theater. Osbourne has also made the statement that the closest Black Sabbath got to black magic was in opening a box of black magic chocolate. In yet another interview he was asked if the name Black Sabbath implied the group's devotion to the occult. Ozzy's answer was, "The Rolling Stones don't cause avalanches."

Black Sabbath has had some strange supernatural happenings in their history. Terry "Geezer" Butler, the bassist, is the band's resident psychic. In dreams of precognition, Butler would often have visions that would many times come true. To better understand his abilities, Butler began researching the occult. It was in the 1970s, and Ozzy gave Geezer a four-hundred-year-old handwritten book on witchcraft and the occult. After he received the antiquated book strange things began happening in Butler's home. The first night he brought the book home, a black cat was said to have appeared in front of him and then simply disappeared. Butler was convinced that what he had just witnessed was an apparition. At this time his studies in the occult lessened significantly.

During the making of the *Sabbath Bloody Sabbath* album, the band stayed in a medieval castle to do some recording and play a concert. One night Ozzy fell asleep in one of the rooms and a burning coal fell from the fireplace and started a fire in the room. Ozzy awoke in the smoke-filled bedroom and made his way to safety just in time. The band left the castle shortly after this episode.

In the United States during the same time period, rumors surfaced that the Ohio rock group Cheap Trick was led to its name by consulting an Ouija board. Theatrical rocker Vincent Furnier was also said to have chosen the name Alice Cooper as a stage name after conferring with an Ouija board. This urban legend states that Furnier was in contact with a seventeenth-century witch who was condemned and executed for witchcraft. After he had become the father of shock-rock, Alice Cooper's performances ghoulishly contained scenes with him being hanged and later beheaded upon a guillotine as the crowd roared its enthusiastic approval.

It was also during this time period that comedian Flip Wilson coined a phrase that places all our faults and failures upon the proper guilty party: "The devil made me do it!" In 1966, Anton Szandor LaVey, a former assistant lion tamer with the Clyde Beatty Circus, began his Church of Satan in San Francisco, California. LaVey chose the night of April 30, 1966, as the birth of his "Magic Circle." Symbolically, the night of April 30 (Walpurgisnacht) is the witches' sabbath celebrating the spring equinox. Since this sabbath is very close to Easter it is rumored to be a night when all evil forces are at the height of their powers. It is ironic that April 30 is also the date of Adolf Hitler's suicide in his bunker in 1945. Perhaps it is only appropriate that Hitler, who had a keen interest in the occult, died on the very night when demonic forces were to be given full sway. (Then again, it may represent another coincidence that the name LaVey sounds very similar that of Eliphas Levi.) LaVey proclaimed the year of the birth of his church as the Age of Fire and *Annus Satanas*—the first year of the reign of Satan.[1] The so-called Black Pope was born Howard Stanton Levey on April 11, 1930, in Chicago, Illinois. As Aleister Crowley was defined by his enemies, so LaVey defined himself. Stangely enough, he was called "the evilest man in the world," in contrast to Crowley, "the wickedest man alive." Much of LaVey's biography has now been discredited, and it would appear that his whole life has become an urban legend within itself. For instance, Anton LaVey died on October 29, 1997, yet his death announcement was altered to give the date as October 31, 1997. Employment records with the Clyde Beatty Circuses and the San Francisco Police Department also differ greatly from the Anton LaVey published biography. However, Halloween would be the most appropriate time for the death of such a dark force as LaVey.

LaVey was a flamboyant leader who appealed to many of the entertainment figures in Hollywood. It has been rumored that Sammy Davis Jr., Keenan Wynn, Jayne Mansfield, Marilyn Monroe, and singer Marilyn Manson were all linked at one time or another with LaVey. (Some sources claimed that LaVey was involved with Marilyn Monroe in her early years in Hollywood, but this apparently has been discredited by those close to Monroe.) Anton LaVey's teachings detail a lifetime's celebration of total excess. According to the Church of Satan's promotional literature, "The Church of Satan is an eclectic body that traces its origin to many sources—classical voodoo, the Hellfire Club of eighteenth-century England, the ritual magic of Aleister Crowley, and the Black Order of Germany in the 1920s and 1930s. It departs from its predecessors by (1) its organization into a church, and (2) the openness of its magical endeavors." In 1969, Anton LaVey released his teachings through the publication of *The Satanic Bible*. The Black Pope contends that there are nine Satanic statements:

1. Satan represents indulgence, instead of abstinence!
2. Satan represents vital existence, instead of spiritual pipe dreams!
3. Satan represents undefiled wisdom, instead of hypocritical self-deceit!
4. Satan represents kindness to those who deserve it, instead of love wasted on ingrates!
5. Satan represents vengeance, instead of turning the other cheek!
6. Satan represents responsibility to the responsible, instead of concern for psychic vampires!
7. Satan represents man as just another animal, sometimes better, more often worse than those that walk on all fours, who, because of his "divine spiritual and intellectual development," has become the most vicious animal of all!
8. Satan represents all of the so-called sins, as they all lead to physical, mental, or emotional gratifications!
9. Satan has been the best friend the Church has ever had, as he has kept it in business all these years![2]

Each of these supposed virtues represents smashing the weak and following the doctrine of Social Darwinism, the survival of the fittest. It seemed that LaVey's purpose was to establish an organization for "nonjoiners." This fellowship would have weekly meetings and rituals and take the name of the original rebel, Satan, as their patron. To the Satanist, his religion is but an enlightened carryover from the humanistic teachings of the Renaissance. In Blanche Barton's *The Secret Life of a Satanist*, Anton LaVey states, "We don't worship Satan, we worship ourselves using the metaphorical representation of the qualities of Satan. Satan is the name used by Judeo-Christians for that force of individuality and pride within us."

According to his biographers, LaVey, while working with the Clyde Beatty Circus, noticed the circus's male customers eyeing the dancing girls on Saturday night during circus performances, only to watch them come reverently to the Sunday church services with their families the next morning. Anton LaVey played the organ at those services and became convinced of the hypocrisy of man, an indictment of modern religion. Obviously, he must have smiled with delight as "crying ministers" confessed to extramarital affairs with prostitutes, and television ministries crumbled due to fraud and deceit. Yes, Satan is very much alive and well and with us today!

Given his background in the circus, it would be only natural for Anton LaVey to become a great carnival pitchman. Instead of showing bearded ladies and men with two faces, LaVey would offer up naked women lying upon his living altar. Dressed in a costume complete with miniature horns, LaVey would offer up (down?) praises to his infernal lord. There were hints of drugs, sex, and other indescribable behaviors taking place in his grotto (the official name for each licensed church). It appears that the more outrageous the charges, the more publicity the self-named Black Pope received. In the late 1960s, LaVey appeared, complete with shaven head and costume, in newspapers, magazines, and television. It was also at this time that LaVey flashed "the sign of the horns." The sign is made by holding up the little and index fingers of the left hand. The thumb holds the ring and middle fingers down. In Satanic terms this supposedly is a symbol of denying the three (the Holy Trinity) and raising the two (Satan and the Anti-Christ).

I must admit that when Richard Dawson was host of the *Family Feud* television game show and at every show's conclusion raised his hand in what appeared to be the same gesture, I thought to myself, What if? Of course, with the thumb extended it becomes sign language for "I love you." What a strange parallel! This newfound publicity brought LaVey many inquiries as to membership, but for some followers their association with LaVey could prove to be dangerous to their careers. The rumor of a Satanic curse had played throughout the media earlier in 1967. The most startling example of this supposed power concerns the death of the Hollywood star Jayne Mansfield, who was among the early members of LaVey's church.

Following Marilyn Monroe's tragic death, Mansfield was now the new blond bombshell and was specifically groomed by Hollywood to take Monroe's place. As she was making her way up the ladder of success, her lover, an attorney named Sam Brody, approached LaVey and informed the Black Pope that Jayne would be leaving the Church and that she would cut all ties with LaVey. Brody realized that linking Mansfield to black magic and devil worship could very well destroy her now promising career. One photograph actually made its way into publication showing Mansfield kneeling in front of a smiling LaVey drinking from a chalice in what appeared to be some form of dark communion service. It also appears that LaVey was interested in a romantic relationship with Mansfield and several of her friends remember Jayne teasing him on the phone. The interest was obviously one sided.

LaVey told Brody he would see him dead within one year and went through a ritual satanic curse, conjuring up all the forces to destroy him. LaVey also told Jayne that Brody was "under a dark cloud" and warned her not to be alone with him. He especially urged her not to get in a car with Brody. LaVey stoically stated, "I made it clear what would happen."

Several months later, on July 29, 1967, Jayne and Sam

Brody were driving to New Orleans when their car was in a bad crash with a tanker truck spraying for mosquitoes. It was a grisly scene. Preliminary press reports claimed that Mansfield was decapitated, but it now appears that one of the actress's wigs gave that illusion. The San Francisco police showed no interest in pursuing an inquiry of murder by proxy basically because they could never prove it.[3] When LaVey was interviewed following the accident he claimed wryly that he had only cursed Brody. LaVey had also mentioned a strange coincidence that had occurred the morning of the accident. It seemed that while he was cutting out an article on himself from a local newspaper, he just by chance turned the article over and saw that he had mutilated a photo of Jayne Mansfield that was on the other side of the article. With his scissors, Anton LaVey had unintentionally severed the actress's head from her body. This coincidence occurred just hours before the fatal crash. Due to the increase of publicity, membership in the Church of Satan grew to an estimated 18,000 by the end of 1969, a strangely fitting end to the decade of the sixties along with the disaster at Altamont and the Manson murders. Some individuals report that LaVey had placed a curse upon the entire hippie movement of the sixties, due to their careless use of drugs and complete apathy toward life. It is reported that on the night of August 9, 1969, he performed a ritual that would bring the powers of darkness down upon what he referred to as the "psychedelic vermin." Was it yet another coincidence that on this same night the Manson family murdered actress Sharon Tate and a small group of her guests in the so-called "Helter-Skelter" murders? It is true that public opinion radically turned against the flower children, and the "Summer of Love" crashed and burned that summer night in 1969. Strangely enough, one of the murderers, Susan Atkins, had once performed as a topless dancer in one of LaVey's early occult-influenced sideshows before he had founded the Church of Satan.

The newfound notoriety of Anton LaVey enabled him to accept a number of film roles as well as technical advisor. In fellow Satanist Kenneth Anger's film *Invocation of My Demon Brother,* LaVey played the role of Satan. The role of Lucifer was played by Manson family member Bobby Beausoleil. Anton LaVey's biography claimed that he was then hired as a technical consultant to Roman Polanski's film adaptation of *Rosemary's Baby,* concerning modern-day Satanism in New York. In this film LaVey was also said to be have been given a walk-on role as the devil. But in the autobiography *Step Right Up! I'm Gonna Scare the Pants off America* by William Castle, the film's producer, there is no mention of LaVey being hired as a technical consultant or having any role in the film whatsoever. The role of the devil was obviously played by John Cassavetes in makeup, and a small male dancer wore the rubber devil's suit in another scene. Shortly following the release of this film, Roman Polanski's wife, actress Sharon Tate, was viciously murdered by the Manson cult in California. (Polanski's life was destined to be filled with tragedy. His mother died in a concentration camp and in one incident, when he was but a child, he was used as target practice for German soldiers. In 1974, he received great acclaim as the director of *Chinatown.* However, in 1979, Polanski was arrested for sex with a minor and fled when he was released on bond. To this day he has avoided the United States, and his latest film, *The Pianist,* has brought him even greater commendation.)

Anton LaVey would be hired as a technical director and actor in which he led a group of Satanists in a ceremony in *The Devil's Rain.* This 1975 film stared such established stars as William Shatner and Ernest Borgnine, and rumors of strange, unexplained occurrences on the set followed the film's debut across the country. The same hysteria would later be relived when *The Exorcist* was released. Rumors of mysterious fires, and the eminent death of some of the film's actors, continued the urban legends of the occult and its consequences. Of course, the untimely deaths of several of the actors who played roles in the *Poltergeist* film series has now continued yet another strange chapter in film tragedy and urban legendry.

Anton LaVey continued to flout middle-class values by performing a Satanic funeral service for one of his members in San Francisco. In one vivid photograph, carried by newspapers throughout the world, LaVey performed a baptismal ceremony using his three-year-old daughter, Zeena, as the initiate. The child sat dressed in a red robe upon the living altar adorned with a naked woman, while her father, wearing his ceremonial robes, administered the rites of baptism. To many this was completely appalling, but for the Church of Satan the article provided world-wide publicity and requests for membership came in from around the world.

LaVey's carefully planned but covert transition into the music business was revealed in Blanche Burton's 1990 publication, *The Church of Satan*. LaVey decided auditoriums and stadiums could be used to spread the word to new followers through what was described as "Black Metal concerts." The newly staged concerts had the power of a religious crusade. At this time, rumors of backward tracks and so-called satanic messages being hidden in recordings filled the media. Some bands placed warning labels on their releases claiming that some of their songs contained secret backward tracks. The effectiveness of these backward messages affecting people on a subliminal basis has been disputed by psychologists. The brain typically does not recognize backward phonemes and cannot rearrange them into words that would have any influence on human thoughts and behavior.

The main element behind Black Metal was to generate enough publicity to bring Satanism into the mainline press. Many young fans took to the music and carved their new heroes' names on their notebooks as well as on their flesh. The band's image was paramount and the message was true rebellion. LaVey points to young people adopting the salute of "two thumbs," which was now more popular than the Mason's handshake.[4]

With the release of *Hotel California* even the Eagles were placed under closer scrutiny. Some listeners suggested that the name for the LP came from the street address of the Church of Satan in San Francisco. The church was formed from a remodeled brothel and was said to be located upon California Avenue. This became what some fanatics considered to be a strong indication that some members of the Eagles had now become willing initiates into the dark side. Singer/drummer Don Henley composed the lyrics of the title song, which took on a strange *Twilight Zone*–like atmosphere. The story line that concerned "steely knives," "kill the beast," and "you can check out any time you like, but you can never leave" provided references that some believed were influenced by occult practices. Did the "steely knives" represent sacrifice? Did not being able to "leave" conjure forth the tragic story of Jayne Mansfield, the former member of the Church of Satan, who in her leaving only hastened her own terrible death? Another lyric that stated "We've not had that spirit here since 1969" brought back terrible memories of Altamont and the Manson murders. It was also the very year that *The Satanic Bible* was first printed.

Another puzzling scene from *Hotel California* deals with an album photo showing the Eagles standing in the lobby of a crowed hotel. A living sea of humanity surrounds them, but upon the balcony, a figure half hidden by the darkness gazes down upon the crowd. The figure sports what appears to be a cleanly shaven head and neatly trimmed black goatee, resembling none other than Anton LaVey himself. The Eagles have denied any reference to Satan or the occult within the song and have suggested that the mysterious figure upon the balcony was only an extra who had simply been in the wrong place at the time of the photo shoot. Nearly twenty years after the release of *Hotel California,* and the original breakup of the Eagles, the band re-formed for their *Hell Freezes Over* tour. The name for the album and tour came from an expression credited to the band members, who angrily said they would re-form only if hell froze over. Since the re-forming of the Eagles, Henley has taken on Satan once again. In "The Garden Of Allah" Henley has Satan return to earth once more to check on the progress of man. The song title was taken from the name of a scandalous Hollywood hotel that was the very picture of decadence. In a 1995 interview with CNN Henley stated, "I think if people listen closely they will see the humor in it. I mean the devil shows up in a seersucker suit and gets angry because it's so hot here that it reminds him of home and he's all sweaty." Henley even persuaded Kirk Douglas to play the role of Satan in the rock video. Douglas agreed, but only after consulting his rabbi.

With the development of theatrical rock throughout the 1970s, concert attendance continued to soar. Many rock groups then decided to wrap themselves in the mantle of the occult. It was at this time that KISS appeared in complete makeup. Their stage antics included spitting up blood and blowing fire, and in many cases seeing their performance was like going to the circus. KISS bassist Gene Simmons once stated, "We wanted to look like we crawled out from under a rock in Hell. We wanted parents to look at us and instantly want to throw up."[5] The legions of their fans multiplied as many followers appeared at KISS concerts dressed in the same costumes as their idols. It wasn't long after KISS's popularity rose until rumors started to appear stating that KISS was an anagram for something much more sinister. It was suggested that the group's name actually stood for "Knights in Satan's Service." KISS vocalist Paul Stanley challenged this accusation by sarcastically saying that the group's name actually stood for "Kids In Sunday School." Some music insiders claimed that the letters of the group's name actually represented their formula to success: "Keep It Simple Stupid!"

The lightning bolt double S's were said to be Satanic S's. I didn't know that a Satanic alphabet existed, but the two letters bear a striking resemblance to the insignia worn by Hitler's elite SS troops. Of course, Hitler and Goebbels were no strangers to the occult, crafting the very swastika as a symbol of occult powers. The Nazi legend mentions that Heinrich Himmler's fascination with the occult led him to create the SS insignia based upon an ancient Teutonic runic symbol found in an archaeological dig.

Other metal acts were also placed under closer scrutiny. The group W.A.S.P. was said to be an anagram for "We Are Satan's People." You can imagine the relief when W.A.S.P. founder Blackie Lawless set the record straight. He calmly insisted that the name W.A.S.P. actually stood for "We Are Sexual Perverts." I'm sure that shortly after this announcement many parents gave a heartfelt sigh of relief!

Another rock group that was said to be one of Satan's minions was the popular group AC/DC. The group's name was said to be a "hidden reference" to "Anti-Christ/Devil's Children," or "Anti-Christ/Devil's Crusade," or even stranger yet, "After Christ the Devil Comes." Perhaps the most logical reference relates to the properties of electrical power, AC (alternating current) and DC (direct current). The lightning bolt between the lettering reinforces the insignia of electrical power. Of course, it takes thousands of volts to provide the massive sound system and the stacks of Marshall amplifiers with the decibel force needed to conjure forth the gods of rock and roll. Perhaps this explanation was not sinister enough for AC/DC's detractors. To some observers, the lightning bolt bore a resemblance to a satanic S, that of the hated Nazis SS insignia. An interpretation for the lightning bolt was even said to be explained in the book of Luke: "And he said unto them, 'I beheld Satan as lightning fall from heaven'"(Luke 10:18).

Less dramatically, some insiders claim that it was band members Angus and Malcolm Young's sister Margaret who gave the band its name after viewing the word *ac/dc* on the electrical information of her sewing machine. Angus has also claimed that he spotted the word on his mother's vacuum cleaner. I'm sure that some detractors will remember a specific make of vacuum that has the name "devil" associated with it to further lay claim to a hidden Satanic purpose.

The highlight of an AC/DC concert has always been the onstage antics of guitarist Angus Young. Young, dressed in his schoolboy uniform complete with short pants, struts across the stage as a demented Chuck Berry, and falls to the stage kicking and writhing as if caught in the throes of an epileptic seizure. The concept of the outfit is derived from Angus showing up for band practice immediately after school. He just practiced in his uniform. The short pants allowed the guitarist to keep cool as he was constantly in perpetual motion throughout a performance. Angus also hints of a strange transformation that takes place when he dons his stage clothes. "'It's the suit,' insisted Angus. 'I'm normally the laziest person you'd ever want to meet. But when I put on that school suit, it gets me full of beans. There's something about it. I put it on, and it's probably a bit schizophrenic, but it lets me become someone else for a couple of hours. It never fails to amaze me. When I put it on, I look in the mirror, and I'm afraid.'"[6]

A number of AC/DC's songs seemed to hint at an alliance with the dark powers. The first major hit for the band was *Highway to Hell*. The album was released with Angus wearing his customary schoolboy uniform. On his head can be seen devil horns, and he holds a forked tail as he sneers directly into the camera. Though there is mention that the band has paid its dues, the meaning behind the song was given by Angus in an interview with the *Los Angeles Times* in which he discussed the rigors of the band's early torturous years on the road: "It has nothing to do with devil worship. We toured four years at a stretch with no break. A guy asked how would you best describe our tours. We said, 'A highway to hell.' The phrase stuck with us. All we'd done is describe what it is like to be on the road for four years. When you're sleeping with the singer's socks two inches from your nose, believe me, that's pretty close to hell."[7]

The song "Highway to Hell" was also used as a "secret weapon" by the United States Armed Forces in their invasion of Panama in January of 1989. The U.S. troops played the AC/DC anthem at full volume to help hasten the surrender of Panamanian Manuel Noriega, who was in hiding at Panama's Vatican Embassy. When told of the U.S. military strategy Angus Young replied, "They were trying to aggravate him so he couldn't get a restful sleep. It was pretty funny for us. I figure if our music is good enough for the U.S. Army, it's good enough for anybody, I guess." Singer Brian Johnson answered, "When I heard that my first thought was, now we'll never play for the pope."[8]

Other songs by AC/DC were also said to contain Satanic allusions, such as "Rock 'n' Roll Damnation," "Hell's Bells," "C.O.D." (Care of the Devil), and "Hell Ain't a Bad Place to Be." In considering "Hell Ain't a Bad Place to Be," Angus Young stated, "That song is a joke. We're saying if you've got a choice between heaven and hell, you might pick hell. In heaven you have harp music and in hell there's a good rockin' band and rocking songs. That's what we'd choose. So hell ain't a bad place to be. It's all in fun."[9]

There are incidents that AC/DC has faced that have not been all in fun. The first tragedy to strike the band occurred when lead singer Bon Scott died following an all-night drinking binge at a club called the Music Machine in London's Camden Town.

Scott was with his friend Alistair Kinnear and the pair left the club at approximately 3:00 A.M. According to eyewitnesses, Scott had consumed seven double whiskeys. Apparently, Bon Scott had managed this feat before on several other occasions and it was an ordinary night with a return to Scott's flat. Kinnear was unable to wake Bon, who was now unconscious and sleeping soundly. Kinnear then drove to his own home but was still unable to awaken his passenger, so he wrapped some blankets around Scott and left him in the car to sleep it off. "After sleeping for about fifteen hours, Kinnear woke and checked Bon at about 7:45 on the evening of the twenty-first, and discovered that Scott was dead. The singer was pronounced dead on arrival at London's King's College Hospital . . . An initial report recorded the cause of death as acute alcohol poisoning, but it was determined that Scott had moved in his sleep, vomited and choked to death. At a coroner's inquest, at which the singer's bandmates offered testimony, the coroner reported that Scott's stomach had contained the 'equivalent of half a bottle of whisky' when he died and officially designated Bon's demise as death by misadventure."[10] Scott's drinking ability was legendary. In 1979, following an Atlantic Records party, Bon Scott had to have his stomach pumped before he could appear on stage. He was yet another victim of his own excesses.

Bon Scott was cremated and the funeral service was held at Fremantle, Australia, on March 1, 1980. In a bizarre twist of fate, shortly following his funeral, Bon Scott's many friends started to receive Christmas cards addressed to them personally by the fallen singer. It appears that Bon had not placed the proper postage on the envelopes and this had resulted in their delay.

Replacing a singer of Bon Scott's ability would be no easy feat, but after acquiring Brian Johnson, AC/DC was yet again on its thunderous way. The release of *Back in Black* in 1980 reestablished the band as rock superstars with their most successful album, but yet again many overzealous individuals saw what they took to be hidden offerings to Satan. The album title was merely a salute to the memory of Bon Scott, but to the new inquisitors it became easy to suggest that AC/DC had returned with the backing of the forces of darkness. The evidence offered to support this view was found in the melancholy sounds of the ringing bells found in the opening track of "Hell's Bells." The mention of "If you do evil you're a friend of mine," "If God's on the left then I'm sticking to the right," and "Got my bell I'm gonna drag you to hell" provided yet more ammunition to accuse the band of promoting the occult. Singer Brian Johnson retorted, "Those God-bothers mention the devil more than we do. They're trying to scare people. The big idea with us isn't Satanic messages. It's trying to get one line to rhyme with the next." Angus Young also joined in the discussion by stating, "We're not black magic Satanists. I don't drink blood. I may wear black underpants now and again, but that's it." In turn Johnson also attacked the bands' detractors by mentioning their "designer churches." Johnson exclaimed, "And I saw this other guy who openly said, 'I saw God last night—He came to me in a dream, and He talked with me.' That's blasphemy! If God was gonna come down and talk to somebody, the last person He'd talk to is a guy with a fleet of Cadillacs, who claims to have had a runnin' conversation with Him for the last fifteen years." [11] Unknown to the band, this would be the easiest accusation to overcome.

With the revelation of the "Night Stalker" murders in California, new emphasis was placed upon rock and roll's occult influences. On August 31, 1985, Los Angeles police arrested Richard Ramirez, the "Night Stalker," and placed him on trial for at least a dozen murders in a serial killing spree that had haunted the Los Angeles area. His victims ranged from a sixteen-year-old teenager to a seventy-nine-year-old grandmother. This bloody reign of terror produced references to Satanism, inverted pentagrams, and Ramirez's personal meeting with Anton LaVey. LaVey denied any responsibility for the murders, saying that Ramirez appeared only to be a well-mannered young man. The Black Pope also commented that if any individual came to his church claiming to be sent by Satan that LaVey would personally give that individual the "bum's rush." Not only was evidence introduced concerning Ramirez's Satanic practices, but it also became public knowledge that the "Night Stalker" was obsessed with what he believed to be Satanic symbols found on the *Highway to Hell* album jacket. He especially enjoyed the song "Night Prowler." The lyrics to this song about a "peeping tom" may very well have resulted in Ramirez's naming himself the "Night Stalker." When this information was leaked to the public AC/DC became yet again the popular target of the zealots. Concerts were canceled. Other concerts were picketed by some churches, and AC/DC was yet again in the crosshairs of intolerance.

The Ramirez trial lasted fourteen months. During the trial one juror was murdered by her boyfriend and yet another female juror sent Ramirez a Valentine's Day cupcake that read "I Love You." The "Night Stalker" was nevertheless convicted and sentenced to nineteen death sentences. He was also sentenced to over 198 years in prison on other charges. At the end of his trial Ramirez displayed an inverted pentagram on the palm of his hand and shouted "Hail, Satan" as he was being taken away. On October 3, 1996, Richard Ramirez was married in a fifteen-minute prison ceremony to a forty-one-year-old freelance magazine editor. He is awaiting an appeal to his sentence.

Tragedy struck AC/DC a third time at a concert on January 18, 1991, in Salt Lake City, Utah. Three teenage fans were crushed to death as fellow fans rushed toward the stage. This was eerily like an earlier Who concert in which several of their fans were crushed and trampled by the surging mob as they fought to get the best positions near the stage. With such tragedy many cities placed bans upon so-called festival seating appearances. In fairness to performing bands, it is impossible to see into an audience with thousands of watts of lighting shining in your eyes. It is also impossible to hear what is going on with the thunderous roar of the sound systems that numb the sense of hearing into complete submission.

With the resurgence of heavy metal in the late 1980s, new metal bands took upon themselves the challenge of shocking their audiences with actual hymns to Satan and a complete acceptance of the left-hand path. For instance, metal groups including Venom, Possessed, Sad Iron, Manowar, Morbid Angel, and Slayer flashed a constant motif of Satanic themes. This was accomplished openly throughout their lyrics. The group Acheron in their album titled *The Rites of the Black Mass* actually included the reading of the Black Mass by Peter Gilmore of the Church of Satan.

Undoubtedly, the current leader in the field of shock rock is Marilyn Manson. Marilyn Manson, whose real name is Brian Warner, states that not only is he a card-carrying member of the Church of Satan but that he has also been ordained as a Satanic priest. Manson once told *Seconds* magazine, "Dr. Anton Szandor LaVey expressed that he felt Marilyn Manson was one of the more Satanic bands to come along in our time." Anyone can argue that membership in the Church of Satan can be obtained by simply paying a one-time $100 initiation fee. The member then receives a subscription to the church newsletter *The Cloven Hoof* as well as a membership card, suitable for framing. Of course, if an individual is only slightly curious he or she could pay a nominal fee and attend a gathering at one of the grottoes. LaVey even charges members of the media the same fee if they should wish to observe the rituals. In the December issue of *Details* magazine Marilyn Manson told interviewer Brantley Bardin that "the story of Lucifer, the fallen angel, is my favorite story of all time. Maybe with the new record *Anti-Christ Superstar*, I can show people that the character isn't such a bad guy—it's just that history is written by winners. In the Bible's case, the winner is God."

Ironically, Marilyn Manson was educated in a Christian school, and he once told MTV News (*The Week in Rock,* January 17, 1997) about "being a thirteen-year-old kid, and having someone tell you on a daily basis that this is the final hour and that the Antichrist was coming and it was going to be the end of the world. You know, I would stay up every night and have nightmares about this and then finally 1984 passed, and all those years that they said was going to be the end, I developed a real hard shell, you know, that really became what Marilyn Manson is, it was resentment." In a *Rolling Stone* interview Manson continued, "My mother used to tell me, 'If you curse at nighttime the devil's going to come to you when you're sleeping.' I was never afraid of what was under the bed. I wanted it. And I never got it, I just became it."

The paradox of Manson's early Christian education and his rebellion from the same principles is evident in his chosen name Marilyn Manson. He took the first name Marilyn from Marilyn Monroe, the beautiful sex goddess whose life ended in suicide—far from the happy ending she so desperately wanted—and of course his last name Manson from Charles Manson, the leader of the notorious family who murdered Sharon Tate and a few other helpless victims. Following this formula, each of Marilyn Manson's fellow group members adopted the same strange pairing of names. The first name was from a famous actress or model while the last name would be taken from a convicted serial killer. The names were not taken lightly. Not only did the last name have to be that of a killer, but that killer also had to be associated with the Satanic movement, or a convicted child murderer. Group members adopted names that included: Daisy Berkowitz, Twiggy Ramirez, Madonna Wayne Gacy, Sara Lee Lucas. (Guitarist Zim Zum does not fit the mold; however, some followers believe the secret to his name is found in the mystical Cabalistic teachings. Possibly, the name is derived from *tzimtzum*—this is interpreted as the mystical place that God willed his presence to help make room for the creation of the universe and of man.) The pairing of the names seems to suggest the Eastern philosophy of Yin-Yang, that there is evil in good and good in evil. Of course, this becomes the everyday struggle that confronts man.

As far as teachings go, Manson stated, "I go by the attitude 'do what you will' that is the whole of the law (Crowley, *The Book of the Law*). And I will do exactly that. Satanism is not about a devil. It's about realizing, much like Nietzsche said, that you are your own god. I guess a word for it is 'me-ism,' because it's a very selfish philosophy."[12] Manson also says he suffers from "the delusion of the self." As he told *Details*, "It's when you feel that everything is related and all circumstances have something to do with one another. I just think of it as a higher plane of awareness." Already urban folklore has produced many Marilyn Manson legends. Did he really have three ribs removed? Does he throw live puppies into the audience to be killed before each of his concerts begins? Are he and his band planning on committing suicide in front of their audience on their 666th performance? Or will he commit suicide on a Halloween performance? Is he actually an actor who once was featured in a starring role in *The Wonder Years*? These rumors continue to add to the band's Gothic mystique.

It is interesting to note that Marilyn Manson, like other so-called Satanic heavy-metal bands, thrives on publicity. They rejoice in having churches protest their concerts since this only brings about more publicity, and of course publicity equals greater record sales. I have always thought that parental warnings on recordings serve as a double-edged sword. They do purport to keep "offensive" recordings out of the hands of children, but in actuality they only attract more attention to a questionable recording. It is only human nature, and that old vice curiosity, that makes each of us wonder what is it that they (record companies, governmental bodies, etc.) do not want us to see or hear. I would like to see some numbers on the sales of albums both before they were stamped with a parental warning and afterward. My guess is the sales were much higher after the warnings were added, but we always have that age-old excuse, "The devil made me buy it."

Apparently, there will always be a number of individuals who take things too seriously. The success of role-playing games such as Goth may make it hard for some of its followers to separate fact from fantasy. There are reported crimes linked to overzealous believers in the occult. In Knoxville, Tennessee, a Job Corps student was brutally tortured and murdered. A pentagram was carved into her chest and her skull was crushed with a block of asphalt. Her killer allegedly carried away a small piece of her skull both as a souvenir and in the belief that the victim's spirit would always be forced to remain trapped within her lifeless body. Other teenage murderers include cults of role-playing Goths who actually play the role of real-life vampires and in some extreme cases commit terrible murders that grab the evening news headlines.

It is important to note that regardless of sensational television programming, the FBI claims that there is absolutely no direct evidence of a national or international Satanic underground that produces sacrifices to Satan. There may well be too much credit given to the small number of hard rock acts who adopt strange stage personas in order to help sell records and not enough attention to the eroding of the basic family unit that unfortunately preaches the same commandment of "do what thou wilt." If Satan were good business for rock and roll each of the so-called Satanic metal bands would be with major labels, bringing in millions of dollars of revenue each year. The radio airwaves do not electrify their listeners with a daily playlist of black metal. The simple but undeniable facts are that the outrageous heavy metal bands are not generating mass income for the record companies. Most of these bands perform on obscure labels with very limited distribution, and the only way to increase sales is through any publicity that calls attention to the band. In this case, the more outrageous the act, the better. It seems that recently Marilyn Manson has come under attack by some of his fellow Satanists in that Manson seems to not fit the description of Anton LaVey's concept of "one part outrage, nine parts social respectability." To most listeners, death metal is only an orchestrated fad that will simply be replaced by the next one, another in a series of acts thrown upon the trash heap of the continuous but inevitable cycle of rock and roll history.

8. THE BACKWARD MASK AND OTHER HIDDEN MESSAGES

Do you see yonder cloud that's almost in shape of a camel?
—Shakespeare, *Hamlet*, 3.2

And you know sometimes words have two meanings
—Led Zeppelin, "Stairway to Heaven"

If a man wishes to practice magick he must train himself to think backward by external means, as set forth here following, let him learn to write backward, let him learn to walk backward, let him constantly watch, if convenient, films and listen to records reversed.
—Aleister Crowley

'Tis the eye of childhood that fears a painted devil.
—Shakespeare, *Macbeth*, 2.2

ARE THERE REALLY HIDDEN MESSAGES IN ROCK SONGS? The answer is a resounding yes! In order to gain full appreciation of the topic, it is important to realize that the phenomenon of hidden messages is in no way limited to rock music. Long before the advent of rock and roll, human beings were perplexed by a deep and burning question: What lies beneath the surface? Hidden messages pique a morbid curiosity in mankind, filled with whys and what ifs. Images of conspiracy, cryptic allusions, sinister purposes, and things that aren't always what they seem on the surface flood our minds. What *does* lie beneath the surface? It is a fascinating question, full of intrigue, mystery, and enigma. No form of media—books, movies, advertising, and especially music—has been exempt from the question. Were we as a culture not so perplexed by our own mortality, these theories would never have received such intense scrutiny. The search remains a part of our never-ending quest for truth. Rock music has indeed had its fair share of allegations and speculation from its beginnings. However, even seemingly innocent works, such as the Bible, have fallen prey to the search for human meaning.

It is obvious that one of the most cryptic works is the Holy Bible. The early influences of the Chaldeans and Persians upon the Hebrew prophets created and maintained a keen interest in astronomy. Seers would then interpret the movement of the heavenly spheres as predictions of man's fate. Comets referred to the future death of kings and the fall of empires while a blazing star signaled the birth of the Messiah. The New Testament, appropriately, ends with the Book of Revelation, which undoubtedly is the most curious and interpreted book of the Bible.

Since the Book of Revelation is open to so many fascinating interpretations, it will always serve as the ultimate biblical mystery. There may be another hidden message in the Bible of which you may not be aware. We know through English history that King James I commissioned the English translation of the Bible.

A committee of fifty-four scholars was put together to translate the scriptures from the surviving ancient Hebrew, Greek, and Aramaic manuscripts. This followed the well-worn path of the Reformation, and the biblical scholars were selected from Oxford, Cambridge, and Westminister Abbey. The beautiful Book of Psalms required the touch of a poet. Was it possible that King James had appointed Shakespeare as one of the chosen translators? The biblical translation began in earnest in 1610 and William Shakespeare had just celebrated his forty-sixth birthday. This brings us to an incredible coincidence. To solve this hidden mystery we must first examine the evidence. In this case, let's take a look at Psalm 46:

> *God is our refuge and strength, a very present*
> *help in trouble.*
> *Therefore will not we fear, though the earth*
> *be removed, and though the mountains be carried*
> *into the midst of the sea;*
> *Though the waters thereof roar and be troubled,*
> *though the mountains shake with the swelling*
> *thereof. Selah.*
> *There is a river, the streams whereof shall*
> *make glad the city of God, the holy place of the*
> *tabernacles of the most High.*
> *God is in the midst of her; she shall not be*
> *moved: God shall help her, and that right early.*
> *The heathen raged, the kingdoms were moved:*
> *he uttered his voice, the earth melted.*
> *The Lord of hosts is with us; the God of*
> *Jacob is our refuge. Selah.*
> *Come, behold the works of the Lord, what*
> *desolations he hath made in the earth.*
> *He maketh wars to cease unto the end of the*

earth; he breaketh the bow, and cutteth the spear
in sunder; he burneth the chariot in the fire.
Be still, and know that I am God: I will be
exalted among the heathen, I will be exalted
in the earth.
The Lord of hosts is with us; the God of
Jacob is our refuge. Selah.

Many Shakespearean scholars claim that Shakespeare's name is placed critically in the Psalm 46. If you count forty-six words from the beginning you find the word "shake." Count forty-six words from the end of the Psalm (do not count the word "Selah" since it is not an English translation), and you will find the word "spear." It is also curious that Shakespeare's plays were written in a circle pattern. They end very much as they begin. For instance, at the beginning of Shakespeare's *Macbeth* Scotland is torn by a civil war resulting in a treasonous act by the Thane of Cawdor. The play concludes with Scotland being involved in yet another civil war brought about by the treason by Macbeth, ironically named the Thane of Cawdor by his cousin and later victim, King Duncan.

William Shakespeare and King James I were involved in a rather close relationship. James was a patron of Shakespeare's acting company, the King's Men, and Shakespeare wrote *Macbeth* in honor of James's rise to the throne. Actually, Shakespeare distorted Scottish history by conveniently forgetting that James's ancestor, Banquo (upon whom the very Stuart monarchy was based) helped murder King Duncan. It would be terrible to mention that King James's forefather had helped in usurping the Scottish throne. When the Great Chain of Being was shattered, terrible calamities would strike the people. Some scholars claim that if William Shakespeare was not a translator then he was bestowed this great honor by King James on Shakespeare's forty-sixth birthday at Westminister Abbey. Since one of Shakespeare's sonnet themes was immortality through verse, this gift would allow King James's favorite playwright the honor of having his name cryptically placed in one of the greatest works of mankind. Though I'm sure that some would question why a man of Shakespeare's questionable reputation would be given this high honor, I feel that the answer may lay in the character of King James.

In our time, during the investigation into the death of pageant queen JonBenet Ramsey, the Ramseys' attorneys mentioned that there may be a link in the ransom note that demanded a $118,000 payment to Psalm 118 from the King James Bible. The attorneys noted that there was a strange parallel to the twenty-seventh verse, as follows: "God is the Lord, which hath shewed us light: bind the sacrifice with cords, even unto the horns of the altar." Since JonBenet's body was found bound in cords, did this become some bizarre stretch to serve as a connection to the actual killer? Or, is it just another case of trying to make things fit into yet another dark conspiracy theory?

In the 1950s another unseen terror silently made its way into American consciousness. This predator was invisible and was found in movie theaters. Its name was subliminal advertising. It was suggested that some movie houses spliced several frames showing popcorn, soft drinks, and other food items into a feature reel. The splices were said to be placed at certain intervals; as each frame rhythmically made its presence known through the unconscious mind, the pattern supposedly created hunger pangs within each viewer. Like mindless zombies the theater's patrons would purchase more and more popcorn and soft drinks. Some theaters reported that their sales of food items skyrocketed. Some movies warned that they contained subliminal pictures of skulls and other horrible objects that would transfix the viewers with fear. Promoters would place doctors and nurses in the movie houses to help care for patrons who would be literally "scared to death." As far as I know, not one person died of a heart attack during one of these films. Another favorite example of a hidden subliminal in a popular movie is found in the 1960 thriller *Psycho*. Alfred Hitchcock placed a hidden subliminal at the end of the film and this occurs when Norman Bates says that he "wouldn't raise his hand to hurt a fly." If a video of the film is viewed in the slow mode, one frame at a time, right before the car is pulled from the swamp, the mummified face of the mother appears over Norman's smiling face. This is a fantastic effect, but the matricide rate did not soar, nor was there any increase in the sale of taxidermy kits. Today, however, there are some individuals who claim that hidden messages are found in—of all places—Walt Disney animated films! Does *The Little Mermaid* contain phallic drawings of towers? No. It is just a coincidence and a vivid imagination. Is there a minister in the wedding scene from *The Little Mermaid* who becomes "sexually aroused"? No. Look closely and you will see his knee. In *Aladdin,* doesn't the title character say "Good teenagers, take off your clothes"? Actually he says "Good Kitty, get up and go." In *The Lion King,* does the word "SEX" form in a cloud of dust? If you look long enough at an angle, with a little guidance, you could see anything. Does Jessica Rabbit have a nude scene in *Who Framed Roger Rabbit?* See the answer to the cloud of dust.

Other popular films were said to contain strange supernatural images. *Three Men and a Baby* was said to contain the ghostly apparition of a young boy who supposedly committed suicide with a pump shotgun in the house leased by the film company to complete the film. When Ted Danson moves in front of one window it is said that an inverted shotgun can be seen in the window. When he passes by the window a second time the shadowy shotgun disappears and is replaced by the ghost of a small boy who watches emotionlessly from the same window. According to the cast, the scene was shot on a movie set, not in a house. The figure of the small boy is actually a cardboard cutout of Ted Danson that was placed in the window by one of the crew. Again, the ghostly apparition is certainly open to speculation.

Another rumor of hidden messages in a popular film was revealed when two DJs in a *Globe* magazine article (September 3, 1996) claimed that John Travolta's hit film *Phenomenon* contains several subliminal messages dealing with the Scientologist beliefs. Travolta's character is able to absorb massive amounts of printed information and keeps saying "he sees things much clearer." This is said to be an ultimate goal of Scientology. The DJs, from Flint, Michigan, also claim that when the theme song, sung by Peter Gabriel, is played backward an eerie voices asks, "Don't you miss Ron?" To followers of Scientology this supposedly refers to the founder of Scientology, L. Ron Hubbard: "According to Peter Gabriel's publicist, the rocker is 'not and never has been a Scientologist.' Travolta's spokeswoman Michelle Bega says there is no Scientology message in the movie's theme song, but DJ Mitch stands by his findings. 'Play it backward,' he says, 'and it's clear as a bell, "Don't you miss Ron?" It's spooky.' "

As is evidenced in the Globe article, people are still playing their records backward, a trend that began in the 1960s. What started this wave of hysteria? How does one listen to a hidden or backward track? Why are hidden or backward tracks placed on recordings? What records are said to contain hidden messages?

It is appropriate that we begin with the Beatles. After all, they were the first to introduce the technique known as backward masking. It was during the recording of "Rain" that John Lennon first became inspired to try a backward vocal track. Lennon mentioned to David Sheff in *The Playboy Interviews with John Lennon and Yoko Ono,* "I got home from the studio and I was stoned out of my mind on marijuana and, as I usually do, I listened to what I recorded that day. Somehow I got it on backward and I sat there transfixed, with the earphones on, with a big hash joint. I ran in the next day and said, 'I know what to do with it, I know . . . listen to this!' So I made them play it backward. The fade is me actually singing backward with the guitars going backward. 'Sharethsmnowthsmeaness.'"[1]

Many individuals may ask why anyone would place a backward track on a record. One answer is that the new sound results in a texture that will embellish the recording. An example of this would be in the recording of cymbals and in their being played backward to help layer a recording. Now that you know one reason for using this technique, it may be important to explain that there are two types of backward recording. The first is a true backward mask where a singer has previously recorded a lyric and at the mixdown that one track is reversed and mixed into the song. An example of this is found in the Beatles' "Rain." This track is an actual hidden message whose meaning can hardly be called a coincidence. The second type of backward recording is a phonetic reversal. Each letter creates a basic sound called a phoneme. When a simple letter containing one syllable is reversed sometimes it creates a two-syllable sound. This technique is found in the Beatles "Revolution 9" when the test engineer's voice stating "number 9" is reversed and the message seems to say "Turn me on dead man." This is also the recording method used to determine the backward message said to be contained in "Stairway to Heaven." This is a much more subjective approach. The swirling sounds can be and usually are interpreted to be anything that the listener wants to hear, usually after some guided listening by a friend who hears the "hidden message." This may well work in a pattern similar to the famous Rorschach test. The subject is shown a series of ten inkblots placed in a particular order by the psychologist and encouraged to explain what he sees in great detail.

The psychologist sits a little to the side and behind the subject and constantly writes notes detailing each answer. According to the theory behind this test, the basic ego defense mechanisms, including repressed memories, are brought out in patterns and interpreted by the psychologist. Hidden fears and compulsions are then brought to the surface and dealt with in counseling. In many ways, individuals who hear many backward messages in phonetic reversals are actually facing their own hidden demons and repressions.

I suppose a prudent question at this time would be "How do you play a record backward?" There are many ways. If you own a turntable that has a neutral position you can spin the record backward and by varying the speed the listener can discern the hidden messages. WARNING: This can destroy the turntable's motor and the needle, and ruin a valuable vinyl recording. Obviously this is not the best answer. A second way to listen to a backward track is by opening a cassette's plastic case and reversing the tape itself. Then you reassemble the cassette case and play the tape normally. This works, but it takes a great deal of time and in some cases destroys the cassette.

If you have a generous friend with a multitrack recorder, you can record all four tracks on one side of the cassette and then simply turn the recorded tape over and listen to the entire track backward. This is very easy, but expensive if you have to purchase the tape deck.

With the development of computers and the sound card it has now become very simple to sample a backward track. For instance with Windows 95, click Start, go to Programs, and find Accessories. Click on Accessories and open Multimedia. Open the Sound Recorder icon and you are just about ready to sample your own backward tracks. Place a CD in your CD-ROM drive and record the questionable section. After the recording, go to Effects and chose the Reverse mode. The recorded section will now be played backward and the "hidden messages" section can be analyzed. Simply save the file as a .wav file and then play it back-

ROBERT JOHNSON Robert Johnson, "The King of the Delta Blues." His haunting voice and unique playing style convinced many of his contemporaries that he had struck a bargain with the devil at a deserted country crossroads in Mississippi. Strangely, a number of rock stars have died at the age of twenty-seven—the age that Robert Johnson met his fate, unleashing what is now known as "The Curse of 27."

Newspaper ad for Buddy Holly's last concert.

Buddy Holly proved to be a pioneer of the early rock and roll movement. His untimely death in 1959 is often referred to as "The day the music died." Tragedy followed a number of musicians who shared a relationship with Holly and his backing band, the Crickets.

RITCHIE VALENS *(below, right)* A seventeen-year-old Ritchie Valens overcame his fear of flying to join Buddy Holly on the Winter Dance Party tour. A coin toss won him the only remaining seat in the doomed plane.

J.P. RICHARDSON *(inset)* "The Big Bopper" traded his new sleeping bag to Waylon Jennings in an attempt to escape another night on a freezing school bus during the Winter Dance Party tour.

EDDIE COCHRAN Eddie Cochran was a brilliant guitarist whose "Summertime Blues" and "C'mon Everybody" served as teenage anthems. Following Buddy Holly's death, Cochran recorded an emotional "Three Stars," a tribute to Holly, Valens, and the Big Bopper. Coincidentally, Cochran's last song was titled "Three Steps to Heaven."

EDDIE COCHRAN
The wrecked taxi in which rock and roll singer Eddie Cochran, age twenty-one of Hollywood, suffered fatal injuries. The taxi is shown at a London garage after the accident. Cochran and three companions were dashing to a London airport for their flight home to Los Angeles when the taxi's tire blew out and they smashed into a lamppost.

BOBBY FULLER His bizarre death is still one of rock and roll's greatest mysteries. His life had many similarities to Buddy Holly's. His last recording was a Holly composition titled "Love's Made a Fool of You."

ALLMAN BROTHERS BAND The Allman Brothers Band has faced many tragedies. In a strange kind of déjà vu, both Barry Oakley *(top)* and Duane Allman *(center front row)* would perish in the same manner a little more than a year apart.

LYNYRD SKYNYRD Lynyrd Skynyrd's lineup at the time of the crash.

LYNYRD SKYNYRD
The *Street Survivors* album was released three days before the crash of the *Freebird*. This cover, showing the band in flames, was replaced with a black cover in tribute to the fallen band.

OZZY OSBOURNE AND RANDY RHOADS The great and powerful Ozz with guitar virtuoso Randy Rhoads.

THE ROLLING STONES Keith Richards, Brian Jones, Mick Jagger: The three creative energies who developed the Rolling Stones' sound.

BRIAN JONES Brian Jones with a woman reported to be femme fatale model Suki Poitier. Poitier's premonition that three of her lovers would meet an early demise became reality: First was Tara Brown, Guinness heir who "blew his mind out in a car," and later, Brian Jones and Jimi Hendrix.

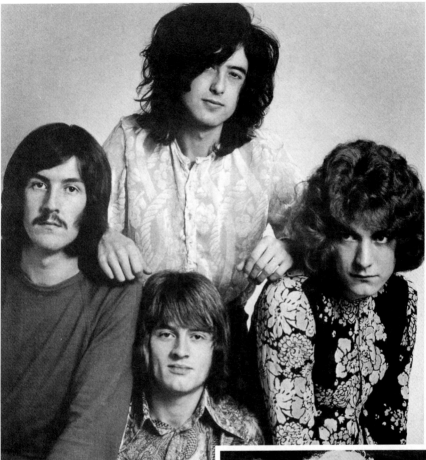

LED ZEPPELIN (group photo, *above*): The meteoric journey of Led Zeppelin followed in the path of the 1930s Robert Johnson myth. Jimmy Page's involvement with Aleister Crowley memorabilia, and rumors of a blood pact became the stuff of legends.

LED ZEPPELIN Jimmy Page and Robert Plant *(right)*: The duo's release of "Walking into Clarksdale" invoked memories of blues great Robert Johnson and was perhaps a reference to a meeting at an infamous crossroads.

Guitar great Jimi Hendrix's search for enlightenment led him into the realms of UFOs and numerology. The exact circumstances of his tragic death may never be known.

JOHN LENNON Lennon once said, "Nothing just happens." His belief in numerology convinced him that the number 9 ruled his life—and death.

JIM MORRISON Jim Morrison was one of rock and roll's greatest poets. When hearing of the deaths of Jimi Hendrix and Janis Joplin he exclaimed, "You're drinking with number three." Many fans still wonder if Morrison managed to fake his own death.

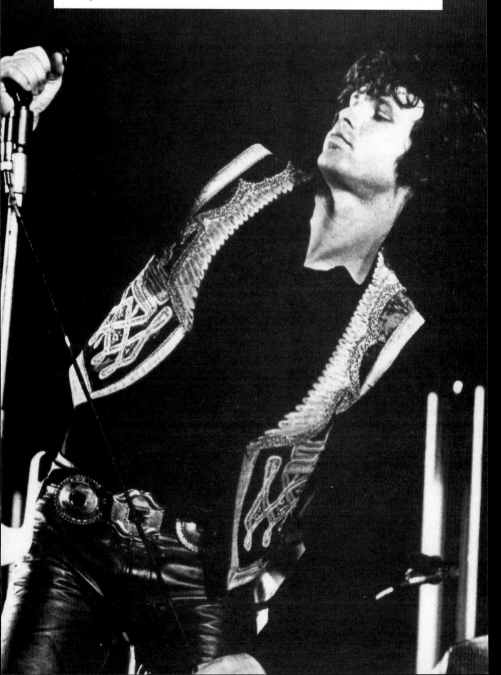

JANIS JOPLIN Janis Joplin sang the blues with incredible power. Shortly before her death she contributed funds for a tombstone for blues great Bessie Smith. Joplin's will was completed the day she died, leaving money for her friends to have a drink on Pearl.

BADFINGER Badfinger was one of rock's most tragic bands. They rarely received payment for royalties, which contributed to the suicide of two of its members, Pete Ham and Tom Evans (Ham *upper right*, Evans *lower right*).

KURT COBAIN Kurt Cobain was the creative force behind Nirvana. Following his suicide his mother stated, "Now he's gone and joined that stupid club." Cobain was another tragic victim of "The Curse of 27."

ward. This is the simplest way. Of course each operating system is different, but once the file is saved there should be a way to reverse it. After experimenting with your setup you will now be able to embark on an adventure that just may make you never listen to your favorite song the same way again. Maybe the best time to try this would be late at night in a dimly lit room whose only light is the glow from your computer's monitor. After all, the proper preparation is everything.

Though many have questioned the use of subliminal messages, nothing created the hysteria of hidden messages like the *CBS Evening News* on April 28, 1982. Dan Rather ran a report commenting on the discovery of supposedly hidden Satanic messages in pop songs. He played the infamous Led Zeppelin "Stairway to Heaven" backward track as well as sections of songs by Electric Light Orchestra and Styx. Many viewers were shocked by what they thought they heard. Many fundamentalist groups raised questions as to a hidden plot by the recording companies to create a Satanic conspiracy. This hysteria resulted in House Bill 6363 being introduced by Representative Robert K. Dornan (R-CA) to label records that fell under suspicion: "Warning: This record contains backward masking that makes a verbal statement which is audible when this record is played backward and which may be perceptible at a subliminal level when the record is played forward."

When we look to discover the true art of the current backward mask we should begin with Electric Light Orchestra. ELO actually have a number of recordings that contain hidden messages. The first example is found on the album *Face the Music,* at the beginning of the song "Fire on High." The track begins with an obvious backward track that sounds rather foreboding. When the track is reversed the actual message can be heard complete with a major complement of studio reverb. The track says, "The music is reversible, but time is not. Turn back! Turn back! Turn back!" Since we all agree that we can't turn back time, what is the meaning of the phrase "Turn back"? It has been suggested that ELO founder Jeff Lynne simply meant that if you don't turn back, your phono needle will jump off the record. The B-52's used the same approach at subliminal humor by placing a backward track on "Detour Through Your Mind" from the LP *Bouncing Off the Satellites*. When the track is reversed, the listener can hear Fred Schneider's voice saying, "I buried my parakeet in the backyard. No, no, you're playing the record backward. Watch out, you might ruin your needle." ELO, however, was one of the first bands accused of having a "hidden Satanic message" placed in one of their early songs. The song entitled "Eldorado" was said to contain a phonetic reversal that states, "He is the nasty one. Christ you're infernal. It is said we're dead men. All who have the mark will live." To find this track, you must listen for the phrase "on a voyage of no return . . ." and record this passage. If you listen carefully and follow along with a printout of the hidden message you may hear some of the words. Was it intentional? Jeff Lynne in one radio interview claimed, "It is absolutely manufactured by whoever said, 'That's what it said.' It doesn't say anything of the sort. And, that was totally manufactured by the person who said it said that. Because, anybody who can write a song forward and have it say something else backwards, has got to be some kind of genius and that I ain't. And I was upset at first by the accusation by that. But now I think it's kind of funny. I was just going to say again, categorically, that we are totally innocent of all those claims of devil stuff, it's a load of rubbish, and we're all God-fearing chaps."

The fun obviously continued for ELO with the release of the *Secret Messages* album. This LP was an evident parody of the entire phenomena of backward masking. On the back cover, the viewer will notice a series of ads including the following names: "F. Y. J. Ennel, T. D. Ryan, V. Nabbe, and G. U. Ruttock." These purported names are actually a series of anagrams that, when properly arranged, become the proper names of ELO members. For instance: "F. Y. J. Ennel" is Jeff Lynne, "T. D. Ryan" becomes R. Tandy, "V. Nabbe" rearranges to B. Bevan, and "G. U. Ruttock" is K. Groucutt. In this way each band member secretly places his name in code that can be deciphered.

The liner notes from the LP contain other hidden messages. The cupid is holding an ELO insignia. From this symbol a series of dots and dashes spells out ELO in Morse code. The opening song of the album is appropriately titled "Secret Messages." At the beginning of the song the listener can hear a keyboard methodically tapping out "ELO" in Morse code to complement the liner note image. (The use of musical instruments to pass along coded messages was also used by John Lennon in "Strawberry Fields Forever," in which he places his own name in code. Many listeners believed that this was John's way of claiming his complete ownership of this rock and roll masterpiece.) After the keyboard section opens "Secret Messages," a backward track can be heard with the phrase "Come again" immediately afterwards. Of course a voice intones secret messages to help the first-time listener discover the location of the backward track. When the track is reversed a voice says, "Welcome to the big show." At the conclusion of the album a voice states, "Welcome to the show," and then there is another backward track. When this track is reversed, the hidden message is "Come again." During "Rock 'n' Roll Is King" another backward track is heard. This message played backward simply becomes a very cordial "Thank you for listening." And finally, in the song "Danger Ahead," a hidden message can be reversed, stating "Look out there's danger ahead." It was apparent that Jeff Lynne and the ELO were having a great deal of fun with those individuals with little more to do than play their records looking for secret messages. The *Secret Messages* LP in Great Britain included a tongue-in-cheek warning to youths about secret hidden messages contained within the album. The American distributors were said to have become so upset that they deleted the warning for all American releases. Perhaps the British thought that only in America would people spin their records backward looking for hidden messages or clues for yet another conspiracy. Perhaps this is why the "Paul is dead" rumors were regarded in England as an altogether American phenomenon.

Not everyone saw the humor in *Secret Messages*. Those individuals who had always blamed the excesses of rock and roll for all of society's ills produced the twentieth-century equivalent of spectral evidence when the reversed word salad of phonetic sounds was put on display as hymns to Satan. No popular song was safe. The Eagles were accused of hiding a Satanic message in the pop classic "Hotel California." When the lyric "This could be heaven or this could be hell" is reversed some listeners claim that the backward track proclaims, "Yeah Satan. How he organized his own religion. Yeah, well he knows he should. How nice!" Of course to the detractors who believed the bizarre rumor that "Hotel California" was merely a code word for "the Church of Satan," this was yet more proof of a hidden Satanic agenda.

When the original House Bill 6363 was first read, the group Styx was also accused of being minions of Satan. Supposedly, "Snowblind" (a song against drug abuse) contained a hidden message that stated "Satan move through our voices." Listen as closely as possible and there is no way that this message can be understood! With the release of *Kilroy Was Here,* a red sticker proclaimed "By Order of the Majority for Musical Morality, this album contains secret backward messages . . ." Styx, true to their word, includes a backward track at the beginning of "Heavy Metal Poisoning." When reversed, the "mysterious" message becomes the Latin phrase *Annuit coeptis. Novus ordo seclorum.* This message is not from a Black Mass but is found instead upon the back of the one-dollar bill. The translation? "God has favored our undertakings. A new order for the ages." Of course this message referred to the founding of the United States government, and our new order was based upon our belief in democracy. The other occult symbols upon the dollar bill, the unfinished pyramid of Solomon and the eye of the Universal Architect, are apparent references to the ancient rite of Freemasonry. To some conspiracy buffs these very symbols represent the mysterious Illuminati, an organization said to be dedicated to a one-world government and blamed for every revolution and injustice suffered by the human race.

Another ludicrous charge was made that Satanists were summoned to recording studios to place hidden chants within the recordings to conjure forth demons. A character whose name is given only as Elaine gave this testimony: "I was, for seventeen years, a servant of Satan. . . . I attended special ceremonies at varying recording studios throughout the U.S. for the specific purpose of placing Satanic blessings on the rock music recorded. We did incantations which placed demons on *every* record and tape of rock music that was sold. At times we also called up special demons who spoke on the recordings—the various back masked messages."[2] It's hard to imagine that if a conspiracy of this magnitude existed, nothing has been documented to prove these absurd allegations. If it were true, it would only make sense that these newfound agents of supernatural powers would have taken each recording to the top of the charts. This apparently didn't take place; however, these sensational charges could be just the thing to trigger an appearance on a tabloid television show.

It was not only the heavy-metal bands that were condemned for backward masking. In the Plasmatics' "Coup d'État" a backward message states "Consensus programming is dangerous to your health. The brainwashed do not know they are brainwashed." Perhaps this message was a political statement that warned us to not become the Winston Smiths of George Orwell's

1984 and question whether Big Brother was now in firm control of our government and media.

The pop band Cheap Trick was also placed under fire. Some listeners became convinced that a backward mask in "Gonna Raise Hell" actually exclaimed, "Satan holds the keys." On Cheap Trick's *Heaven Tonight* the track "How Are You?" contains a high-speed subliminal message that rushes by during the lyrics that begin "I heard your voice I couldn't stand it you know you talk too much," and when this high-speed gibberish is slowed down, the hidden message becomes "The Lord's Prayer," in this case a very appropriate reference to an album entitled *Heaven Tonight*. The Christian rock act (many fundamentalists would consider this an oxymoron) Petra includes a backward track on their *More Power to You* LP. The track is found just before "Judas Kiss." When the track is reversed a voice states, "What are you looking for the devil for? When you ought to be looking for the Lord?"

The rock star formerly known as Prince (yet another hidden message) contains a religious reversal following the risqué "Darling Nikki." The backward track is found at the conclusion of the track amid the musical swells, and when reversed declares "Hello. How are you? I'm fine. 'Cause I know that the Lord is coming soon. Coming. Coming soon." Of course this may relate to Prince's belief that the world would end in the year 2000. Remember the lyrics from "1999"? "Two thousand zero, zero, party over/Oops out of time/So tonight I'm gonna party like it's 1999."

Other groups accused of placing hidden Satanic messages by way of the backward mask included the following: the Cars, whose "Shoo Be Doo" reversed was supposed to state "Satan" eleven times; Jefferson Starship's "A Child Is Coming," supposedly contained the hidden message "son of Satan" when the lyric "It's getting better" is played backward; Black Oak Arkansas's "When Electricity Came to Arkansas" from the live album *Raunch and Roll* was said to contain a backward subliminal that exclaims "Satan, Satan, Satan, Satan, Satan. He is god. He is god." What is surprising about this is that the album was recorded live and the grunting syllables would have to be well thought out in advance and pronounced very clearly and phonetically to give the hidden message. Not surprisingly, I find it very hard to hear anything that would effectively prove that this message, as well as many others mentioned here, actually exists and is not simply in the ear of the beholder.

Another band that seems to get a laugh out of placing hidden messages in their music is none other than Pink Floyd. In their *Animals* LP, released in 1977, Pink Floyd included a parody of Psalm 23. This was accomplished by using a synthesized voice, probably a Vocoder, and if you listen carefully the following message becomes rather plain:

> *The Lord is my Shepherd, I shall not want*
> *He makes me down to lie through pastures green*
> *He leadeth me the silent waters by*
> *With bright knives he releaseth my soul*
> *He maketh me to hang on hooks in high places*
> *He converteth me to lamb cutlets*
> *For lo, He hath great power and great hunger*
> *When cometh the day we lowly ones*
> *Through quite reflection and great dedication*
> *Master the art of karate Lo, we shall rise up*
> *And then we'll make the bugger's eyes water.*

The release of Pink Floyd's *The Wall* in 1979 contains a true backward mask. The track is found at the beginning of "Empty Spaces," just after the fadeout of "Good-bye Blue Sky." When the track is reversed, the listener can hear a voice stating "Congratulations. You have just discovered the secret message. Please send your answer to Old Pink, care of the funny farm,

Chaford [Chalfont?]" Another voice is heard to say, "Roger, Car-
olyn's on the phone." Some fans believed the reference to Old
Pink was directed toward Pink Floyd founding member Keith
(Syd) Barrett. Barrett had devised the band's name from two
Georgia bluesmen: Pink Anderson and Floyd Council. With
Barrett at its head the group explored the fertile musical fields of
psychedelia. Outrageous stage shows were perfected with the
first extensive use of lighting. It was the era of acid rock, and
Barrett became a victim of his own excesses. As he consumed
more and more LSD he would stare transfixed at the audience
and at times would only repeat the same chord throughout the
duration of each song, as the group was bathed in the eerie glow
of projected moving liquid slides. On April 6, 1968, Barrett left
the band and was temporarily hospitalized. Rumors of a "mental
breakdown" followed the band. In this case the reference to Old
Pink at the funny farm may be an affectionate accolade given to
Barrett by fellow founding member Roger Waters. In 1975 the
Pink Floyd album *Wish You Were Here* was another tribute to Syd
Barrett. The LP opens and closes with "Shine On You Crazy Di-
amond," which is also dedicated to Barrett. With the release of
The Wall in 1979, Pink Floyd's brilliant thematic album concerns the story of a rock star driven into madness and become
"Comfortably Numb." By this time, the group, under the creative control of Roger Waters (David Gilmour had replaced Barrett in 1968) began its Orwellian journey into the nothingness of
life. We each become victims of a unrelenting society personified
by sadistic schoolmasters who practice mind control, or in the
case of the earlier release *Animals,* a society divided and controlled by three groups: the Dogs, the Pigs, and the Sheep. This
was a fable or allegory dedicated to the exploitation of the classes
until "the sheep learn karate" and fight back against their oppres-
sors (the dogs) and those that represent the materialistic society

(the pigs). Some messages do not always have to be hidden in a backward mask.

Those individuals who are determined to find all the hidden messages of the past thirty years may be interested in taking another look at Pink Floyd's *Dark Side of the Moon*. Recently there have been reports that this Pink Floyd masterpiece is actually keyed as a sound track to MGM's *The Wizard of Oz*. Incredible as this may sound, there are a number of rather interesting coincidences when the album is played along with the movie. An article by Helen Kennedy from the *New York Daily News* May 13, 1997 states "When deejay George Taylor Morris at WZLX-FM in Boston first mentioned the phenomenon on the air six weeks ago, he touched off a frenzy. 'The phones just blew off the wall. It started on a Friday, and that first weekend you couldn't get a copy of *The Wizard of Oz* anywhere in Boston,' he said, 'because everyone knows the movie, everyone was staying at home to check it out.' . . . Dave Herman at WNEW-FM in New York mentioned the buzz a few weeks ago. The response—more than 2,000 letters—was the biggest ever in the deejay's 25-year on-air career." All right, are you ready to begin? To make sure the LP and film are in proper sync, the album needs to be started with the third roar of the famous MGM lion (don't get this confused with the Cowardly Lion). Why the third roar? How many times did Dorothy click her heels and say "There's no place like home, there's no place like home, . . ." This may take a few tries but you'll notice some strange coincidences that include:

*   During "Breathe," Dorothy is balancing on a fence at the time of the lyric "balanced on the biggest wave."
*   As Dorothy falls from the fence, "On the Run" starts.
*   At the sound of bells and chimes, "Miss Gulch" appears riding her bicycle.

- During "Time," Dorothy begins to run during the lyric "No one told you when to run."
- Also during the "Time" selection the fortune-teller is first seen with a sign that reads "Past present and future" (the three states of time).
- When Dorothy leaves the fortune-teller to return to Auntie Em's farm, the album is playing "home, home again" from "Breathe Reprise."
- When the tornado is seen in the background, the line "And I am not afraid of dying" can be heard (strangely, the tornado may be the Gig in the Sky). The tornado also seems to pulsate in time with the musical track.
- The female vocalist quiets down as the window frame hits Dorothy's head.
- As the house is in the sky, "The Great Gig in the Sky" continues.
- Side one of the LP ends at the exact time as the black-and-white section of the film.
- When Dorothy opens the door and beholds Oz in glorious color, the cash register rings and signals the beginning of "Money." The "yellow brick road" and "Emerald City" could represent a materialistic society based upon gold and paperback currency.
- Glenda, the good witch, appears in her bubble with the lyric "Don't give me that do-goody good bullshit."
- The Munchkins appear to be dancing in perfect time to "Us and Them."
- At the sound of "Forward he cried from the rear" Dorothy abruptly turns forward.
- During the repeated phrase "black . . black . . black," the Wicked Witch of the West appears, and on "blue . . . blue . . . blue," the camera shows Dorothy, who just happens to be wearing a blue dress.

- The phrase "And who knows which is which and who is who" occurs as the Wicked Witch of the West gazes down upon her recently deceased sister, The Wicked Witch of the East. This could be taken as an obvious play on the word "witch."

- With the line "Out . . . out . . . out," the Good Witch of the North leaves.

- "Brain Damage" begins at about the same time as the Scarecrow starts to sing "If I Only Had a Brain."

- During the lyric "The lunatic is on the grass," the Scarecrow frolics across the green meadow. (The line "And if the band you're in starts playing different tunes/I'll see you on the dark side of the moon" probably relates to Syd Barrett.)

- As the LP ends with "Eclipse," the most interesting coincidence occurs as Dorothy places her ear against the Tin Woodsman's chest to listen for a heartbeat. It is at this time that a heartbeat is heard on the album.

- Another coincidence concerns the album cover. The cover shows a triangular-shaped prism (like the dinner bell at Auntie Em's) set against a black background. A white beam of light strikes the triangle, and passing through the prism the beam is transformed into a brilliant rainbow. Does this hint at the movie, which also undergoes a transformation from black-and-white into color? Of course, it is only appropriate that the rainbow makes its appearance on the cover, since Judy Garland's timeless "Over the Rainbow" is from the same film.

After these clues were brought up across the country from local classic rock stations to MTV, listeners wanted to know if this was an incredibly planned stunt or simply a coincidence. Pink Floyd keyboardist Richard Wright swore on his family that it indeed was only a strange coincidence. *Dark Side of the Moon* engineer Alan Parsons, in an interview with Dave Herman on WNEW-FM in New York, denied any intentional parallels and said that the whole thing was mere chance. Still, those who believe in the theory feel that Roger Waters had the necessary skills needed to choreograph a sound track to the popular movie since he had worked on movie scores earlier in his musical career. What does all this mean? In the worst-case scenario, it gives music fans the opportunity to enjoy two classic works in a way probably not thought possible before.

In retrospect, I suppose we haven't come too far since everyone was looking for "Paul is dead" clues. From what I'm told, many people are still looking. Recordings by Beck, Metallica, and of course Marilyn Manson are now being played backward for hints of current hidden messages.

It is also refreshing when one of rock and roll's great classic albums is given new life by yet a new generation of fans. It is also amazing to many of us that looking at a cloud, or into the ebony swirls of an inkblot, so many of us see our own anxieties and fears. There is a scene in Shakespeare's *Hamlet* where the Prince of Denmark asks Polonius if a certain painted cloud was in the shape of a weasel? A camel? Or a whale? Of course, the foolish chancellor is only too happy to agree that he sees the shapes that Hamlet has shown him. Perhaps it is only the need to agree to become one of the insiders that allows us to see the hidden shapes that someone points out to us. How many individuals constantly stand staring into a "Magic Eye" drawing waiting for the image to leap out from the frame in all its 3-D glory? We want to see and we would like to believe. And just at that moment, when the first obscure mass becomes more and more intelligible and we finally recognize that certain familiar image or sound, the icy pinpricks rush up our spines and we give that knowing little shiver of complete recognition. We may never listen to that song or see that picture in quite the same way, because it has now expanded our perception.

Obviously, at least two points can be made concerning the

search for hidden meanings. First of all, many of us would agree that anyone who spends so much time playing records backward, putting albums in sync with classic movies, and searching endlessly for the meaning for each minute detail contained within an album's cover artwork probably simply has too much time on his hands. But on the other hand, wasn't it Einstein who said "Imagination is more important than knowledge"? It is fun to look back over your old album collection and think, "Why didn't I think of that? It was always right in front of my face." So, the pure entertainment value alone is worthwhile, if the listener remembers that it is all in fun.

The second point in dealing with the hidden messages phenomenon concerns those individuals and groups who carefully dissect musical passages looking for a hidden conspiracy, Satanic or otherwise, and announce their findings as valid and not open to discussion. For example, I was shocked while reading *The Satan Hunter* to discover that the book's publisher was located at 666 Dundee Road. I couldn't help but notice the irony in this. I also find irony in the sensational court cases that have been brought against Judas Priest and Ozzy Osbourne.

Did a hidden subliminal message in Judas Priest's "Stained Glass Window" lead two youths to commit suicide? *Variety* magazine (December 31, 1986) ran an article on this sensational trial. The original lawsuit claimed that Judas Priest and CBS Records were responsible for the two youths attempting suicide by shooting themselves in the head in a church parking lot. The victims allegedly spent six hours listening to an album by the band. The legal argument deals with the "hypnotic" quality of the ever-present beat. Additionally, the lyrics were argued to have an effect on the listener, especially those with "emotional problems," that would lead them to "reject society and commit suicide." One point was obvious. Rock and roll music has always rejected society. It is another matter, however, to prove that it leads to suicide.

The boys' attorney, Kenneth McKenna, claimed that the combination of the "intonation of the music" and suggestive lyrics led to the "mesmerism" of the plaintiffs, making them believe that the solution to life's many problems is death.

Lawyers for the band claimed that the individual members of Judas Priest were protected by their First Amendment rights to freedom of expression. It was also argued that it would be unrealistic to claim any form of monetary damages and the band could not be held liable for any damages.

Jerry Whitehead, the Washoe district judge in Nevada who heard the case, denied a defense motion to dismiss the suit against Judas Priest. He said under Nevada law a lawsuit could not be dismissed unless "every factual claim made by the plaintiff could be considered true and there could still be no basis for damages." There was no statement issued concerning the proper interpretation of the First Amendment. "McKenna said [the two youths] had been listening to the album *Stained Glass* in Belknap's bedroom. He said they had been drinking 'some' and smoking marijuana."[3]

The hidden subliminal message is said to be found in "Better by You, Better Than Me" and when played backward simply states "Do it." The actual sound seems to be formed from the breathing of one of the singers and a reversed guitar sound. "The 1990 trial in Reno was a media circus, complete with members of Judas Priest, groupies, subliminal junk-science extraordinaire Wilson Bryan Key, and the national press. Rob Halford [lead singer] of Judas Priest and CBS Records insisted that they had no intention whatsoever of exterminating their markets."[4] During the trial, Halford did admit to placing one subliminal message in the Judas Priest song "Love Bites" from the album *Defenders of the Faith*. Halford claimed that the well-hidden message stated "In the dead of the night, love bites." Even with this admission the judge ruled against the plaintiff's case.

A similar California suit against filed against hard rocker Ozzy Osbourne and CBS Records was also dismissed in another courtroom. The song in question was "Suicide Solution" and a claim that a twenty-seven-second subliminal message existed. The message was alleged to say, "All right now people, you really know what it is about. You've got it. Why try? Why try? Take the gun and try it. Try it. Shoot. Shoot. Go on."[5] Ironically, the true message behind "Suicide Solution" is antisuicide and was written by Osbourne shortly after the death of AC/DC's lead singer Bon Scott.

In looking back at the hidden-message phenomenon of the early 1980s we must ask ourselves, were the Plasmatics right in the backward warning given in "Coup d'État"? Were we the brainwashed? Or is the entire concept of the dangers of backward masking a modern-day Tituba placing the blame on a new generation of accused disciples of Satan? This new spectral evidence does not contain invisible yellow birds representing witches' familiars but rather the inconstant gibberish of phonetic word salad open only to the interpretation of the faithful. Fortunately for many unjustly accused musicians and companies, the gallows and stake were not prepared in order to purge their souls from the perceived foul touch of Satan. As the backward message craze grew more and more outlandish, the embarrassed public quickly turned away from the accusations. It took the visionary girls from Salem, accusing the wife of Massachusetts's governor of witchcraft, to end the witch craze in that time period. Perhaps it was the accusation of a hidden Satanic message in Bing Crosby's traditional Christmas rendering of "Silver Bells" that may now help the public see through the lunacy of declaring that many songs are being filled with cryptic messages. It was suggested that when "Silver Bells" was played backward a listener could hear "Agents of evil they're listening . . . they are longing." When Christmas classics and religious hymns can be brought into question, surely the madness must end here. To some extent it has, but rumors still persist as to the placement of hidden messages.

At the height of the congressional hearings on back masking and the Tipper Gore findings, comedian Bob "Bobcat" Goldthwait recorded a live comedy album, *Meat Bob,* that made fun of many of these supposed hidden messages. As his album ends, the listener can't help but hear a garbled message that indicates the presence of a concealed track. As researchers recorded the passage to determine the meaning, they were shocked to determine its true message. What did it say? What was this secret demonic message? Only this: "Obey your parents, be nice, don't eat snacks, and go to church. Umm, give money to Jerry Falwell. Bye."

9. "IF 6 WAS 9"

There are more things in Heaven and earth, Horatio, than are
dreamt of in your philosophy.
—Shakespeare, *Hamlet* (1.5.187–88)

Nothing ever just happens.
—John Lennon

If I don't see you any more in this world,
I'll see you in the next one so don't be late.
—Jimi Hendrix "Voodoo Chile"

THROUGHOUT HISTORY MAN HAS SOUGHT THE ANSWERS to his inevitable destiny. In the dawn of the ancient Chaldean empire the movement of the stars and other heavenly bodies gave birth to the study of astrology. Seers looked into the heavens in order to find their place in the universal order of things. From the heavens man has witnessed omens from the skies. Written history has chronicled "flaming stones [falling] from the skies. The Israelites witnessed their enemies, the Egyptians, being plagued by fiery hail. Aristotle recorded the fall of a meteorite at Aegosotami. Meteorites showered on southern France in 1790. A single meteorite, which fell in Siberia in 1908, filled the sky with debris for two years. The Indians spoke of red-hot stones being hurled down from the heavens. Oil rained down on Arabia. The Portuguese say that it rained blood in Lisbon in 1551.

". . . In the Middle Ages, flaming crosses fell several times. Stone hatchets were showered on Sumatra. Flaming planks blasted down on Touraine. Fish fell without warning from the sky in many places, most notably in Singapore in 1861. Also in the skies luminous visions have appeared. To the children of Israel there appeared a pillar of fire by night and a cloud by day. Constantine saw a lighted cross appear in the sky. Visionaries through the ages have spoken with angels and have whirled up into the clouds. Winged beings appeared in Palermo, Italy, in 1880. Winged beings also appeared over the battlefield of Mons in 1914. They appeared to the English soldiers below as English bowmen, and they were led by St. George."[1]

As man continually searches the heavens he also quietly casts an introspective eye within his own being. Desperately, he searches for the true meaning of his existence and his purpose for being. He probes for some hidden key to bring about his eventual enlightened state. Nothing can be taken for granted. The mathematical laws of nature all must be examined as to their meaning and significance. This search for meaning can also add to tragedy. The rules of the universe are simple. No one is guaranteed to live happily ever after, not even a rock star.

Guitar great Jimi Hendrix was in a constant search for some cosmic meaning to life. His songs strongly suggested his belief in UFOs ("Up From the Skies," "Castles Made of Sand," "House Burning Down"), Transcendental Meditation, and reincarnation. He believed that rainbows were actually bridges that linked the world of the living to the unseen spirit world of the dead. His dreams were often filled with vivid colors and images of being underwater. His trademark guitar classic, "Purple Haze," was at first considered a drug song. The title was mistakenly cast as a tribute to LSD, or in the opinion of some listeners, amphetamine tablets called "purple hearts." According to the late Monika Dannemann, Hendrix's lover at the time of his death, the actual meaning of the song was based upon a very long manuscript whose actual working title was "Purple Haze—Jesus Saves." In this manuscript Hendrix stated that the entire meaning of the song came from a dream he had: "In this dream he looked down on earth and saw an unborn fetus waiting for its birth as if it were pointing at the time for it to be born. At the same time he saw spirits of the dead leaving earth. Later in the dream he went on a journey through the dimensions, and was walking under the sea. Part of the song was about the purple haze which surrounded him, engulfed him, and in which he got lost. He told me later what a traumatic experience this had been, but that in the dream his faith in Jesus had saved him."[2] Some sources, though, including Keith Altham in an article from the magazine *Univibes,* claim that the title "Purple Haze" actually came from a sci-fi novel concerning a futuristic weapon that emitted pulsating purple beams of light. Altham claims that Hendrix's vision was based upon Philip José Farmer's *Night of Light,* published in 1957. It was also in 1957 that the American sci-fi pulp magazine *Fantasy and Sci-*

ence Fiction ran a short story derived from the same novel. This may well have served as the inspiration behind the song's title. Jimi Hendrix, however, seemed to corroborate Dannemann's claim when he mentioned in an interview with John King for *New Musical Express* (January 1967): "I dreamt a lot and I put a lot of my dreams down as songs. I wrote one called 'First Look Around the Corner' and another called 'The Purple Haze,' which was all about a dream I had that I was walking under the sea." (The lyric "'scuse me while I kiss the sky" was said to refer to a drowning man bursting through the water's surface to fill his collapsed lungs with life-sustaining oxygen.) .

Jimi Hendrix's underwater dreams continued with his vision of the lost continent Atlantis in "1983 (A Merman I Should Turn to Be)." In this selection Hendrix and his lover, Catherina, walk peacefully into the sea, away from the war-torn earth, to be reborn as higher spiritual beings and make their way to the undersea colony of Atlantis to live forever in complete spiritual awareness. The irony involving Hendrix's dreams seems to relate to a premonition of his premature death. Jimi Hendrix died by asphyxiation caused by inhaling his own vomit while he slept. Earlier that evening Hendrix had drunk some wine and taken nine sleeping pills to help him sleep. When he was rushed to the hospital his lungs were filled with a combination of vomit and wine. Sadly, the press rushed to the incorrect verdict that Jimi Hendrix had died of a drug overdose. "He [Hendrix] regarded taking drugs, drinking alcohol, even smoking cigarettes, as weaknesses and nothing to be proud of."[3]

At least one of Hendrix's most popular songs hinted at his awareness of magic and the supernatural. In "Voodoo Chile (Slight Return)," Hendrix's lyrics suggest that he can chop a mountain down with a wave of his hand. Monika Dannemann comments on Hendrix's suggestion of magic and voodoo: "I asked him why he called himself a 'voodoo child,' because for me voodoo had always meant something to do with black magic. He explained that the word came from Africa, and just meant magic in general, and that originally voodoo was a religion in which magic is used, as it is in many other religions. Depending on the purpose for which this magic is used, it can be positive or negative. Voodoo was meant to be a positive force."[4] In the opening lyric to "Voodoo Chile," Hendrix sings

> *The night I was born the moon turned a fire red*
> *My poor mother cried out, "well, the gypsy was right"*
> *And I seen her fall down right dead*

Once while performing at the Royal Albert Hall in 1969, Hendrix introduced Dave Mason, Chris Wood, and African percussionist Kwasi Dzidzornu, who was called "Rocki" by his fellow musicians, and invited them to join the Experience on stage and perform "Room Full of Mirrors." Hendrix enjoyed composing his songs against a background of different drum sounds. They helped serve as his inspiration: "Rocki's father was a voodoo priest and the chief drummer of a village in Ghana, West Africa. . . . One of the first things Rocki asked Jimi was where he got that voodoo rhythm from? When Jimi demurred, Rocki went on to explain in his halting English that many of the signature rhythms Jimi played on the guitar were very often the same rhythms that his father played in voodoo ceremonies. The way Jimi danced to the rhythms of his playing reminded Rocki of the ceremonial dances to the rhythms his father played to Oxun, the god of thunder and lightning. The ceremony is called *voodoshi*. As a child in the village, Rocki would carve wooden representations of the gods. They also represented his ancestors. These were the gods they worshiped.

"They would jam a lot in Jimi's house. One time they were jamming and Jimi stopped and asked Rocki point blank, 'You communicate with God, do you?' Rocki said, 'Yes, I communicate with God.'"⁵ It is ironic that Oxun would be the god of "thunder and lightning," since the roaring wailing feedback of the guitar icon's trademark Fender Stratocaster guitars duplicated the tumultuous sounds of the tempest and the deafening howl of the gale. To a great extent human existence relies on rhythms. The pounding of the blood through the arteries and veins determines a fine-tuned pulse. The pulsating and throbbing of the heart forces the life-giving blood throughout the body in a sweeping cadence. As the heart ceases to beat, life comes to an end. The first musical rhythms to inspire a young Jimi Hendrix were the driving gospel rhythms of the black Pentecostal churches in which he grew up.

Jimi Hendrix was also proud of his Native American ancestry. His great-grandmother was a full-blooded Cherokee. Though Jimi's actual birth name was given as Johnny Allen Hendrix, Jimi's father decided to change his son's name to James Marshall Hendrix when young Jimi was four years old. However, "There's an old superstition among certain Native American tribes that it is unwise to name a child twice because it splits his eternal spirit in two, half of it ascending into Heaven and half of it going straight to Hell."⁶ In this way, Jimi Hendrix was indeed born a "Voodoo Child." Shortly after his parents' divorce, Jimi remembered a dream concerning his mother: "My mother was being carried away on this camel. It was a big caravan and she's going under these trees and you could see the shade, you know the leaf patterns across her face. She's saying, 'Well, I won't be seeing you too much anymore, you know. I'll see you.' And I said, 'Yeah, but where are you going?' It was about two years later that she died. I will always remember that. There are some dreams you never forget."⁷

Hendrix's fascination with the occult continued with his release of *Axis: Bold As Love:* "The axis is like the Christian cross or the voodoo peristyle—a link between the heavens and earth. The axis of the earth holds everything together. If the axis of the earth were altered, everything would be different. Entirely new continents, new directions for north and south, and seas inundating shores that once laid peaceful . . ." Jimi also felt a record spinning on a turntable was directly related to the Earth's spinning on its axis. At one point he said, "Well, like the axis of the Earth, you know. If it changes, well it changes the whole face of the Earth like every few thousand years, you know. It's like love in a human being if he really falls in love deep enough, it will change him, you know, it might change his whole life . . ." Manly P. Hall once wrote (in *The Secret Teachings of All Ages: An Encyclopedic Outline*), "The Axis is a mysterious individual who, unknown and unsuspected, mingles with mankind and who, according to tradition, has his favorite seat on the roof of the Caaba . . .

"When an 'Axis' quits this earthly existence, he is succeeded by the 'Faithful One,' who has occupied the place at his right hand. . . . For to these holy men, who bear the collective titles of 'Lord of Souls' and 'Directors,' is committed a spiritual supremacy over mankind far exceeding the temporal authority of earthly rulers."[8]

Spiritual awareness is also evident in the study of numerology. Monika Dannemann writes about Hendrix's awareness of numerology and his belief in mysterious powers in her book *The Inner World of Jimi Hendrix.* He believed these powers are found everywhere but specifically in certain words, numbers, and names and felt that there are deep mysteries hidden in some ancient words.

Danneman goes on to explain Hendrix's belief that when positive energy is reversed it becomes negative. To demonstrate this to her, Hendrix wrote GOD and then DOG. He explained that there is duality in Nature and that since he'd discovered this concept he had become much more careful in his choice of words.

He claimed at the time that he tried to avoid the use of the word "God." Next, Hendrix wrote DEVIL and again mentioned that the reverse form spells out LIVED.

Then Jimi gave Monika a lesson in numerology. He wrote the number 8 and explained that for various reasons it is used for evil purposes. He subsequently wrote the number 15 in front of DEVIL, and the sign =. In this case he claimed that 15 equals the Devil. Hendrix then commented on the number 7, and claimed that this number was a very special and positive number. Danneman remembers Jimi stating that 7 is full of mysteries and had many important meanings that were to be revealed. According to Hendrix, the number 7 is the most important number.

Danneman further elaborates on Hendrix's reasoning: "The earth and the spirit are linked strongly with the number 7. Also, every seventh year, there is a change in the body. It's a circle to put things right, and because of this, everything alters and evolves around it. Jimi pointed out to me that in the past other civilizations had to go through these circles connected with the number 7, going through a peak, and then some sacrifices have to be made, some effort gone through, which he symbolized by drawing a cross over each circle. 'That is the way evolution happens,' he said.

"Then Jimi drew four 7s opposing one another, thus forming a spiral of 7s, a symbol which is known as the swastika cross. He explained that it is of vital importance which direction the 7s are pointing in, because this shows whether the symbol has a good or an evil meaning."[9]

Obviously, this was a reference to the Nazi adoption of the swastika in World War II and in Hitler's study and collection of occult artifacts. Hitler was also said to have come in possession of the Spear of Longinus (The Spear of Destiny). This relic was said to be the spear used to pierce Christ's side during the crucifixion and it gave its owner vast amounts of power—in some cases, the power to rule the world. The spear, according to legend, had also been in the possession of Bismarck during his rise to power as German chancellor. Hitler was also in search of other mysterious occult artifacts that would increase his power. This search included the Holy Grail, the goblet used by Christ at the Last Supper and later by Joseph of Arimathea to collect Christ's blood during the crucifixion. According to the legend of the Grail, it has appeared throughout history in various places and to many individuals. Some have actually claimed ownership of the vessel (and I'll bet you thought all those Harrison Ford movies were completely fictitious!). Hitler's belief in the occult was so well-known that it was purported that the "V for Victory" gesture used by Winston Churchill, and adopted by the Allies during World War II, was actually a sign used to ward off evil. It has been insinuated that the gesture was given to the British Prime Minister by none other than Aleister Crowley, the leading master of magic in Great Britain.

Since Jimi Hendrix believed in numerology to such a great extent, let's determine what his numbers reveal about his personality. First of all, according to Richard Cavendish's *The Black Arts*, we have to prepare the proper chart so here we go:

1	2	3	4	5	6	7	8	9
A	B	C	D	E	F	G	H	I
J	K	L	M	N	O	P	Q	R
S	T	U	V	W	X	Y	Z	

To translate Jimi Hendrix's name into its proper numerological form, we first must find the number associated with each of his name's letters. Therefore, J =(1) I= (9) M= (4) I= (9) H=(8)

E=(5) N=(5) D=(4) R=(9) I=(9) X=(6). Now, we add the numbers together 1+9+4+9+8+5+5+4+9+6= 69. The entire numerical value of Hendrix's name is 69. Isn't it strange that these two numbers are represented in "If 6 Was 9" (On the *Axis: Bold as Love* album)? Coincidence? The 6 and 9 are then added together to reach the number 15. Again the 1 and 5 are added together to arrive at the number 6. In this calculation Jimi Hendrix's destiny would be controlled by the number 6. According to Cavendish, "six is a 'perfect' number. A 'perfect' number is one that equals the sum of its proper divisors other than itself. The proper divisors of 6 (apart from 6 itself) are 1, 2, and 3, and 1+2+3=6 . . . 6 is regarded as a balanced, well-integrated, harmonious number, not torn by internal conflict, and so the 6-nature is balanced, well-adjusted, and contented . . . 6 people are affectionate, reliable, and hardworking . . . They may be extremely successful in the arts, because they have the creative power of 3 twice (6=3+3). 'Three' is associated with the Trinity and is a symbol of completeness." [10]

In Louis Stewart's *Life Forces,* the author says that to determine our destiny we must first calculate our "life-path number." Jimi Hendrix was born on November 27, 1942. November is the eleventh month (11), on the twenty-seventh day (27), in the year 1942. Now, if we search for the life-path number, 11+27+1942= 1980; 1+9+8+0=18; 1+8=9. The numeral 9 now becomes the life-path for the guitar great. A 9 life path leads to "A cosmopolitan life, full of achievement but also of sacrifice. People born as 9 are especially open-minded, but at the same time they tend to be ironic and cold. They can be sure that whatever happens to them will be intense." [11] There is no doubting that Jimi Hendrix's life was "intense." However, reading a book on numerology is much like looking at a horoscope and seeing a general pattern that you can adapt to your present-day life. It is much easier predicting the future when you know the outcome. Still, in looking at the repetition of the number values found in Jimi Hendrix's name, you can't help but notice that the number 9 is dominant in that it is repeated three times. The next repeated numeral is the 5. According to books on numerology, the number 5 represents a sensual person, since we have five senses. It is also is said to denote "a life of adventure, travel, and sudden changes. There's often a strong emphasis on sex. Some '5' people become entirely too adventuresome and unattached; then there's a danger of alcoholism, drug addiction, and repetitious sex." [12]

As far as the number 9 is concerned with Jimi Hendrix's fate, remember that he was born on November 27 (2+7=9) in 1942, and he died on September 18, 1970. He was pronounced dead at 11:25 P.M. Now Hendrix's life had indeed come full circle. He was born on the twenty-seventh, which equals 9 and died in September (ninth month) on the eighteenth (1+8=9) at 11:25 P.M. (1+1+2+5=9). The immediate cause of death was given as "inhalation of vomit," possibly due to Jimi Hendrix's taking *nine* Vesperax sleeping pills. When Monika finally called for an ambulance she dialed the emergency prefix 999. He died at the age of twenty-seven (2+7=9), the exact age of his mother when she died in 1958. Following Hendrix's death, "The two persons closest to him on a personal and a business level, Devon Wilson [former girlfriend] and Michael Jeffrey [manager], both died strange and violent deaths soon after he left this world, Devon in an ambiguous plunge from the upper stories of the Chelsea Hotel in New York City and Jeffrey in an exploding commercial airliner. Other close associates died, got strung out, or went mad soon after his death." [13] In this case we can see that Hendrix's fate was peculiarly tied to the numerals 6 and 9, just as "If 6 Was 9" suggests.

Other numbers have been tied to various rock stars' fates, but probably none more bizarre than in the case of John Lennon and the number 9. In the great Ray Coleman's definitive biography, *Lennon,* the author lists a number of unusual coincidences involving John Lennon and the number 9. John was aware that the number 9 seemed to have a powerful connection to his life. He was born at 6:30 P.M. (six plus three makes nine) on October 9, 1940. His mother's address was 9 Newcastle (nine letters) Road, Wavertree (nine letters), Liverpool. Sadly, his mother was killed when she was struck by a car driven by an off-duty policeman. The car's registration number was LKF 630 (nine) and the police constable's badge number was 126 (nine). Familiar locations in Liverpool included Penny Lane (nine) in postal district 18 (nine) in Liverpool (nine). The bus John rode to school each day was number 72 (nine). John also attempted nine General Certificate of Education Exams but failed each of them.

Many of the people who touched John's life had nine letters in their names, including his beloved aunt Mimi Smith, Bob Wooler at the Cavern, the Maharishi, Bill Harry of *Mersey Beat* newspaper, John's best friend Stu Sutcliffe, and songwriting partner Paul McCartney.

John's musical career was also rife with the number 9. John's first group was the Quarrymen (nine). The Beatles began with the addition of Paul McCartney and the group played such Liverpool venues as Jacaranda, the Blue Angel, and Cassanova (all containing nine letters). Brian Epstein first introduced himself to the Beatles at the Cavern on November 9, 1961, and nine years later in 1970 the Beatles officially broke up. Epstein died on August 27 (nine), 1967. The Beatles received their recording contract with E.M.I. Records on May 9, 1962 and produced many of their greatest recordings at Abbey Road (nine) Studios. The Beatles made their first appearance in America on *The Ed Sullivan Show* on February 9, 1964.

When John first met his future wife Cynthia Powell she was living at 18 (nine) Trinity Road, Hoylake. John and Cynthia's son, Julian, was born at Sefton General Hospital, 126 (nine) Smithdown (nine) Road, Liverpool. Ironically, both John's mother and stepfather were pronounced dead there. John's second son, Sean, was born on John's birthday on October 9, 1975.

A number of Lennon's recordings featured the number 9 prominently, including "The One after 909," "Revolution 9," and "Number Nine Dream." Lennon told Coleman that one of his most important songs contained nine key words: "All we are saying is give peace a chance."

John met his soul mate, Yoko Ono, on November 9, 1966 (strangely the same date of the "mysterious" car crash in the Paul is Dead rumors). He changed his name to John Ono Lennon so that the combination with Yoko Ono Lennon would feature the letter O nine times. In 1971, John and Yoko moved to New York City, and nine years later John Lennon would be murdered. The Lennons lived in an apartment at the Dakota, located at 72nd Street. Their original apartment number was also number 72. John had once received a death threat while performing with the Beatles in Paris in 1964, and became very nervous when the written threat mentioned that "I am going to shoot you at nine tonight." Tragically, John Lennon was shot to death on 72nd Street outside the Dakota—the time of the shooting was given as 10:50 P.M. on December 8, 1980. However, due to the five-hour time difference between New York and his native Liverpool, Lennon's death was announced in Great Britain on December 9, 1980. John was rushed by ambulance to Roosevelt (nine) Hospital, which is located on Ninth Avenue, Manhattan. John Lennon was pronounced dead at 11:07 (nine).[14]

There are other references to the number nine in John Lennon's life. In *The Last Days of John Lennon,* by Frederick Seaman (Seaman was hired as John Lennon's personal assistant), the author describes the front gate of the Dakota: "Over the front gate is an Indian head carved in stone and surrounded by the digits 1-8-8-1. [1+8=9; 8+1=9; 9+9=18; 1+8=9] To a casual observer, those numbers indicate the year in which the Dakota was built, but after I had spent a couple of years working for the Lennons, I would begin to contemplate them in a very different light: Eight plus one is nine, the highest number, denoting change and spirituality; if you add 99 to 1881, you get 1980—the year in which John Lennon was struck down by a hail of bullets in this very spot; when your good luck runs out, eight-minus-one minus eight-minus-one equals zero."[15]

John Lennon and Yoko Ono were fascinated by the occult. At times John would buy out the entire sections of occult literature in bookstores. He was intrigued by divination and sought the advice of tarot readers and psychics. During the evenings he would follow the example of James Joyce and read seven pages from seven different books before falling asleep: "John read voraciously, often on weighty matters, as if he were researching some challenging subject. He was always giving me lists of books to purchase. Many dealt with religion, psychic phenomena, the occult, and especially death. Other favorite subjects were ancient history, anthropology, and anything having to do with the sea.

"A typical list of books included *Color and Personality* by Dr. Audrey Carger; *Rebel in the Soul* by Bika Reed; *The Secret Science* by Ischa Schwaller de Lubitz; *Drawing Down the Moon* by Margot Adler; *A Slaver's Logbook* by Captain Theophilus Conmean; *The Anatomy of Swearing* by Ashley Montagu; *Working* by Studs Terkel; *The Manila Galleon*, a history of Spanish galleon trading between Manila and Acapulco; . . . and *How to be Really With It*, by Father Bernard Basser, S.J."[16]

One of the most surprising aspects of the Lennons' stay in New York was in how they acquired their apartment at the Dakota. Stephen Birmingham of the Independent News Alliance describes the unsavory history of the Dakota in an article entitled "The Dakota: John Lennon Murder Adds to Often Bizarre Legacy of Century-Old Apartment Building" (December 13, 1980). The dark brooding Dakota has long had a reputation for being haunted. One legendary ghost is said to be that of a young girl who appears in nineteenth-century dress. One worker mentioned seeing the spirit a few years before the Lennons moved in. She calmly bounced a ball and excitedly told the worker, "Today's my birthday." When the astonished man told his fellow workers about the mysterious little girl, they searched for her identity. No child at the Dakota matched her description. A few days later, the workman tragically fell to his death down an open stairwell. When the Lennons moved into the Dakota they lived on the seventh floor in apartment 72 [nine]. John Lennon became so upset about the stairwell outside his apartment that he laced it shut with heavy clothesline to keep Sean from falling through the opening.

Another phantom stalking the Dakota is a figure of a "man with a wig" who would appear at times and threaten workmen. Insiders say the ghost resembles Edward Clark, who built what was described as "the most beautiful apartment house in the world" in 1884. He died before seeing it completed, but strangely records showed that this eccentric millionaire wore a wig and bore a strong resemblance to the ghostly shape that walks the halls of the Dakota.

Perhaps the living inhabitants who occupied apartments within the shadowy walls of the prestigious dwelling are more fearful than the ghostly spirits. First there was Miss Leo, who stuffed one of her carriage horses and put it on display within her parlor. At the ripe old age of 100 she would walk the halls completely naked, singing songs as her long dyed-red hair billowed out behind her. Only in the imaginative world of William Faulkner could the following story emerge. Miss Leo's neighbors became very curious about an odd odor that came from within her apartment. It seemed that Miss Leo lived all alone with her bachelor brother. When the puzzling odor became a stench the neighbors entered the room to find the corpse of her brother still sitting in his favorite chair. He had been dead for days but Miss Leo could not bear to part with him.

The Dakota was a gathering place for celebrities. Judy Garland had lived there, as had Edward R. Murrow. Lauren Bacall, Rex Reed, Leonard Bernstein, and Roberta Flack were also familiar patrons of the Dakota. Of course, some tenants died there. The list of celebrities who "shuffled off this mortal coil" and made their way through the seldom opened Undertaker's Gate on Seventy-third Street included Boris Karloff, Judy Holiday, and actor Robert Ryan and his wife Jessie.

"Apartment 72 is the Ryans' old apartment, and when the Lennons moved in they decided to hire a medium to investigate the possibility of any resident spirits. Promptly contacted was the late Jessie Ryan, who announced that she was happy to share her home with John and Yoko, and promised to cause them no trouble.

"Yoko Lennon decided that it would be a good idea to let the Ryans' daughter, Lisa, know of her mother's whereabouts in the Beyond.

"Lisa Ryan was not exactly thrilled with the news."*

Still another sinister history permeated the history of the seventh floor of the Dakota apartments. The Roman Polanski horror film *Rosemary's Baby* was filmed in a series of apartments that were bought by the Lennons. Of course, shortly after the release of this occult thriller, Polanski's wife Sharon Tate was brutally murdered in Los Angeles by the Manson family. It was even suggested by Seaman that Lennon had written "Helter Skelter" on one of the apartment walls within his Dakota offices.

When Yoko became pregnant with Sean it was determined that the baby would be delivered by caesarean on John's thirty-

* Birmingham, "The Dakota," Independent News Alliance, December 13, 1980.

fifth birthday, October 9, 1975. "It was not until much later, when I learned that among the many superstitions John and Yoko shared was an ancient Hindu belief that a son born on his father's birthday inherits his soul when the father dies, that I finally understood why Yoko would go to such lengths to deliver a child on John's birthday." [17] In *Dakota Days,* the Lennons' tarot reader John Green, who was known to them as Charlie Swan, relates this story with Yoko speaking: "'This baby is going to change the world. If a messiah were going to be reborn today, he would choose rock stars as parents so he could have access to the media . . . Our baby can't be normal! We would hate a normal baby! No, she has to be perfect.'

"'She?'

"'Now don't be stubborn, Charlie. I know that you said 'a boy,' but this time the Messiah has to be a woman. It makes sense, doesn't it? Last time a man, this time a woman. That's the economy of the universe.'" [18]

Of course the baby was a boy and his name was chosen in the following fashion. John is speaking: "'Yeah, we decided on Sean. It means John in Irish or Gaelic or something . . . Yoko wanted to name him John, but as I already got a son named John—John Julian—I thought having two sons with the same name a bit redundant. And Taro, that's his middle name. That's for you, like the cards . . . No, you're right. It's John in Japanese or something, but I thought the similarity was fun.'" [19]

John Green (Charlie) also recalls a trip with Yoko to consult a *bruja* [witch] in Colombia for protection against her enemies and for Sean's continued good health. After Yoko went through a series of purification rituals, it was time for the blood sacrifice. A dove was displayed as Nora, the witch, pierced its tiny brain with a sharpened stick. When the witch asked Yoko to sign her name in blood to seal the pact, Yoko suddenly became terrified and asked if it would be all right if John were to sign it for her, but to sign his own name and not hers. Green signed the pact but only after warning Yoko of the dire consequences of trying to mislead supernatural forces. When this was completed the ceremony ended.

Yoko was so relieved that she exclaimed, "'That was very brave of you, Charlie. Thank you. I'm sure that you will be all right. You have lots of protections and things. John and I will take care of you for this. You had to do it. I couldn't. I just couldn't. That was very brave signing your name like that.'

"'My name? Why Yoko, I didn't sign *my* name.'

"'But you must have! You had to! Otherwise I won't get the things I wished for! You must have signed your name or . . . Whose name was it? Charlie, you didn't! Not my name! Not mine!' I turned away so that she couldn't see me smiling. I decided that I would wait awhile before I answered that particular question."[20]

Mick Jagger and model Jerry Hall underwent a very similar ceremony to protect them from their enemies and bless their new marriage in Bali in 1979: "The black chicken was the first to be sacrificed. The flashing blade splashed crimson blood on to the floor of the small wood-carver's house in the thickly wooded Ubud district of Bali.

"Then the white chicken was slaughtered and its sad little body placed to protect Mick and Jerry from evil from the East. A yellow chicken was killed to protect from the West. A black one offered protection from the North, a red fowl for the South and a multi-colored chicken was killed for protection from the centre . . . The first part of the ceremony consisted of Mick and Jerry changing their religion to Hinduism. Dressed in rainbow-colored sarongs and yellow brocade tops, called kebayas, they vowed their belief in the Holy Soul, in reincarnation, and the Supreme Being. They talked of Liberation, the tenet which says that all people are equal spiritual beings, and that their occupation and material situation are irrelevant."[21]

Though John Lennon had claimed that he was a "born-again pagan" and, according to Ray Coleman, once professed to having sold his soul to the devil, he was far removed from the trappings of devil worship. When John and Yoko asked John Green to perform a pagan wedding service for them on their approaching anniversary, Lennon was sent throughout New York City to find the "special ingredients" for the ceremony. He went into a shop specializing in occult objects but leaning more to black magic. According to John as he left the shop he shouted, "'May the Good Lord bless and keep you.' God got them fuming. I loved it. Just what the assholes deserve. Maybe you should check and see if they cursed me, Charles."[22]

Of course, on the *Sgt. Pepper's Lonely Hearts Club Band* album cover the Beatles chose to place a scowling Aleister Crowley within the crowd of their admired celebrities. Some strange coincidences can be seen by some individuals with very active imaginations. First of all, Crowley is pictured on the "left-hand path" in the photo. His head is shaved and some observers say that they can see three distinct sixes displayed across his scalp. Secondly, *Sgt. Pepper's* was released in 1967, and in the opening song the singer mentions that "It was twenty years ago today Sgt. Pepper taught the band to play." Aleister Crowley died in 1947, twenty years before the release of *Sgt. Pepper's*. The final Crowley coincidence lies in the selection of the name *Sgt. Pepper's*. "Sergeant" contains the exact number of letters as "Aleister," whereas "Pepper's" contains the exact number of letters as "Crowley." This incredible coincidence is used as evidence by some misguided sleuths to suggest that *Sgt. Pepper's* was a revolutionary New Age album whose purpose was to propagate Crowley's mysticism on an unsuspecting public. (Of course the word "evangelist" can also be an anagram for "evils agent.")

Lennon seemed convinced that he would suffer an early death. He had his personal assistant Fred Seaman search his genealogy for the cause of his ancestors' deaths. In a number of his recordings there are disturbing coincidences that hint at his tragic death at an early age. In "I Am the Walrus" the song ends with a burial scene from Shakespeare's *King Lear.* One voice in the fade-out states "Bury my body." Another voice exclaims, "Oh, untimely death!" while the last actor softly mutters, "What? Is he dead?" John's death was indeed untimely at he age of forty. There was even a mistaken "Paul is dead" clue stating that "Walrus" was Greek for "corpse." Of course this is not true, but is yet another strange coincidence, since "I Am the Walrus" begins with a keyboard simulation of an English ambulance siren.

Perhaps the most chilling hint of his untimely death is found within the *Magical Mystery Tour* LP booklet. John is standing next to a sign that states "The Best Way to Go is by M & D Co." To the "Paul is dead" fans the mysterious M & D Company was said to be a funeral home in London; however, the sickening revelation is that MDC are also the exact initials of Lennon's assassin, Mark David Chapman.

Fred Seaman relates that "John talked about 'weird' recurring dreams in which he suffered a violent death. Sounding grim and apprehensive, John said that he assumed that because he had led a life filled with violence, both in thought and in deed, he was destined to die a violent death. He told me he often fantasized about getting shot, which, he said, was a modern form of crucifixion, a rather elegant means of moving on to the next life with a clean karmatic slate. He was very serious, very impersonal, and spoke without any visible feelings—it was if he were thinking out loud."[23] Strangely enough, there were other coincidences concerning John Lennon and Christianity that became even more ironic due to his misinterpreted remark comparing the Beatles' popularity to that of Christ. John had first met Paul at a function at St. Peter's Church Hall in Woolton, Liverpool. The Beatles recorded their brilliant music at Abbey Road Studios. Of course, an abbey is a building inhabited by either monks or nuns who are completely devoted to the church. Since the Beatles' last recorded album was simply entitled *Abbey Road* it would appear that the group had completed a cycle within their musical careers. The Beatles began at a church function and ended with yet another reference to a holy place.

In John's last interview with David Sheff in *The Playboy Interviews with John Lennon and Yoko Ono,* a shrill scream is heard outside the apartment. John responds with "Oh, another murder at rue Dakota." [24] The Dakota had been standing for almost one century when John Lennon was murdered in its Gothic gateway. In all its sordid past there has only been one murder that took place on its grounds, and that murder occurred on the night of December 8, 1980, and the victim was John Lennon. In another strange reference to *Rosemary's Baby,* there is a scene where a young woman jumps to her death. Rosemary then becomes the object of the cult's desire to make her the mother of the Anti-Christ. The scene was played out in the film at the exact location John Lennon would be murdered by Chapman.

John also theorized that in death, "one's life would simply flash by in reverse chronological order. In death, explained John, the movie of one's life is played backward with the more recent 'reels' shown first." [25] Lennon, in a conversation with his older son Julian concerning metaphysics and life after death, promised to float a white feather across the room as proof of the afterlife if indeed it existed.

There are also a number of chilling coincidences concerning the *Double Fantasy* album: "The back cover showed John and Yoko standing grim-faced on the corner of Central Park West and Seventy-second Street. Both photos had been taken by the Japanese photographer Kishin Shinoyama, who was famous for taking the last photos of Yukio Mishima. (John referred to this prominent Japanese novelist, who committed hara-kari after a failed coup attempt, as 'that kamikaze writer.')"[26] Of course, John's life ended when he was gunned down on Seventy-second Street the night of December 8, 1980.

The strangest phenomenon in the death of John Lennon deals with his assassin, Mark David Chapman. Chapman first claimed that he murdered Lennon because of Lennon's statement in 1966 that the Beatles were more popular than Christ. He later admitted that he felt like the character Holden Caulfield from J. D. Salinger's *The Catcher in the Rye.* Like Caulfield, Chapman claimed to be protecting the innocence of childhood. Mark David Chapman stalked Lennon and even adopted John's name for a short while. He would lead church youth-group sing-alongs including a take-off on "Imagine," where Chapman would sing "Imagine there's no John Lennon." In Jack Jones's haunting *Let Me Take You Down,* the author describes a scene that took place in Hawaii shortly before Mark David Chapman set out on his journey to end the life of the great dreamer: "Slowly, ritualistically, he [Chapman] began removing his clothes. At last he sat before the record player, naked except for a pair of headphones clamped across his skull.

"'Hear me, Satan,' he prayed softly, bowing his head. 'Accept these pearls of my evil and my rage. Accept these things from deep within me. In return, I ask only that you give me the power,' he continued rocking gently in time to the Lennon song 'Lucy in the Sky With Diamonds,' '. . . the power to kill John Lennon. Give me the power of darkness. Give me the power of death. Let me be a somebody for once in my life. Give me the life of John Lennon.'"[27] An article printed in *The Globe* newspaper (December 30, 1980, p. 23) stated that six weeks before the murder of John Lennon, Chapman attended a film lecture in Hawaii given by Kenneth Anger. It was reported that Chapman stayed after the lecture to ask Anger many questions concerning the filmmaker's knowledge of John and Yoko.

On the night of December 8, 1980, Mark Chapman, with his newfound faith, managed to end the life of John Lennon. To continue the saga of the number nine, Lennon was taken to Roosevelt [nine letters] Hospital on Ninth Avenue, where he was pronounced dead: "John's remains were taken in a body bag from the morgue to the Frank E. Campbell funeral chapel at Madison Avenue and Eighty-first Street [nine]. From there it would go to the Ferncliff [nine] Mortuary in Hartsdale [nine], New York."[28] A series of hearses was to leave the funeral home at the same time to keep the media unaware of where John's cremation would take place.

In the later 1980s a made-for-television movie was commissioned to tell John and Yoko's story. The special was called simply *John and Yoko: A Love Story*. The sad, sick irony found its way back to the Lennons when the actor who was to have played John in the special was replaced. The reason behind this was simple. The actor's real name was Mark Chapman.

Have there been other and more recent examples of performers whose lives have been determined by numbers, fate, and premonitions? Take the case of the tragic death of Tupac Shakur. Tupac Shakur's last album was entitled *Makaveli: The Don Killuminati: The 7 Day Theory*. The corruption of Niccolò Machiavelli's name has some significance. Machiavelli's *Prince* has always served as the ultimate teaching tool to acquire and keep power. The message would be the same from the Renaissance to modern gang warfare. The lessons are: 1) The ends justify the means, and 2) It is better to be feared than loved. Simply put, if you want something badly enough, whatever you do to obtain it is justified. Morality has no place in the struggle for power. The second precept states that fear is the only force that keeps a ruler safe and secure. When enemies fear a reprisal, they will never attack.

The inventive spelling of *Don Killuminati* suggests the age-old mystery group the dreaded Illuminati. According to history the Illuminati was a secret society that came into existence in Bavaria on May 1, 1776. It was founded by Adam Weishaupt. The very word Illuminati would be translated as "illuminated" or "intellectually inspired." Notice the founding date coincides with the beginning of the American Revolution. The Illuminati have been accused of starting every major revolution in history. Today's believers in conspiracy place the Illuminati at the head of a powerful political organization devoted to the establishment of a one-world government. The very word *Illuminati* could suggest the most powerful secret gang in existence, an organization that any gang seeking the ultimate power would want to emulate.

The concept of the "7 Day Theory" may well be Tupac Shakur's premonition of early death. Shakur was shot on Saturday, September 7, 1996 (the seventh day). He was taken into surgery but managed to live until the next Friday (seven days); Shakur was twenty-five when he died (2+5=7) and he was pronounced dead at 4:03 P.M. (4+3=7). The irony suggests the fateful number seven is in play here. Also it is ironic that Tupac was shot on Buddy Holly's birthday, September 7.

The cover to the *Makaveli* CD portrays Shakur as Christ being crucified. Strangely, Tupac Shakur died on a Friday the thirteenth. In legend it has been assumed that Christ was crucified on a Friday the thirteenth (Good Friday). There were thirteen shots fired into the car, with four hitting Shakur. Some fans believe that Shakur's bullet wounds can be seen on the *Makaveli* cover. If Shakur had been hit five times it would also parallel the five wounds of Christ at his crucifixion, but sometimes fate can simply get a little too close. Another coincidence is in the fact that the number thirteen is also portrayed in the message at the bottom of the cover: "In no way is this portrait an expression of disrespect for Jesus Christ"(thirteen words).

Urban folklore has now suggested that Shakur faked his death much as some Elvis Presley fans believed in the early 1980s.

The Christ scene, to many fans, implies a possible resurrection, and the adoption of a new name, Makaveli, may suggest an alias with a new identity. As in any great rock rumor, there has to be just that small shred of evidence that has to be manufactured. In this case it is the suggestion that Niccolò Machiavelli faked his own death (Elvis and Morrison maybe, but Machiavelli?). This is where the theory is shot down. How could enemies fear a ruler who is dead? To be strong does not mean to continuously fight wars with your own armies. That leads to weakness and defeat. The best time for an attack would be in the confusion brought about in a transfer of power following the death of a monarch.

Besides the seven-day theory and the repetition of the number thirteen, the most ironic occurrence before the death of Tupac Shakur lies in the release of his last music video, "I Ain't Mad at 'Cha." This video was delivered just days before the fatal shooting and shows Tupac Shakur being gunned down and making his way to rock and roll heaven. There he meets Jimi Hendrix and the other stars who preceded him in death. This is a chilling commentary. It is also ironic that Shakur's recording label was Death Row Records.

On March 9, 1997, rap star Christopher Wallace, the "Notorious B.I.G.," was gunned down on a city street much in the same way as Tupac Shakur. Many observers feel that Wallace's death was gang-related (East Coast vs. West Coast) and was in revenge for the death of Shakur. The Notorious B.I.G.'s last album was simply entitled *Life After Death . . . 'Til Death Do Us Part.*

Since the bizarre grip of fate plays no favorites, it seems that even country music performers are not safe from the foul clutch of chance. In the beginning, rock and roll and country and western music were born at the same crossroads. The blues has always played a major role in the development of country music. The first country performer to become a victim of his own excesses would have to be the great Hank Williams. Williams's bouts with alcohol and prescription drugs are legendary. His songs reflected the complete extent of human emotion. Even his death is marred in mystery: "Hank died either in the late night of December 31, 1952, or the early morning hours of January 1, 1953, in the back seat of his new powder-blue Cadillac convertible. He was being driven by a teenage chauffeur to two shows scheduled for December 31 in Charleston, West Virginia, and January 1, in Canton, Ohio. They tried to fly out of Knoxville on December 31 to Charleston, but the weather was bad and the plane turned back. They spent several hours in a hotel in Knoxville and then left for Canton, but not before a physician was called to the hotel and injected Hank, already very drunk, with two shots of vitamin B-12 laced with morphine (an addiction he had developed from his back pain). According to a report filed by the investigating police officer, Hank was probably already dead when he was carried out of the hotel late that night and laid in the back of the car for the trip to Canton. He was officially declared dead at 7:00 A.M. on January 1, 1953, at the Oak Hill Hospital in Oak Hill, West Virginia."[29] The last recording by Hank Williams was appropriately entitled "I'll Never Get Out of This World Alive."

Later in 1953, a young country singer whose name was Johnny Horton married Hank Williams's widow, Billie Jean. Horton was a somewhat reluctant performer whose greatest hit was the crossover classic "The Battle of New Orleans" in 1959. His new wife, Billie Jean, had received a lump-sum settlement from Hank Williams's first wife, Audrey Williams, in return for Billie Jean not performing under the stage name Mrs. Hank Williams. It seemed that Horton had also inherited a strange appointment with chance. He had recurring dreams and visions of being killed by a drunken driver. He feared playing on the road, but finally agreed to appear at Austin's Skyline Club: "After playing two sets, Johnny drove his car the 220 miles back to Shreveport, Louisiana, accompanied by [members of his band]. Suddenly, in the early hours of

November 5, 1960, a drunk driver hit Horton's car head on and Johnny was killed.

"The funeral was a bizarre affair, with Horton's psychic counselor, Bernard Ricks, handing out fish drawings which intimated that the singer was in Heaven. Standing before the casket, Johnny's brother, Frank, a professional gambler, found Jesus and vowed to change his ways."[30] Not only had Horton inherited Hank Williams's wife, but his last show was performed at the Austin Skylight Club, the same club where Hank Williams had made his final performance in 1952, eight years earlier.

When the role of fate and bitter irony can be discerned in the lives and works of mankind it may do well for each of us to remember some advice from the great William Shakespeare. As we play out our predetermined roles in this soap opera called life only to find that we are bound together by the simple whims of fate and chance along with the influence of heavenly spheres, then surely we are no longer "passion's slaves" but merely "fortune's fools."

10. THE CLUB

Now he's gone and joined that stupid club. I told him not to join that stupid club.
—Kurt Cobain's mother following her son's apparent suicide

Hope I die before I get old.
—The Who, "My Generation"

So, you want to be a rock and roll star?
—The Byrds, "So You Want to Be a Rock and Roll Star"

All our lives we sweat and save, building for a shallow grave.
—Jim Morrison, "The Soft Parade"

It's better to burn out 'cause rust never sleeps,
The king is gone but he's not forgotten.
—Neil Young, "Hey Hey, My My (Into the Black)"

IN ANCIENT GREEK HISTORY, Alexander the Great often spoke of a compact he had made with Zeus-Ammon, the most powerful of all the Greek gods. In this agreement, Alexander faced two choices. The first choice was to die young and achieve everlasting fame and fortune, while his second choice would be to live to a ripe old age but never tasting glory. According to Alexander, it was the same offer presented to Achilles during the Trojan War. Obviously, the decision took but little consideration. Alexander chose the short life and conquered the known ancient world by the time he was but thirty-three years of age. One legend stated that he sat upon a rock and cried because there were no more worlds for him to conquer. Ironically, Alexander died that same year from a fever. His body was encased in solid gold and carried throughout his conquered provinces so that his subjects could pay homage to the fallen conqueror. He was buried secretly and to this day his tomb has not been discovered. The Egyptians worshiped Alexander as a living god in the same manner as they did the ancient pharaohs. Did he make the right choice? In the words of the modern-day prophets Def Leppard, it is "better to burn out than fade away." James Dean was said to have once commented that the true purpose in life was to "live fast, die young, and leave a good-looking corpse."

Sadly, throughout literary history a great number of the most creative writers may well have entered into Alexander's untimely pact. The English Romantic poets are a prime example: John Keats died at the age of twenty-five, Percy Bysshe Shelley died at the age of twenty-nine, Lord Byron met his death at the age of thirty-six, each poet dying at the height of his poetic powers.

In this chapter we will examine a number of musical giants who accepted Alexander's challenge and died in the full bloom of youth and have now become legends in pop music. In this manner they are all members of "the club." The membership requirement is simple. The initiation occurs when the subject reaches the age of twenty-seven and the length of membership is eternity.

The founder of the club was bluesman Robert Johnson (see Chapter 1). Johnson became the catalyst in the musical melting pot of spirituals, country, and blues. He was the master alchemist who used a black cat's bone and the wailing sounds of his slide guitar to serve as his philosopher's stone. Throw in a little mojo, and rock and roll was born at this crossroads situated between deep-rooted faith and backwoods superstition. Johnson's premature death at the age of twenty-seven seems to have developed a bizarre pattern that would later claim many of rock's legendary performers, and like Johnson, some of those deaths hint at "murder most foul."

In a two-year period beginning with July 3, 1969, and ending exactly upon July 3, 1971, a total of five major rock icons would die tragically and all at the age of twenty-seven. The first rock victim to follow in Robert Johnson's fatal footsteps was British blues disciple and founder of the Rolling Stones, Brian Jones. Jones had been replaced by the Stones shortly after the *Beggars Banquet* album. In the days that were to precede his death, Brian's friends reported that he was never happier, and that he was putting his own band together to play his own music. He suggested that both John Lennon and Jimi Hendrix were eager to join his band. Jones had always felt that his musical numbers had been completely ignored by Jagger and Richards and that this would serve as his chance to again take control of his musical destiny. Brian Jones had recently purchased Cotchford Farm in Sussex. This had once served as the residence of A. A. Milne during his writing of *Winnie-the-Pooh*. The ex-Stones guitarist had hoped to build his own studio and start production with his new group as soon as possible. Sadly, this was not to be. The very farmhouse that created the innocent Pooh series would soon serve as the stage for violent death.

Once in late 1966 while discussing the tragic death of Tara Browne, the Guinness heir and friend of both the Stones and the Beatles, Keith Richards looked at Brian Jones and said, "You'll never make thirty, man." Jones answered, "I know."[1] The whole discussion had concerned the role of fate in choosing young victims. Of course, these victims usually cooperated by living their lives in the pursuit of excess. Brian Jones more than fit this pattern of self-destruction. Marianne Faithfull, a longtime friend of Jones, recalled a strange story surrounding an event she remembered happening in June of 1969. Faithfull stated, "As 1969 plunged on, I was becoming increasingly worried about Brian. I could feel something very nasty coming. So I suggested to Mick that we throw the I Ching about Brian and see what we should do.

"It was just dusk when I threw the coins. The reading I got was: Death by water. I turned to Mick and said, 'It's very odd, isn't it?' And he said, 'My God, do it again.' I did it again, and I got the same thing. We just looked at one another. Finally, I said, 'Look, this isn't good at all. We've got to do something.' And he said, 'We ought to phone, see if he's all right.' And he actually did. Guilt, maybe."[2] Two weeks later, Brian Jones was dead.

During the night of Wednesday July 2, 1969, Brian had been entertaining a small number of guests at his residence, including Anna Wohlin, Jones's girlfriend; Frank Thorogood, a builder who was overseeing some restoration of Jones's property; and Janet Lawson, Thorogood's guest, who also happened to be a nurse. Sometime approaching 10:30 P.M., Brian Jones announced that he was going for a swim and put on his swimming trunks. Janet Lawson warned him that after he'd been drinking vodka and taking downers it would be extremely dangerous for him to get into the pool. Tragically, Jones did not listen. Anna Wohlin, Janet Lawson, and Frank Thorogood went with him to the pool but they all noticed that Jones appeared a little sluggish. Jones then adjusted the water temperature to a steamy 80° Fahrenheit. Janet

Lawson stayed for a short time but then returned to the house. Shortly after they began swimming, Anna left the pool to answer the telephone. Approximately ten minutes later, Thorogood came to the house looking for a towel and a cigarette. It was then that Lawson came back and found the submerged, still body of Brian Jones face down in the deep end of the pool. Frantically, the guests pulled his body from the water. Janet and Anna started artificial respiration but it was too late. An ambulance was called and Jones was pronounced dead shortly after midnight. Brian Jones was dead at the tender age of twenty-seven.

The coroner's inquest ruled that Jones's death was the result of "immersion in fresh water under the influence of drugs and alcohol" and recorded the tragedy as death by misadventure. It was suggested that the extremely warm water temperature combined with the large amounts of alcohol and barbiturates could result in coma and death. But could all this occur in less than ten minutes? It was also believed that Jones could have had an asthma attack or a seizure that may have led to his untimely death. An inhaler was found by the poolside, but during the autopsy the pathologist stated that there was no sign that asthma had played a role in his death. One of the most puzzling questions was how Brian Jones's lungs could completely fill with water and his body sink completely to the bottom of the pool in such a short time. Then the rumors started.

One rumor suggested suicide. Some of Jones's friends knew of the heartbreak that Brian had gone through when he lost the beautiful Anita Pallenberg to Keith Richards. Some insiders claimed Mick Jagger had taken yet another of Brian's lovers, forcing Jones to take his own life to escape yet another heartbreak. This theory was disputed by Jones's closest friends, who claimed that they had never seen him happier. He was in love with Anna Wohlin and was in the process of putting a new band together.

Surely, these would not be the actions of a man considering suicide.

Another rumor stated that Brian Jones's death was but a Satanic sacrifice, a terrible payment for the Stones' continued success. During his recording of the native drum ceremony in Joujouka, Jones was convinced that during the service a voodoo curse had been placed upon him. The day of his funeral it was estimated that over a half a million people gathered along the roadway to catch a glimpse of the hearse carrying his body. A large crowd also gathered outside the church at Cheltenham where the funeral service was held. Ironically, it was in this same church that a young Brian Jones had earlier served as a choirboy. At the funeral service Canon Hugh Evans Hopkins used his pulpit to condemn the lifestyle of Jones and the Rolling Stones in particular: "He [Jones] was a rebel. He had little patience with authority, convention, and tradition. In this he was typical of many of his generation who have come to see in the Rolling Stones an expression of their whole attitude to life. Much that this ancient church has stood for nine hundred years seems totally irrelevant to them and yet it is not humbug to come today to offer our prayers on this tragic occasion."[3] The Reverend Hopkins also mentioned a suicide attempt by Marianne Faithfull, who had been in a drug-induced coma for two days, and asked for everyone's prayers. Brian Jones's tragic death had driven the beautiful Marianne Faithfull to total despair. Faithfull had claimed that when she looked into a mirror she saw Brian looking back. She cut her hair to resemble his. Her mental state suffered due to her heroin addiction but she was trying to kick her habit by going cold turkey. Marianne's physician had prescribed sodium amytal to help her sleep, but before she went to sleep that night she swallowed 150 tablets. Now she was ready to face death and be with Brian for eternity. In her deathlike coma she claimed that Brian had appeared to her and taken her by the hand. Shortly afterwards, he dropped her hand and told her that she would have to return. She could not go with him. Following this, she soon awoke in the hospital, though the memory still haunts her.

There was a final indignity when Jones's family had to ask permission for Christian burial for their son in the parish church-yard: "Father John Heidt, the present rector of Cheltenham's St. Philip and St. James's, explains, 'You see, Brian ought to have been buried with us, but my precedessor [Hopkins] would not allow it because of the rumor going about at the time of possible suicide.'"[4] Brian Jones had become a modern-day Ophelia. Jones and Shakespeare's tragic heroine did have much in common: Both suffered a lover's rejection, both were alienated from their respective families, and finally both had limited burial rights because their "deaths were doubtful." Brian Jones was buried at Priors Road Cemetery one mile from the churchyard.

Many fans and journalists were quick to accept the explanation of Jones's death being either suicide or accidental death. Still, there were some insiders who believed that there could be one other logical answer—murder. As Keith Richards stated in a *Rolling Stone* interview, "Some very weird things happened that night Brian died . . . there were people there that suddenly disappeared . . . Some of them had a weird hold over Brian . . . It's the same feeling with who killed Kennedy. You can't get to the bottom of it."[5] One of the "weird things" that Richards mentioned was the disappearance of a number of Jones's personal items a few days following his death. Whoever stole these items and planned to resell them at a later date had a key to Brian's house. The items stolen included his guitar collection and a large number of antiques and house furnishings. Another stolen item included Brian Jones's first retirement check from the Rolling Stones made out in the sum of £100,000. The money and furnishings were never recovered. Another strange happening the night of the murder concerned the official statement made by the three witnesses; it appeared that they were each telling different stories concerning the night of the horrible drowning. It was as if they had different recollections of what had actually happened there.

A. E. Hotchner, in his *Blown Away: The Rolling Stones and the Death of the Sixties,* presented a series of interviews collected twenty years after the death of Brian Jones that tell a very different story of what happened that tragic night at Cotchford Farm. One man who claimed to have been present that night was one of the workers hired by Jones to help with his renovations. His story mentions a party in which he and his fellow workmen returned to Jones's estate later that night. The workers were drinking and a number of them were very jealous of Jones and his wealthy lifestyle. A few of their girlfriends seemed to be quite attracted to Brian and watched him as he swam in his pool. It was then that two of the workmen attacked Jones in the pool, holding his head under the water. They continuously kept his head bobbing up and down in the water, paying little or no attention to his gasping and his violent struggle to breathe. When his body became still, the other partygoers left hurriedly. Threats were reportedly made to other witnesses to ensure their silence. This incredible story has been corroborated by at least three others who have now claimed to have been present that night. One of the spectators was said to be a former member of the Walker Brothers (rock group), while another was Nicholas Fitzgerald, a longtime friend of Jones and a member of the Guinness family. Fitzgerald, along with his friend Richard Cadbury, made his way to Jones's home the night of July 2, 1969, to attend a party. Fitzgerald had met with Jones earlier that afternoon and noticed that Brian appeared very upset. Jones had mentioned that there were a number of men hanging about his home and he was convinced that they were up to no good. Brian was upbeat about his future band plans and had been in recent contact with both John Lennon and Jimi Hendrix. He appeared to be excited that both musicians were seriously considering being a part of his new group. Jones had then invited his friend to attend his party later that night. As Fitzgeald approached the house from a wooded area he noticed three men who were standing on the right side of the swimming pool. The middle man fell to his knees and pushed down on a struggling swimmer's head. The head appeared to be very white (Jones had light blond hair). At the opposite end of the pool, a man and woman were standing just staring into the pool. Shortly afterward a third man jumped into the pool, landing on the back of the helpless swimmer. It was then that Fitzgerald and Cadbury were approached by a "burly man wearing glasses. He pushed Richard out of the way. He grabbed my [Fitzgerald's] shoulder. His other hand made a fist, which he put in my face menacingly. 'Get the hell out of here, Fitzgerald, or you'll be the next.'"[6] As the two men hurriedly returned home, a series of strange events were put into motion. When Fitzgerald had tried to contact Cadbury after the strange events of the following night, he was informed that Cadbury had moved and left no forwarding address. Stranger still, another of Brian's friends stated that Anna Wohlin and her best friend Linda Lawrence were told that they were to leave England immediately. Wohlin also stated that Jones had not been using drugs and was in fact an excellent swimmer. Ronni Money, another of Brian's friends, exclaimed, "I believe in ultimate evil now. I do, I've seen it, and I believe in it. And I don't think it's got anything to do with horned people, it's to do with people who can actually loathe you to death."[7]

To make things even more interesting, it has now been reported that in 1993, Frank Thorogood made a deathbed confession in which he admitted to the murder of Brian Jones.[8] (Today, the Thorogood family denies the allegation and claims it was an attempt to sell a new book on the death of Brian Jones.) A few days before his death, Jones had confided in several friends his intention to fire Thorogood. Perhaps Brian had chosen that warm night in July when his drinking had given him just a little more courage to confront Thorogood. In any case this situation could have very well provided a motive for murder. Supposedly, the Sussex police have now reopened the case and are searching for new clues that hopefully will solve one more of the greatest hidden mysteries of rock and roll.

On September 3, 1970, Canned Heat guitarist Al "Blind Owl" Wilson joined the club. Wilson received his peculiar nickname due to his nearsightedness. Wilson graduated with a degree in music from Boston University and, along with singer Bob "Bear" Hite, formed Canned Heat in 1966. Both Wilson and Hite were singers devoted to the blues, but it was Wilson's distinctive high quivering falsetto that was featured on the band's most successful hits, "On the Road Again" and "Going Up the Country." Wilson was said to have suffered from severe bouts with depression, and on the night of his death he was camping out behind Bob Hite's home. The band was to leave on a European tour the next day. His body was found the next morning still wrapped in his sleeping bag. Though the official version of his death was given as a drug overdose, many of his closest friends believe that his premature death was suicide. (Tragedy struck Canned Heat once again in 1981 when Bob "Bear" Hite died of a heart attack following one of the band's performances. He was thirty-six years old.)

Later in that same September, the rock world was stunned once again when word came from London that Jimi Hendrix had died in his girlfriend's apartment. The American guitarist had conquered the musical world through the introduction of his cosmic blues. No one has ever played the guitar like Jimi Hendrix. He played the fretted instrument behind his back and with his teeth. He defined musical showmanship and with his incredible virtuosity laid down the musical challenge for other up and coming guitarists who wanted to claim his throne. After watching Hendrix perform, none chose to challenge him. Though Hendrix crafted an ingenious tonal rainbow of new musical sounds and directions, he always remained true to his first love, the blues. Some of Jimi Hendrix's friends felt that the rock superstar may have sensed his own premature death. That July, before his death, Jimi was said to have told some reporters during his last tour that, "The next time I go back to Seattle it will be in a pine box." He also remarked to one reporter, Anne Bjørnal, that "I've been dead for a long time. I don't think I will live to see twenty-eight."[9] Little did he know that day just how prophetic that last remark would truly become. Following his much too early death, listeners and fans couldn't help but notice some eerie foreshadowing in Hendrix's lyrics. In "I Don't Live Today," Hendrix's song dedicated to the many Native American tribes who lost their freedom as well as their lands, the title becomes self-explanatory. When listening to the song a listener can't help but notice the phrase "No sun coming through my windows, feel like I'm living at the bottom of a grave." In this case the lyric becomes self-prophetic.

I suppose that the most disturbing phrase can be found in the masterful "Voodoo Chile (Slight Return)" when Hendrix sings, "If I don't meet you no more in this world, I'll meet you in the next one, so don't be late." His incredible guitar work and phrasing became the ultimate tribute to the Mississippi Delta and all those who fell under its mystical spell. Jimi Hendrix's invitation is every bit as chilling as Robert Johnson's pronouncement in "Me and the Devil Blues": "I said, hello, Satan, I believe it's time to go." Both musicians talk of escape from a tormenting world by summoning death.

The official version of Hendrix's death states that he was unable to sleep the night of September 17, 1970, and took nine sleeping pills that his girlfriend, Monika Dannemann, had. He obviously didn't realize the strength of the drug or he wouldn't have taken so many. Hendrix's usual dosage was two pills. Early the next morning, Monika left the apartment for a few minutes to buy some cigarettes. When she returned she noticed that Jimi had vomited in his sleep. She then became very alarmed when she couldn't wake him. The first call she made was to Hendrix's friend Eric Burdon, former lead singer of the Animals. Burdon screamed at her to call an ambulance now! She then dialed the emergency phone number and an ambulance was summoned. The attendants arrived in a matter of minutes and began CPR on the unconscious Hendrix. They assured Dannemann that Hendrix was very much alive and that he would be rushed to St. Mary's Abbot Hospital. After a few minutes at the hospital it became futile to continue trying to revive Hendrix. He was pronounced dead and the cause of death was given as asphyxiation due to severe barbiturate intoxication and the inhalation of his own vomit. It appeared that the sleeping pills had blocked Hendrix's gagging reflex, allowing fluid to fill his lungs and in essence drowning him.

At the time reports surfaced saying that Hendrix had died of a drug overdose. There had always been rumors passed around in the media concerning Jimi's alleged use of drugs. Some rumors suggested that Hendrix was addicted to heroin, and that he shot up, sometimes using the veins in his neck, with speedballs (a combination of heroin and cocaine). All of these rumors were completely untrue. Jimi Hendrix was no junkie. Like many in the late 1960s, he experimented with both LSD and marijuana. However, he was never addicted to heroin and his body showed no evidence of the needle marks that signaled the telltale trademark of a serious drug user. However, many questions did remain. First, why did Monika Dannemann wait so long to call an ambulance? She simply stated that she was afraid of a public scandal and that Jimi would become upset with her.

The second question was why Jimi took the nine sleeping tablets. Was it simply a mistake or was it actually suicide? Hendrix's last few concerts were very disappointing to him. At one show after only playing a couple of songs, Jimi apologized to the audience, stating that they "just couldn't get it together." He then left the stage. He was becoming despondent about his financial affairs and complained about being restricted musically. Did suicide provide the escape from this world into the next? A few days after Jimi Hendrix's death, Eric Burdon appeared on a television show in London and suggested that Hendrix had indeed committed suicide. He formed his opinion based upon a five-page poem that Hendrix had written the day of his death. The poem was entitled "The Story of Life." The poem ended with this simple line: "The story of life is hello and good-bye, until we meet again." Was this a restatement of Jimi's invitation to meet us in the next world and for us to not be late? Eric Burdon seemed convinced that his friend had calmly chosen his own exit from this room full of mirrors. Perhaps it is ironic that Hendrix's last poem is called "The Story of Life," since it was written the day that he died. Another irony links him to the poet Shelley, whose last work was "The Triumph of Life." Sadly and coincidentally, both men died by drowning after the completion of their last works saluting the necessary purpose of living.

To some investigators, as well as some of Hendrix's personal friends, there had to be yet one more answer to the mysterious death of the guitar great. There were several missing pieces that were not examined at that time, pieces that when properly assembled might very well hint at foul play. The last few days of Hendrix's life have been shrouded in mystery. Hendrix had told several of his closest friends that he had been forcibly kidnapped, forced into a car, and a knee placed in his back as he was driven to a deserted building. He stated that he was in constant fear for his life. He managed to escape when three men from Michael Jeffrey's management company appeared and set him free. Also, a few hours before his death Monika drove him to an apartment to meet with some unknown friends. Hendrix entered the apartment alone. Monika Dannemann has suggested that he visited his former lover Devon Wilson to ask her to leave Dannemann alone.

When Monika picked Hendrix up from the apartment, he displayed a handful of pills that had been given to him at the party. Some insiders have stated that perhaps Wilson had provided a substance that brought about Hendrix's death. Rumors also circulated about a mysterious phone call that Hendrix was said to have made to his former manager Chas Chandler. The message was left on Chandler's business answering machine and stated simply, "I need help bad, man." Supposedly the call was made shortly before Hendrix left to visit his unnamed friends. Dannemann disputes this rumor and says that Chandler didn't own an answering machine at that time. Rumors also surfaced that Hendrix had died some five hours earlier and in some way tried to blame Monika Dannemann for the delay in calling an ambulance. I suppose the most puzzling questions have to concern the medical treatment Hendrix was given. Why was he placed in a sitting position in the ambulance instead of being placed on his side? It appears that a sitting position would allow his lungs to fill with fluid faster and in that way contribute to his death. The second question is why didn't the doctors perform a tracheotomy to allow Hendrix to breathe? If his windpipe was obstructed it seems that this would be a proper procedure to allow the victim a chance at recovery. A few years following Hendrix's death, one of the attending doctors was removed from the doctors' registry; no reason was given, although there's no evidence it was linked to Hendrix's death.

Of course when any celebrity dies under clandestine circumstances, there are many individuals who automatically assume that a well-organized conspiracy has taken place. Noel Redding, former Experience bassist, in an interview with journalist Chris Welch mentioned that he was not sure of the events that surrounded this tragedy: "I don't know if it was an accident or suicide or murder." Basically, there are two conspiracy theories concerning Hendrix's death. The first theory concerns involvement by the FBI. During the late 1960s and early 1970s a number of files were kept by the government agency concerning the counterculture. Jimi Hendrix may have been considered a threat due to his involvement with the Black Panthers. Ironically, Hendrix, Janis Joplin, and Jim Morrison were all outspoken critics of the American involvement in the Vietnam War and protested against a number of government domestic policies. To those believers in hidden governmental conspiracies, the death of these rock icons would be a way to help silence the voice of protest.

The next theory concerns the role of Hendrix's manager Mike Jeffrey. Jimi was upset that large amounts of his money were missing. He had asked both Chas Chandler and Alan Douglas to take over as his manager. It was rumored that Jeffrey stood to make a greater sum of money with a dead Jimi Hendrix as opposed to a living one. There was also mention of a one-million-dollar insurance policy covering Hendrix's life made out with Jeffrey being the beneficiary. When news spread of Hendrix's death, investigators were stunned to find that Hendrix's residences in England and New York had been broken into. Many of his most personal items were taken, and insiders accuse Jeffrey of selling them for a huge profit.

Mike Jeffrey created a financial empire based upon the posthumous releases of Hendrix's previously unreleased recordings. In Monika Dannemann's *The Inner World of Jimi Hendrix*, the author mentions a series of threats made against her by Jeffrey. He demanded her silence. To make the story even more interesting, as well as bizarre, Mike Jeffrey was killed in a plane crash on March 5, 1973. He was flying from Spain to England to answer a number of questions concerning his financial dealings. There are those who believe that Jeffrey faked his death by using his many contacts to add his name to the passenger list. It seems that there will always be a market for another conspiracy.

Jimi Hendrix's funeral took place on October 1, 1970, in Seattle, Washington, at the Dunlap Baptist Church. Al Hendrix, Jimi's father, received a message from one of Jimi's fans advising the grieving father to go down to the funeral home and check Jimi's body to make sure that he was really dead. The fan believed that Jimi had magical powers and might simply be in a state of suspended animation. Monika also mentioned that Jimi had previously asked her, in the event of his death, to stay with his body for three days to make sure that he was really dead. She was unable to do this since she was not his wife.

Eric Clapton was deeply moved by Jimi's sudden death. (Hendrix once told Chas Chandler, his first manager, who took him to England and started his career, that if he was going to England then Chandler would have to introduce him to Eric Clapton. Jimi loved to hear Clapton play the blues.) Clapton had told many of his friends that he didn't expect to live to see his thirtieth birthday. He told his friends that he "wanted a voice as tortured as the chords he wrenched from his guitar, a voice like Ray Charles at the height of his addiction." When he heard the news of Hendrix's death he stated, "I went out in the garden and cried all day because he left me behind . . . Not because he'd gone, but because he hadn't taken me with him. It made me angry, I wasn't sad, I was just pissed off." [10]

The guitar great had previously mentioned what he intended for his funeral: "I tell you, when I die I'm not going to have a funeral, I'm going to have a jam session. I want people to just play my music, go wild and freak out." [11] After the emotionally moving funeral and burial in Greenwood Memorial Park, Jimi's friends rented a hall and honored his last request. For a guitarist completely devoted to the blues, and especially to Robert Johnson, it has to be a strange twist of fate that the cemetery that holds Hendrix's body has the same name as the town in Mississippi in which Robert Johnson died in 1938. Perhaps Robert Johnson would agree with this statement made by Jimi Hendrix: "You have to die before they think you are worth living." The black cat's bone and the voodoo chile are now forever joined together at the crossroads of eternity.

In Percy Bysshe Shelley's "To a Skylark" the poet mentions that "our sweetest songs are those that tell of saddest thought." Perhaps the greatest blues singer to share her pain through her songs was Janis Joplin. Only two weeks following the death of Jimi Hendrix, on October 4, 1969, word came that Joplin had died of a heroin overdose at the Landmark Hotel in Hollywood, California. Janis had left her Port Arthur, Texas, home at the age of seventeen. She then made her way to San Francisco to make it as a singer but returned home that next year. Back in Port Arthur she awaited a marriage that didn't take place. That was to become the source of her greatest pain, unfulfilled love. At times her fans didn't realize that her hit song "Piece of My Heart" was truly autobiographical. During high school, she was overweight and also had a bad case of acne. Her classmates referred to her as "pig face." During her short college career some reports claimed that her fellow students nominated her for "Ugliest Man on Campus." Janis imagined she could escape from the pain by dulling her senses. Her drinking increased tremendously, but later she would make it a part of her stage act. She was so convincing that she got Southern Comfort to purchase a fur coat for her because of her ringing endorsement of their product. Eventually, she needed much more than hard liquor to buffer her from painful rejection. On that day, she was introduced to "the white lady"—heroin.

In 1967, Joplin left Texas once again, but this time she was to try her hand as the lead vocalist for Big Brother and the Holding Company. Shortly after joining the group, she became a sensation, especially after her performance at the Monterey Pop

Festival. Her powerful voice sent chills throughout the crowd as she belted out her trademark "Ball and Chain." She belted out the blues in the style of her idols, Bessie Smith and Billie Holiday. Sadly, her life would also follow in their tragic footsteps. Everyone in attendance that night knew that a star was born. Ironically, three star-crossed superstars were born at that festival. Otis Redding, Jimi Hendrix, and Janis Joplin burst across the night sky in Monterey, California, like blazing shooting stars, but just as quickly they were gone.

By 1969, Joplin had left Big Brother and formed her own band, the Kosmic Blues Band. During the fall of that year she was happy, even to the extent of calling City Hall to check on a marriage certificate so that she could marry her new boyfriend, Seth Morgan. She was working on a new album with a new band and she appeared to have every reason to live and finally find the happiness that had so coldly eluded her.

Her critics, however, always seemed to mention that she could never capture the magic of her live performances on tape. This time she was sure that the results would be different. Like many other performers, Joplin now turned to heroin to dull her pain. It helped her deal with what she viewed as rejection and a fear of being alone. On the night of October 3, 1969, the hotel clerk remembered Janis asking for some change for the cigarette machine. She had purchased some high-quality heroin earlier in the day and went to her room to mainline the drug into her waiting but already much abused veins. Then she would simply relax and silently drift away from her anxieties.

When she didn't appear for the recording session the next day her band became very concerned and checked the hotel. When they entered her room her body was found. She was pronounced dead at 1:40 A.M. from a heroin overdose. Joplin's body was cremated and her ashes spread about the California coastline. However, there were a few strange ironies concerning her death.

The morning of her death she was to finish a vocal track for what was now to be her last song, "Buried Alive in the Blues." It was never completed. The Landmark Hotel had also earlier been the scene of another rock and roll tragedy. Bobby Fuller ("I Fought the Law") was found dead in a parked car near that same location in 1966. The common thread that joins Janis to the other members of the club was that she had told her friends many times when they begged her to stop using drugs something to the effect of "Let's face it, I'll never see thirty." Tragically, she was dead right.

Cheri Siddons was married to Bill Siddons, the Doors' manager. What she remembered the most about James Douglas Morrison was his irresistible grin. She also remembered what would prove to be a prophetic conversation that she had with Morrison on his birthday: "On his twenty-fifth birthday we were walking down the stairs of the Doors' office and he said to me, 'Well, I made it to twenty-five, do you think I'll make it to thirty?' And we both knew he wouldn't make it to thirty." [12] A year later, after drinking with some friends, Morrison calmly stated, "You're drinking with number three." [13] This was a reference to the tragic deaths of Jimi Hendrix and Janis Joplin that had occurred within seventeen days of each other in the fall of 1970. Curiously, Morrison was in Miami standing trial for obscenity charges when he read of Hendrix's death. He turned to his friends and calmly suggested, "Does anyone believe in omens?" [14]

Jim Morrison loved to experience life by living at the very edge. He was a rock singer, a poet, and some say a shaman. He supposedly was haunted by the vision he had when he was but four years of age. In "Peace Frog" (*Morrison Hotel*) and "Dawn's Highway" (*An American Prayer*), Morrison tells the story about being with his family as they drove through the desert. At dawn they came across a terrible accident that involved a group of Native American workers. At that time, Morrison was able to see one or two of the dead men's spirits: "Is that the souls of the ghosts of those dead Indians? . . . maybe one or two of 'em . . . were just running around freaking out, and they leaped into my soul. And they are still there." At times, Morrison felt that the dying men's spirit inhabited his own body and became his spiritual guides.

During his concerts, Morrison danced and leaped across the stage. At times he was said to have felt the presence of the Indian shamans controlling his movements. On stage, Jim Morrison controlled an audience like no other singer before or after. His lyrics became at times almost hypnotic and when he called for action the crowd responded. Promoters feared that the Doors' concerts could easily be turned into riots as Morrison used the stage as his personal soapbox for the spreading of his opinions upon the ills of society and what he saw as a police state. Due to his appeal to the counterculture, the FBI had a very real interest in the "Lizard King."

The personal side of James Douglas Morrison was very complex. His father was an admiral in the U.S. Navy, but Jim, even at an early age, became a nonconformist. His IQ was rated at 149. He was asked to join the most popular fraternity in high school; however, he declined the invitation. Jim Morrison was a voracious reader. One of his English teachers mentioned that Jim enjoyed reading offbeat books. The teacher wasn't even sure if the books existed, so she asked a fellow teacher who just happened to be going to the Library of Congress to check and see if the books Jim was reading for his reports actually existed: "I suspected he was making them up, as they were English books on sixteenth- and seventeenth-century demonology. I'd never heard of them, but they existed, and I'm convinced from the paper he wrote that he had read them, and the Library of Congress would've been the only source." [15]

Other writers who inspired a young Jim Morrison and played a significant role in the development of the poet's mind included: Nietzsche, Kerouac (*On the Road*), Ginsberg, Ferlinghetti, Plutarch, Dylan Thomas, James Joyce, Balzac, Molière, Cocteau, and the source of his greatest inspiration, Arthur Rimbaud. Rimbaud was a nineteenth-century French poet who believed that poets should live their lives in derangement of the senses. The poet must know all types of love. He must suffer through the most incredible pain. By living a life filled with excess, the poet will then receive his greatest visions. In Rimbaud's "A Season in Hell," the poet states, "Attain death with all your appetites, your selfishness and all the capital sins." Rimbaud also spoke of "the predestined tragedy." This would become the fatal flaw within the poet's life. To some seekers tragedy would come through alcoholism, to others through drug addiction, while still others would be led to madness. Morrison was greatly impressed that Rimbaud completed his poetry by the time he was only nineteen. Like the Beat poets of the 1950s, Rimbaud ran away from home as a youth and followed his teachings. He gladly lived in squalor. Sometimes he slept on the streets and preached revolution and contempt for both the Church and women. He read many books based upon occult themes and studied the works of banned poets. Rimbaud died at thirty-seven. Jim Morrison was faithful to his poetic mentor. After the Doors had achieved great success, Jim lived in the filth of the cheapest hotels, which were always conveniently located near the Doors' business offices. Michael McClure commented on Morrison's acceptance of Rimbaud's teachings in Frank Lisciandro's *Jim Morrison: A Feast of Friends:* "When you arrange to derange the normal balance of your senses, whether you do it with alcohol, or lack of sleep, or with starvation, or whether you do it with sex, or whether you do it with drugs, you not only add to the body of your knowledge but you jar the body of knowledge so that you are looking out in a different way . . . and this is what a young poet really must do, what a meaningful young poet must do—a young poet writing about acts of adventure and consciousness and perception." [16]

In his quest for experience, Morrison wound up at UCLA studying filmmaking. It was there that he met Ray Manzarek and the Doors were formed. Manzarek became the keyboardist who would compose the musical scores for Morrison's poetry. The name for the band came from a combination of a quote from William Blake and a small book published by Aldous Huxley. Blake had written that "If the doors of perception are cleansed everything would appear to man as it is, infinite." Huxley, on the other hand, described his drug experiences with mescaline as "what Adam saw on the morning of creation" in *The Doors of Perception*. Huxley was also one of the first proponents of LSD. When Huxley died on November 23, 1963, the same day that President Kennedy was assassinated, he was reported to have taken LSD for what he knew would be the last time just a few minutes before his death. (Ironically, Huxley is one of the crowd members on the cover of the Beatles' *Sgt. Pepper's Lonely Hearts Club Band*). Jim Morrison also agreed with William Blake's famous quote from "The Marriage of Heaven and Hell": "The road to excess leads to the palace of wisdom." Obviously this quote would also serve as an inspiration to Arthur Rimbaud as well.

One of Morrison's friends, January Jansen, who designed many of Jim's costumes, including his trademark snakeskin pants, remembered Morrison pushing everything to the edge: "He wanted to push everything to the limit. Just like when he was walking on the edge of the ledge [Morrison once walked a building ledge that was at least fifty feet above a busy street]. He wanted to see how far far was." [17] At times, other friends suggested that Morrison had a conscious death wish. They told tales of his drunken "death rides" in automobiles going at high rates of speed, and some became convinced that Jim Morrison would go out in a flaming crash in James Dean style.

Jim Morrison was a complex individual. He was composed of several classic personalities. His first personality was that of the Greek god Dionysus. He well represented the lifestyle of excessive drinking and wild behavior. Appropriately, the first play structure to be developed was the tragedy. The very term "tragedy" comes from the Greek phrase "goat song." This was used to honor the god Dionysus, who was half man with the legs of a goat.

Another classical figure that Morrison admired was Alexander the Great. Jim studied ancient history and developed a great admiration for Alexander. Morrison was so impressed by the Macedonian conqueror that he would pose for photos with his head gently tilted to one side like many of the marble busts of Alexander that appeared in that age. Tragically, Morrison, as well as Rimbaud, accepted Alexander's challenge to die young with glory.

Finally, Morrison would fit a casting call for the brooding, dark melancholy Prince of Denmark, Hamlet. Hamlet and Morrison were the ultimate enigmas. The reader is never able to completely understand Hamlet's motivations and actions compared with a similar Shakespearean hero such as Macbeth or Lear. Perhaps Shakespeare is saying that the character Hamlet is like the mystery of life itself. The purpose of existence can never be completely understood. Man can never come to grips with his own desires or understand his purpose for being. These absolute truths are kept from us. We only explore the grand mystery of life with very limited vision.

Whenever I listen to "The End" I can't help but compare its impact with Hamlet's question of whether to live or die. Both poets form contrasting attitudes concerning death. Of course,

Hamlet is terrified of what may exist in the unknown eternity that follows death, whereas Morrison seems to welcome the passing as a gentle friend. Strangely, the listener can't be sure whether Morrison is welcoming the end for himself or for another. One of Morrison's repeated themes is the "killer on the road" or "the hitchhiker [who] stood by the side of the road and leveled his thumb in the calm calculus of reason." In Morrison's "The Hitchhiker" the poet combines the story of a mysterious stranger who hitches a ride and confesses a murder that he committed in the desert. The structure of the poem combined with "Riders on the Storm" produces a chilling effect. Some fans actually believe that this scene could be autobiographical in that it is only one more of the "cardinal sins" through which the poet must pass to the ultimate understanding of life and death.

Freudian interpretations of Prince Hamlet's character suggest that the grieving prince suffered from an Oedipus complex. Obviously, this can be interpreted in Morrison's creation of the following lines: "Father?" "Yes, Son?" "I want to kill you." "Mother? I want to . . ." What follows next is a series of primal Oedipal screams. These lines could also have suggested Hamlet's conflict between his uncle-father and aunt-mother. It's the answer Hamlet is looking for. He would have the courage to confront his uncle-stepfather and revenge his father's death. His preoccupation with his mother's incest and his warning to "go not to my uncle's bed" would remove his final rival for his mother's attention.

When the Doors were developing their biography, Morrison told the publicists that his parents were dead. When his mother and younger brother attended one of the Doors' performances he refused to greet them. When they were seated in the theater by the Doors' management, he performed the graphic Oedipus scene from "The End" while looking his mother directly in her eyes. In a final comparison to Shakespeare's tragic hero, it would seem that both Hamlet and Morrison were able to grasp reality only through driving themselves to the very brink of madness.

Jim Morrison was a willing student of the occult. At least twice in his all too short life he performed blood-drinking rituals. The first took place in a Wiccan Handfasting Ceremony on June 24, 1970 (Midsummer Day). Patricia Kennealy was not only a practicing witch but also a high priestess in her coven. During the wedding ceremony, both parties drew their own blood and mixed it in a chalice that was partially filled with wine. At the conclusion of the service they both drank from the cup and were thereby joined together.

The second episode occurred when Morrison was having an affair with a beautiful Scandinavian girl whose name was Ingrid. When she suggested that at times she and some of her friends drank their own blood Morrison insisted that they should also do so. She went into the bathroom and produced a razor blade and after five tries managed to cut the fleshy part of her hand. Morrison collected her blood in a champagne glass. All during the remainder of the night they danced in the moonlight, made love, and awoke with Ingrid's dried blood smeared across both of their bodies. Morrison did not contribute his blood to this feast, possibly because he was unable to cut himself at the earlier ceremony and had actually blacked out for a few seconds. Though Morrison was involved with countless women, only Pamela Courson provided a haven for him to replenish his creative powers. She believed in him as a great poet and he felt responsible for her because, as he once said, "she had never grown up." Perhaps she was Wendy caring for Peter Pan in the Never-Never Land existence of a rock and roll wasteland. It was not a perfect relationship. At times the lovers seem determined to bring as much pain upon the other as possible, but love and hate are our two strongest emotions. Out of this antithesis was born a complete symbiotic devotion that lasted throughout both of their short and tragic lives.

Other rumors existed that his reference to being the "Lizard King" and "rid[ing] the snake . . . to the ancient lake" from "The End" could be further references of his involvement in the occult and in particular the practice of black magic. Some fans felt that the snake and lizard symbols represented the Prince of Darkness himself. In "L.A. Woman," Morrison sings a line "Mr. Mojo Risin'." The mentioning of the word "mojo" hints at the dark powers of voodoo; however, the very phrase is also an anagram for Jim Morrison's name.

Ironically, Jim Morrison performed two tributes to fellow rock stars who died young. The first was for Otis Redding after his fateful plane crash. The Doors were booked at the Winterland in San Francisco to perform three shows starting on December 26, 1967. Redding was the headliner due to his amazing performance at the Monterey Pop Festival. Tragically, Otis Redding was killed on December 10, 1967. Morrison had admired Redding greatly and decided to perform a tribute to the fallen singer the first night of the scheduled shows. Morrison ordered two-dozen bloodred roses and carried them out on stage with him for the first performance. As he emerged from the darkness, he was enveloped in the multicolored stage lights. Jim walked calmly to the front of the stage as the Doors began the syncopated rhythm to what was now to be rock and roll's true requiem, "When the Music's Over," and calmly said, "Poor Otis, dead and gone, left me here to sing his song, Pretty little girl with the red dress on, Poor Otis dead and gone." At this point Morrison threw the crimson rose petals into the audience and began singing the distinctive lyrics as a tribute to Redding. The audience of course was mesmerized. Morrison would include his poetic tribute to Otis Redding in the creation of his lyrics to "Runnin' Blue," which was later included on the *Soft Parade* album.[18]

Jim Morrison would yet again compose a final tribute to another rock star dying young when he became aware of Brian Jones's death on July 3, 1967. Morrison once again appealed to his tragic muse and wrote "Ode to L.A. While Thinking of Brian Jones, Deceased." Little did the Lizard King know that on this very date two years hence he would join Brian Jones beyond the metaphysical veil of existence.

The ultimate legend concerning Jim Morrison has to do with the events that led to his death. Morrison had left the United States to live in Paris and concentrate solely upon his poetry. He and Pamela leased an apartment so that Morrison would renew himself as a poet. After all, he had always considered himself a poet first and never seriously regarded himself as a gifted rock singer. The music was to serve as a complement for his poetic outlet. It became a chance for him to display his emotion, and to preach what he saw as the coming revolution.

On the night of July 2, 1971, Jim Morrison had attended a movie, *Pursued,* staring Robert Mitchum (some sources claim that Jim and Pamela went together while other sources claim that Morrison attended the movie alone). Later that night, after he had returned to the apartment with Pam, Morrison complained of chest pains. This may have been due to a respiratory infection that was troubling him at this time. Early the next morning, Pamela Courson found his body still in the tub. The time of death was fixed somewhere near 5:00 A.M. In this scenario, some medical opinions state that a blood clot could have left the lungs and lodged in the singer's heart, killing him instantly. A medical examiner was summoned to the apartment and after checking the body for the telltale signs of needle marks—indicating a possible drug O.D.—the official cause of death was given as "myocardial infarction," a simple heart attack. This was the official version released to the media that followed Morrison's death. Jim's funeral took place on July 8, 1971. Pamela made arrangements to lease a grave for thirty years in the historic Père-Lachaise Cemetery in Paris. Somehow it seemed very appropriate that the American Poet would be placed in eternal rest with other celebrities including Frederic Chopin, Oscar Wilde, Edith Piaf, Honoré de Balzac, and ironically Paul Verlaine, Rimbaud's homosexual lover. Strangely, there were reports that Morrison had visited Père-Lachaise just three days before his own death.

The second version of the strange death of Jim Morrison concerned evidence of a drug overdose. In this version it was not known if Morrison had attended a movie and then made his way to the Rock 'n' Roll Circus, a hangout for heroin addicts, or simply just bypassed the movie. It was rumored that Morrison had purchased some heroin, some say cocaine, and went back to his apartment where he later became sick and died there in his bath. It would appear that the effects of both the heroin and alcohol would thus be increased, with a relatively small amount leading to his death. In Marianne Faithfull's *Faithfull: An Autobiography*, she has stated that she was accused of giving Morrison the fix that had taken his life. She also stated the name of the dealer who had sold Morrison the deadly heroin. Faithfull mentioned seeing the body and noticing a large purple bruise over his heart.

It was also rumored that Morrison may have suspected the white powdery substance, heroin, found with Pam in the apartment to be cocaine. After taking the substance, Jim became sick and later died from the powerful reactions of the heroin mixed with the alcohol he had previously consumed. In *No One Here Gets Out Alive*, Danny Sugarman mentioned how during an interview following Jim's death, Pamela Courson repeated over and over again how it was all her fault. If Morrison died of a drug overdose we will probably never know, because an autopsy was never performed. During the medical investigation at Morrison's apartment, Pamela told the medical examiner that Jim had never taken drugs and that he had a bad respiratory infection. Since there was no physical evidence of drug abuse, such as needle marks, the coroner ruled the death as a result of natural causes.

The story of Jim Morrison's death should have concluded with one of the above explanations; however, it is extremely hard to allow a legend to just simply die. Following the sudden and mysterious death of the Lizard King, many of his devoted fans were actually convinced that Morrison was not dead. At the Fillmore West in 1967, Morrison suggested that the Doors pull off a death hoax to bring the new band more popularity.[19] (It is strange that in this same year the Beatles had just released the *Sgt. Pepper's* album, which later supplied a large number of the "Paul is dead" rumors.) Morrison also talked with a number of close friends and commented upon how he could see himself radically changing his life at any time. He actually told his record officials that if they received a message from a Mr. Mojo Risin' in Africa that the message would actually be from him. The Mr. Mojo Risin' would serve as his new identity. As stated earlier, Morrison deeply respected Arthur Rimbaud. Rimbaud managed to fake his own death; afterward, he disappeared to Africa and became a trader and gunrunner. Doors keyboardist Ray Manzarek once claimed that if anyone could get away with faking his own death it would be Jim. A few days after the announcement of his death, a few fans claimed that they saw Morrison boarding an airplane leaving Paris. Newspapers and fan magazines have reported individuals who claimed to be Jim Morrison cashing checks and buying property. They claimed that the individual's appearance was astonishingly similar to that of the dead singer.

In a "table hopping" interview (December, 1994) with my friend Gary James from Syracuse, New York, Jim Morrison's brother-in-law, Alan Graham, commented that he was not so sure that Jim Morrison was buried in Père-Lachaise Cemetery. He stated that the corpse found in the bathtub had turned blue and was bloated. At first Pamela had not mentioned the true identity of the newly discovered corpse; it was simply suggested that the body was just another long-haired hippie drunk. Eventually, Pam had to produce a passport to identify the body. It was at this time that the American Embassy contacted Jim Morrison's family.

Graham also suggested that the body in the bathtub may have actually belonged to a mysterious German acquaintance of Morrison. This friend borrowed Morrison's jacket and impersonated the American singer. Some insiders actually claimed that this fellow looked so much like Morrison that they could very well have been taken for twins. Graham claimed that there was at least one occurrence when Dieter, the associate's name, was thrown out of a restaurant for trying to impersonate Jim Morrison. Alan Graham found it quite possible to believe that this may have been the body found in the early morning hours of July 3, 1971.

Since the Parisian morgues were closed, the body had to be kept on ice for the next few days. Graham believed that Pamela Courson did not take the time to look at the body, due to its frightful appearance, when it was placed within a coffin. Another puzzling fact concerned the absence of an autopsy. To some of the most imaginative fans, this would suggest a cover-up. Could a doctor have been bribed? Was the coffin empty? Doors manager Bill Siddons flew to Paris after calling Pamela Courson to confirm rumors of Morrison's death. Siddons was familiar with the rumors. Early in the Doors' career, Siddons had heard many unconfirmed rumors of Morrison's death. In some accounts Jim was killed in a car crash. Other accounts had the rock singer falling from an apartment building into the street as he walked along a narrow ledge. As Bill's heart would sink with each report, Jim would always appear and ask the same question, "How did I die this time?" This time would be different.

Siddons arrived in Paris on July 6, 1971, three days after Morrison's death. He was taken to Pamela's apartment, where he found a sealed coffin and a death certificate signed by one doctor.

The death certificate was filed with the U.S. Embassy the next day, and on the afternoon of July 8, 1971, Jim Morrison was buried at Père-Lachaise Cemetery. "Five mourners were present: Pamela, Siddons, Alan Ronay, Agnès Varda, and Robin Wertle. They threw flowers on the grave and said their goodbyes . . . Siddons said in a prepared statement released after his return to the United States, 'I have just returned from Paris, where I attended the funeral of Jim Morrison, . . . Jim was buried in a simple ceremony, with only a few close friends present. The initial news of his death and funeral was kept quiet because those of us who knew him intimately and loved him as a person wanted to avoid all the notoriety and circus-like atmosphere that surrounded the deaths of such other rock personalities as Janis Joplin and Jimi Hendrix.

"'I can say Jim died peacefully of natural causes—he had been in Paris since March with his wife, Pam. He had seen a doctor in Paris about a respiratory problem and had complained of his problem on Saturday—the day of his death.'"[20] Siddons at no time asked that the coffin be opened to view the body. Maybe there wasn't a reason to do this, but just maybe the last thing that Ray Manzarek said to Bill Siddons before the manager left for Morrison's funeral may haunt Siddons just a bit: "'Oh, Bill,' Ray added, 'I don't mean to sound morbid, but please make sure.'

"'Make sure of what, Ray?'

"'I don't know, man, just make *sure*.'"[21]

On April 25, 1974, Pamela Courson, "just another lost angel . . . city of night," died of a heroin overdose while living in an apartment in Hollywood, California. Her parents had her remains cremated and one legend claimed that her ashes were flown to Paris and buried with Jim at Père-Lachaise. Though her final resting place is reported to be Père-Lachaise, the tremendous costs of transporting a burial urn to Paris and the red tape that surely would have resulted in a long delay for a proper burial forced her parents to have their daughter buried in California instead. If Jim Morrison had indeed faked his own death and escaped to Africa or some other location, surely Pamela Courson would have known. In an interview with Danny Sugarman, Pamela stated, "If Jim were alive he would call." If this was the case, Pamela took the secret to her grave. Perhaps Morrison had written her epitaph earlier within his lyrics to "L.A. Woman" when he mentioned the "little girls in their Hollywood bungalows." The most poignant line, which would certainly refer to Pam, was Jim's description of "just another lost angel . . . city of night." In this case, the star-crossed lovers have both managed to finally break on through to the other side, together.

Some fans claimed that the tragic death of James Douglas Morrison involved the occult. There were suggestions that he had been killed supernaturally. A voodoo doll sent by a spurned lover was one explanation. One grisly account mentioned Morrison being killed with his eyes being removed by his killer to release the dead poet's spirit or demon. Another theory suggested that the death announcement and funeral service were put off five days in order for Morrison's spiritual presence to properly leave his lifeless body in some hidden ritual. Hadn't Morrison been involved with the occult? Hadn't Patricia Kennealy stated that Jim Morrison was interested in undergoing the witches' initiation ceremony and becoming a witch himself? Morrison was deeply interested in the blues and like Robert Johnson mentions a certain happening at a crossroads in "The Soft Parade." Morrison sings that he and a friend should "slay a few animals at the crossroads . . . we need someone new, something else to get us through." Maybe a number of the ancient bluesmen who marveled at Robert Johnson's whispered pact with Satan could mistake Morrison's meeting "someone new" after a symbolic sacrifice at the crossroads in exchange for "something else to get us through" as his own confession that had now placed a hellhound on his trail. As you can see, it's not all that difficult to create a modern-day urban legend.

A small minority of fans have suggested that Morrison was murdered, just another piece of a massive conspiracy led by U.S. government agencies whose purpose was to destroy the counter-culture. Their targets were obviously Jimi Hendrix, Janis Joplin, and Jim Morrison. Strangely, an eerie line from "Hyacinth House" mentions, "I see the bathroom is clear. I think somebody's near, I'm sure that someone is following me, oh yeah." For these conspiracy buffs, it may suggest that in those above lines Jim Morrison may have foreseen his own murder. This theory is really a little too bizarre, but in the United States we seem to have a great affection for unsolved mysteries and conspiracies.

The first time I visited Père-Lachaise in July of 1993, I found myself entering the cemetery gates on a drizzling, chilly Sunday morning. This particular setting seemed strange since Paris is usually very sultry in July. I had read earlier about the riots that had taken place within the cemetery walls upon the twenti-eth anniversary of Morrison's death so I wasn't quite sure what I would see. I had an audiocassette of John Densmore's book about the Doors, *Riders on the Storm,* playing softly within my Walk-man as I made my search for the final resting place of "Le Roi d'Rock."

The jutting Gothic sepulchers inched silently upward to the dark gray sky as I made my way through the winding maze of the stiller town. I noticed a marker, much like those found in a shop-ping mall directing customers to their favorite stores, with com-plete directions to a number of celebrity graves. I visited Chopin, Balzac, and Oscar Wilde. I noted that there were no directions to Jim Morrison's final resting place. It was then that I noticed the simple graffiti that directed me to my destination. It was fascinat-ing to follow the signs: JIM [right arrow]. As I got closer, another message informed me that I was walking the "King's Highway."

Within a few minutes, which actually seemed much closer to an eternity, I was there. Morrison's grave was a very simple plot of earth. The fabled bust had long since been stolen. Behind the simple marker, a large crypt wall bore the inscription, "Morrison's Hotel." I knew my long search had now ended. I gazed at the headstone that contained this inscription: James Douglas Morrison. A Greek epitaph followed which stated, "KATA TON ΔAIMONA EAYTOY." I have heard that the translation is "True to his Spirit." John Densmore was right. This grave appeared to be much too small for someone of Jim Morrison's height.

For a long while after his death, Morrison's grave stood bare and desolate among the highly figured palaces of eternity. Pamela Courson was said to have asked the surviving members of the Doors to contribute for an appropriate marker denoting the eternal lair of the Lizard King. The marker was never purchased, which led drummer John Densmore to accuse Courson of "putting the money up her arm." Eventually, Jim Morrison's family paid for the dead poet's monument. Unfortunately, the family still is forced to pay security costs and cleaning fees that are associated with removing the perpetual layers of graffiti left by two generations paying homage to the rebel poet. As I stood silently by the grave, I noticed that a group of spectators had assembled. This small patch of broken earth was the only gravesite that was literally enveloped by curious onlookers. One at a time they posed for the camera, each standing smiling by the tombstone either alone or in small groups. One young bystander with tears streaming down his face sat solemnly and quietly at the foot of the grave. It appeared that he had lost his best friend. Sadly, I remembered that before the current headstone was in place a simple plastic marker identified the grave. It was engraved with just one word, "Ami." In this case Jim and his music have continued to attract a new feast of friends. Upon the grave fans had paid homage to the fallen star. One had left a Snickers candy bar. A small clay seal rested unperturbed upon the damp earth. An eight by ten color photo of the young Dionysus from early 1967 glanced back at the crowd from its vigil alongside the headstone. To the right of the burial plot, I noticed a playing card pushed down into the soft dirt; appropriately, it was the Jack of Hearts. Again I smiled and thought once again just how appropriate the lyrics to "Hyacinth House" fit this occasion. In this song Morrison includes the line, "Why did you throw the Jack of Hearts away? It was the only card in the deck that I had left to play." Now, the card was finally returned to its rightful owner.

During the summer of 1996, I returned to Père-Lachaise. I couldn't help but notice the inscribed directions that would once again lead me to Morrison's resting place. This time, however, it was to be very different. Bright fluorescent yellow ribbons of police tape surrounded the grave. The curious tourists were there with their cameras recording the scene for hundreds of scrapbooks back home. The graffiti had been washed from the surrounding monuments. A police guard informed us that only one at a time could approach the grave. No camcorders could be used. At this time I remembered Alan Graham's final remarks to my friend Gary James. Pamela Courson had only leased the burial site for thirty years. It was said that many relatives of the dead that surround Morrison's grave have demanded the removal of Jim Morrison's body at the earliest possible time. The lease expired on July 8, 2001, and apparently will not be renewed. In this case Morrison would be exhumed and his body flown to the United States for final burial. It was also rumored that Los Angeles would be his final resting place. Graham hinted that at that time the coffin might be opened and, for some fans, a much overdue final identification made of the electric shaman's body.

On July 8, 2001, I was back in Paris and again made my way to the resting place of James Douglas Morrison. As I walked through the gothic monuments I noticed that something was different. Gone was the graffiti that signaled the "King's Highway," and freshly scrubbed curbs gave no clues as to the direction of Morrison's grave. The yellow police tape was also removed from the gravesite and there were no policemen on duty. It is rumored that the Morrison estate has agreed to pay for upkeep and keep the neighboring headstones graffiti-free and there are whispers about security devices in and around Jim's grave. Morrison is now a permanent resident of Père-Lachaise, and the curious legend of the unopened coffin remains. The crowds will still come and stand by the gravesite but at this time it appears that we may never know the final secret of the Lizard King.

Membership in the club did not end with the death of Jim Morrison. In 1973, the Grateful Dead's keyboardist Ron "Pigpen" McKernan became the club's next member. McKernan was devoted to the blues. He sang, played the harmonica and keyboards, and, along with Jerry Garcia, founded the lineup that would become the Grateful Dead. The long, spirited band jams and constant drinking took their toll on Pigpen. At times he was much too weak to perform as liver disease swept through his body. The band hired Keith Godchaux as a backup keyboardist and Godchaux's wife Donna as a backup singer. For some shows McKernan, on a very limited basis, and Godchaux would perform together with the band. Though he had quit drinking for the last year of his life, McKernan's liver disease continued to progress. On March 8, 1973, his landlord discovered his body next to his bed. It appeared that he had been dead for two days: "The official autopsy results mentioned that Pigpen had died of a 'massive gastrointestinal hemorrhage.' He also was found to have suffered from a 'massively enlarged spleen' and some 'pulmonary edema.' Ron 'Pigpen' McKernan was dead at the age of twenty-seven."[22]

Though no other members of the Grateful Dead were admitted as members of the club, fickle Fate still made sure that at least three other band members would follow in the tradition of the band's name. In 1979, the Godchauxs left due to undisclosed musical differences within the band. Keith Godchaux was replaced with Brent Mydland. One year later on July 23, 1980, Keith Godchaux was killed in a motor vehicle accident. The band continued to perform to enthusiastic crowds of "Deadheads" throughout the 1980s until Brent Mydland died of a drug overdose on July 26, 1990. Ironically, his death was almost exactly one year to the day of the death of former keyboardist Keith Godchaux. Without a doubt the Grateful Dead seemed to produce an extremely high mortality rate for its keyboardists.

The "long strange trip" ended for the Grateful Dead when band founder Jerry Garcia died from complications associated with a drug overdose on August 9, 1995. Garcia's death occurred eight days past his fifty-third birthday and six days before the twenty-six-year anniversary of Woodstock. It would appear that Garcia's life had come almost full circle. The Grateful Dead performed at Woodstock on August 16 (on the anniversary of the death of Robert Johnson). This concert is generally considered to be the last hurrah for the Flower Child movement. Woodstock served as the apex, the highest moment in which a half million members of the counterculture gathered in a sea of mud, with inadequate facilities, and with very little food to attend an event that exhibited no acts of violent crime either at the scene of the performances or in the nearby towns that lay along the way.

The Grateful Dead, also by a strange twist of fate, managed to perform at Altamont with the Stones. It has been speculated that Garcia suggested the concept of the Stones performing a free concert in San Francisco to draw a crowd larger than Woodstock for the conclusion of the Rolling Stones' American tour. The Dead were also said to have suggested the hiring of the Hell's Angels for the Stones' security at the show. The tragedy at the Altamont concert, along with the Manson murders, proved to be the nadir of the hippie movement. Jerry Garcia and the Dead had come full circle with the birth and death of the Woodstock generation.

Rock Scully, the Grateful Dead's manager and close friend of Jerry Garcia, commented on just how superstitious Jerry was concerning death: "He would never say the word or allow himself to be photographed in front of a tombstone, and was always pained when promoters came up with graveyard scenes to advertise the band.

"When Pigpen died, Jerry and I went to the funeral together. Lying in an open casket in his blue-jean jacket covered with his pins and buttons, Pig looked a lot better than he had in some time. But Jerry was appalled. 'Don't ever let that happen to me,' he said as we walked away from the coffin. 'There are just two things I want you to promise me: Don't ever find me in the back of a record store signing records and don't bury me in an open casket.'" [23] Obviously, one promise was not kept. According to press reports covering Garcia's death and funeral, Jerry's body was viewed in an open casket on Thursday, August 10, at St. Stephen's Episcopal Church. (Ironically, one of the Dead's classic songs is entitled "St. Stephen.") He was dressed simply in a black T-shirt and sweatpants. Jerry Garcia's funeral service was held on August 11, 1995. Jerry Garcia's last number performed with the Grateful Dead was said to be Bob Dylan's "Knocking on Heaven's Door." The long strange journey had now ended.

Badfinger was another rock band that contributed one of its members to the club. The British band signed with the Beatles' Apple Records and produced a number of hit songs throughout the world. They were more popular in America than in Great Britain and in some ways this led to tragedy for the band. After signing a management contract with an American promoter, the band began its steady decline. First, the band lost its recording contract with Apple but was signed instead to Warner Bros.

Records for $3 million for a six-album deal. The band received nothing of the advance, which was used up by the band's production expenses. With their financial affairs crumbling, band member Pete Ham committed suicide by hanging himself in his garage on April 23, 1975. He was despondent over his financial state and became worried about the birth of his first child. He was twenty-seven years old.

The band continued, but after a promised tour of America fell through a few years later that forced even more financial worries, band member Tom Evans committed suicide by hanging himself in his backyard. He was thirty-six years old. Ham and Evans were consummate pop songwriters whose haunting "Without You" became a hit song for Harry Nilsson as well as several other artists. Perhaps this song of despair best sums up the careers of two artists destined by fate to follow Alexander's short path.

At times, membership in the club often involves bizarre and unexplained circumstances as a prerequisite. For instance, Roger Lee Durham of Bloodstone entered the club at the height of the band's popularity in October of 1973. His death was credited to unknown circumstances. However, membership in the club often occurs through natural and very explainable reasons. Two members, Chris Bell of Big Star and Dennis Dale Boon of the Minutemen, complied with the membership guidelines when they were both killed in two separate auto accidents. Chris Bell was killed in Memphis when the car he was driving struck a telephone pole on the night of December 27, 1978. Boon was killed in a car crash in Arizona on December 23, 1985.

The next rock superstar to fulfill the requirements for exclusive membership into the club was Kurt Cobain. Cobain was the guitarist, lead vocalist, and cofounder of Nirvana. With the release of *Nevermind*, Nirvana exploded onto the music scene with a primal vengeance. Cobain's lyrics reflected themes of isolation and alienation, and became a rallying cry for Generation X. Due to his fame, Kurt Cobain took his seat upon the rock and roll roller coaster. The highs were associated with the band's deserved critical acclaim, his marriage to Courtney Love, and the birth of his daughter, Frances. Unfortunately, the lows were just as devastating. Cobain turned to heroin to provide an escape from what he saw as his own creative failures. He constantly complained about intense stomach pain. The pain was so severe that alcohol and heroin became his ambivalent antidote by which he exorcized his own demons.

In March of 1994, six weeks before his terrible death, Kurt Cobain was rushed to a hospital in Rome while on tour with Nirvana. It was reported in the media that Cobain had suffered from an apparent drug overdose. Nirvana's management released a statement claiming that the overdose was accidental due to the improper mixing of champagne and tranquilizers. Cobain sank deep into a tranquilizer-induced coma but managed to survive this ordeal. Some insiders, however, claimed that this was his first attempt at suicide.

Following his return to Seattle, Courtney Love summoned police to his home. She had reported that Cobain had locked himself within a room with a loaded gun. Once again she feared that the distraught singer would try suicide. When the police arrived they found "four revolvers, twenty-five boxes of ammunition, and an assortment of pills."[24] After this traumatic episode, Courtney Love and a number of Kurt Cobain's closest friends persuaded the singer to enter a drug rehab program in Los Angeles. Cobain agreed, but checked himself out after only forty-eight hours and returned to Seattle. Though his mother had filed a missing person's report with the police, the singer was not discovered until a repairman, hired to install a home security system, found his body in a room above Cobain's garage. A shotgun was found lying on his chest as well as a nearby suicide note that quoted Neil Young's maxim, "It's better to burn out than fade away." In short, Kurt Cobain had become the Richard Cory of his own generation. In Edwin Arlington Robinson's poem "Richard Cory," Richard Cory was a man that everyone wishes he could become. Cory was rich, handsome, and to all practical observers seemed to have it made: "And Richard Cory, one calm summer night,/Went home and put a bullet through his head." A practical observer may very well notice all outward characteristics that hint at success and happiness, but the victim's inner world may well be filled with horrors compared to which our own trivial fears would pale. This seemed to be the tragic case of Kurt Cobain.

Cobain was born in 1967. This was the same year that the Beatles released *Sgt. Pepper's* as a fitting beginning of the "Summer of Love." His very life would cruelly serve to be an antithesis. Like John Lennon, Kurt Cobain would prove to be a prophet for his generation. His poetic voice exclaimed a new generation's rage, but in the end he was consumed by his own fears and inadequacies. The painful mourning of his death resulted in a few tragic copycat suicides. This was to be a final tribute given at the altar of rock and roll. One of the more introspective songs written by Cobain was the ghoulish-sounding "I Hate Myself and Want to Die." In one interview, Cobain said that the song title was actually a parody of how some individuals pictured him. Sadly, the song proved to be a fitting epitaph. Again, this attempt to explain his introspection seems to parallel John Lennon's "Yer Blues." In this song Lennon included lyrics that stated, "Yes, I'm lonely, wanna die . . . feel so suicidal even hate my rock and roll." Through the use of these lyrics, John Lennon obviously became a kindred spirit to Cobain. From one working-class hero to another, the secret of discontent is passed down much like a ceremonial sword for the next generation to achieve purpose and meaning. Perhaps the ultimate irony with Curt Cobain's death concerned the relationship with the band's name. Webster's dictionary defines Nirvana as "1. *Hinduism:* a blowing out, or extinction of the flame of life through reunion with Brahma. 2. *Buddhism:* the state of perfect blessedness achieved by the extinction of individual existence and by the absorption of the soul into the supreme spirit, or by the extinction of all desires and passions. 3. Any place or condition of great peace or bliss." Perhaps, in this case, the band's name was chosen very wisely.

When I first heard of Kurt Cobain's death I was flooded with the all too familiar feelings that brought back memories of Brian Jones, Jimi Hendrix, Janis Joplin, and Jim Morrison. I was struck by a comment that Cobain's mother, Wendy O'Connor, had made to the media shortly following her son's apparent suicide. She was quoted in *Newsweek* magazine (April 18, 1994): "Now he's gone and joined that stupid club. I told him not to join that stupid club." Obviously, Cobain was very aware of the "Twenty-Seven Club." Did this awareness suggest that he had carefully planned his own exit? Some fans may think so, but there are some who hint at murder. It is just too simple to bury a star. As in the case of Morrison, Hendrix, and Brian Jones, the subtle hint of a hidden conspiracy expands what could very well be a terrible tragic death into infinite rock and roll folklore. Some of the most puzzling questions haunting Internet websites include: Why would anyone committing suicide place three shells in a shotgun? It is reported that Cobain had injected himself with three times the amount of heroin needed to provide a lethal dose. Why would he shoot himself after this lethal injection? And, after giving himself the dosage, would he still be able to pull the trigger? There were reports of someone trying to use one of Cobain's credit cards two days after his established death (the medical examiner placed the time of death on April 6, 1994). When his body was discovered all attempts at using the card stopped. Is it true that the police did not find fingerprints on the shotgun? Curiously, these questions may never be answered and exist only in the uncertain and unjustified realm of innuendo. This is true of all pertinent folklore and in this case, yet once again, the name will not die with the man.

On June 16, 1994, in Seattle, Washington, the body of Kristen Pfaff, the bassist for Hole, was found in her bathtub. Pfaff was from Minneapolis and had moved to Seattle to become a member of Hole and part of the new music scene that was developing there. After the making of Hole's *Live Through This,* she had gone back home to Minneapolis and had rejoined her old band Janitor Joe for a European tour. It was after the tour, and following Kurt Cobain's death, that Kristen became very despondent. Pfaff decided to return to Seattle and pack up her belongings in a U-Haul truck and head back home to Minneapolis. She was well aware of the drug environment in Seattle. She had entered a drug treatment program earlier but now she was clean. Strangely enough it was Kurt Cobain who had first introduced her to heroin. She had no idea that she would join him in death a few short months after his suicide.

She was excited about returning home and leaving an environment in Seattle that reeked of death and self-destruction. She was now ready to make a complete break. Paul Erickson was a fellow musician in Seattle and offered to help her pack the U-Haul. He volunteered to sleep next to the loaded truck all night to watch over her prized possessions. The night of June 15, 1994, Kristen decided to take a long hot bath. This was something she enjoyed and it wasn't unusual for her to take a nap or eat dinner while she bathed. When Erickson returned later that night he heard her snoring in the bath. Thinking nothing of this he went to sleep. The next morning he became concerned that there was no answer from Kristen as he knocked loudly on the bathroom door. It was then that he kicked the door open and found Kristen curled up in the tub. On the floor in her purse was the all too common drug paraphernalia of the user. The syringes gave proof that this was another drug-related death in grim Seattle.

Kristen's body was taken back to Minneapolis, and when Geffen Records asked permission for the members of Hole to attend Kristen's funeral, the Pfaff family refused to allow them to attend. That was one side of her life that needed no celebration, according to her parents. A number of people were puzzled that Kristen Pfaff would ever use heroin again. This was the reason she was leaving Seattle. Why would she become a junkie again after rehab? There are some who say the event is likely a murder and not just another simple drug overdose by another musician. Perhaps Kristen Pfaff's mother was right when she stated, "I don't know what's going on in that Seattle scene, but there is something wrong, terribly wrong." Kristen Pfaff was twenty-seven when she died and is now a member of the club in good standing.

Jason Thirsk was the bassist for the punk-rock band Pennywise. He contributed to four of the band's albums, but in 1995 realized that he had a drinking problem and entered rehab. It wasn't the first time he had tried rehab and he was unable to come to grips with his excesses. On July 29, 1996, Thirsk entered the club at the age of twenty-seven. He was firing a gun into his house and into his refrigerator. Suddenly, he turned the gun on himself and fired a bullet into his own chest. He later bled to death. The police in Hermosa Beach, California, ruled his death a suicide.

Richard Cavendish believes that "The strange patterns of Fate seem to suggest that death at the age of twenty-seven holds some mysterious reason. In life as well as science there are rhythms that are determined by twenty-eight day cycles (e.g., female menstrual, lunar cycles, etc)." Followers of numerology would be quick to point out that the sum of twenty-seven is nine. The numeral nine suggests completeness, since it takes nine months for a baby to fully develop. Nine is also given as "the number of initiation, the end of one stage of spiritual development and the beginning of a new one." [25] Nine also suggests the number with the highest power. After nine the numbers repeat themselves. Also, any single digit multiplied by nine, and added together, will equal nine (for example, 9x2=18, 1+8=9; 9x9=81, 1+8=9; 9x4=36, 3+6=9). Of all nine numerals, this is the only case in which this factor occurs.

In the field of astrology the belief is that each individual goes through a series of twenty-seven-year cycles. Each cycle presents an opportunity for growth and enlightenment. The number 27 can also be explained by looking at each of the specific numbers. The number "2" is associated with individuals who seek love and acceptance, whereas the number "7" is associated with individuals who tend to be escapists. Of course, a number of musicians' deaths were brought about by lethal overdoses of drugs and alcohol to escape from their personal issues.

If each of the members of the club accepted Alexander the Great's challenge and chose an early death filled with fame and glory as opposed to simple fading away, then each would probably agree with this far-reaching adage: "Death is the ultimate trip. That's why they save it for last." Alexander's age at the time of his death? Thirty-three, 3x3=9.

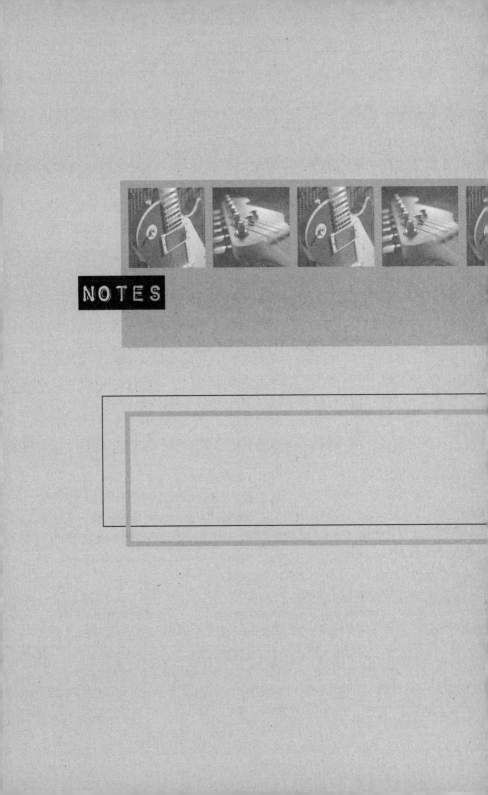

NOTES

INTRODUCTION

1. Timothy White, *Rock Lives: Profiles and Interviews* (New York: Henry Holt & Company 1990), 32.
2. Nick Tosches, *Hellfire: The Jerry Lee Lewis Story* (New York: Delacorte Press, 1982), 27.
3. Jeff Pike, *The Death of Rock 'n' Roll* (Boston and London: Faber and Faber, 1993), 54.
4. Pike, *The Death of Rock 'n' Roll,* 89.

1: WAITING AT THE CROSSROADS

1. Francis Davis, *The History of the Blues: The Roots, the Music, the People—From Charley Patton to Robert Cray* (New York: Hyperion, 1995), 105.
2. Davis, *The History of the Blues,* 105.

2: THE BUDDY HOLLY CURSE?

1. Martin Huxley and Quinton Skinner, *Behind the Music: The Day the Music Died* (New York: Simon & Schuster, 2000), 35.
2. Ellis Amburn, *Buddy Holly: A Biography* (New York: St. Martin's Press, 1996) 271.
3. Huxley and Skinner, *Behind the Music,* 29.
4. Amburn, *Buddy Holly,* 252–53.
5. Phillip Norman, *Sympathy for the Devil: The Rolling Stones Story* (New York: Dell, 1984), 256.
6. Norman, *Sympathy for the Devil,* 257.
7. John Repsch, *The Legendary Joe Meek: The Telstar Man* (London: Cherry Red Books, 2000), 57.
8. Norman, *Sympathy for the Devil,* 303.
9. Dave Thompson, *Better to Burn Out: The Cult of Death in Rock 'n' Roll* (New York: Thunder's Mouth Press, 1999), 9.
10. Alan Mann, *The A–Z of Buddy Holly* (London: Aurum Press, 1996), 26.
11. Jim Driver, ed., *The Mammoth Book of Sex, Drugs, and Rock 'n' Roll* (New York: Carroll and Graff, 2001), 577.

3: "THE DEVIL WENT DOWN TO GEORGIA"

1. Scott Freeman, *Midnight Riders: The Story of the Allman Brothers Band* (Boston: Little, Brown & Company, 1995), 29.
2. Ibid., 111.
3. Ibid., 142.
4. Ibid.
5. Ibid.
6. Marley Brant, *Freebirds: The Lynyrd Skynyrd Story* (New York: Billboard Books, 2002), 151.
7. Ibid., 162.
8. Ibid., 173.
9. Ibid., 229.

4: "MR. CROWLEY"

1. Michael Newton, *Raising Hell: An Encyclopedia of Devil Worship and Satanic Crime* (New York: Avon Books, 1993), 116.
2. John Parker, *At the Heart of Darkness: Witchcraft, Black Magic, and Satanism Today* (New York: Citadel Press, 1993), 175.
3. Parker, *At the Heart of Darkness,* 179.
4. Richard Cavendish, *The Black Arts* (New York: Perigee Books, 1983), 31.
5. Newton, *Raising Hell,* 225.
6. Cavendish, *The Black Arts,* 38.
7. Davis, *The History of the Blues,* 106.
8. Martin Gardner, *On the Wild Side* (New York: Prometheus Books, 1992), 198.
9. Cavendish, *The Black Arts,* 248–49.
10. Newton, *Raising Hell,* 121.
11. Cavendish, *The Black Arts,* 40.
12. Parker, *At the Heart of Darkness,* 184.
13. Ibid., 190.
14. Ibid., 193.
15. Timothy White, *Rock Lives: Profiles and Interviews* (New York: Henry Holt, 1990), 584.
16. Ibid., 584–94.

5: "SYMPATHY FOR THE DEVIL"

1. White, *Rock Lives: Profiles and Interviews* (New York: Henry Holt, 1990), 177.
2. Ibid.
3. Ibid., 189.
4. Christopher Sandford, *Mick Jagger: Primitive Cool* (New York: St. Martin's Press, 1993), 120.
5. Marianne Faithfull, with David Dalton, *Faithfull: An Autobiography* (Boston: Little, Brown & Co., 1994), 207–08.
6. Faithfull, *Faithfull: An Autobiography*, 208.
7. A. E. Hotchner, *Blown Away: The Rolling Stones and the Death of the Sixties* (New York: Simon & Schuster, 1990), 184.
8. White, *Rock Lives: Profiles and Interviews*, 191.
9. Hotchner, *Blown Away*, 182–83.
10. Ibid., 183–84.
11. Tony Sanchez, *Up and Down with the Rolling Stones* (London: Blake, 1994), 145.
12. Sanchez, *Up and Down*, 177.
13. Ibid., 149.
14. Ibid., 151.
15. Ibid., 111.
16. Hotchner, *Blown Away*, 317.
17. Ibid., 318.
18. Sanchez, *Up and Down*, 178.
19. Ibid., 263.
20. Hotchner, *Blown Away*, 27.
21. Sanchez, *Up and Down*, 189.

6: THE SORCERER'S APPRENTICE

1. Ritchie Yorke, *Led Zeppelin: The Definitive Biography* (Novato, CA: Underwood-Miller, 1993), 25.
2. Yorke, *Led Zeppelin: The Definitive Biography*, 33.
3. Ibid., 84.
4. Ibid., 70.
5. Ibid., 81.
6. Richard Cole, *Stairway to Heaven: Led Zeppelin Uncensored* (New York: HarperCollins, 1992), 11.

7. Lewis Spence, *An Encyclopedia of Occultism* (New York: Citadeal Books, 1996), 107.

8. Cole, *Stairway to Heaven,* 256.

9. Davis, *The History of the Blues,* 95.

10. Yorke, *Led Zeppelin: The Definitive Biography,* 150.

11. Cavendish, *The Black Arts,* 255–56.

12. Yorke, *Led Zeppelin: The Definitive Biography,* 117–18.

13. Ibid., 117.

14. Cole, *Stairway to Heaven,* 182.

15. Yorke, *Led Zeppelin: The Definitive Biography,* 132.

16. Ibid.

17. Ibid.

18. Ibid., 129.

19. Davis, *The History of the Blues,* 142.

20. Aleister Crowley, *Magick in Theory and Practice* (Seacaucus, NJ: Castle Books, 1991), 417.

21. Yorke, *Led Zeppelin: The Definitive Biography,* 192.

22. Ibid., 193.

23. Davis, *The History of the Blues,* 211.

24. Ibid.

25. Cole, *Stairway to Heaven,* 324.

26. Ibid., 390.

27. Yorke, *Led Zeppelin: The Definitive Biography,* 200.

28. Ibid., 198.

29. Ibid., 199.

30. Ibid., 199–200.

31. Ibid., 211.

32. Davis, *The History of the Blues,* 286.

33. Cole, *Stairway to Heaven,* 10.

34. Yorke, *Led Zeppelin: The Definitive Biography,* 214.

35. Cole, *Stairway to Heaven,* 402.

36. Ibid.

37. Davis, *The History of the Blues,* 303.

7: "WELCOME TO THE HOTEL CALIFORNIA"

1. Parker, *At the Heart of Darkness*, 256.
2. Anton Szandor LaVey, *The Satanic Bible* (New York: Avon Books, 1976), 25.
3. Parker, *At the Heart of Darkness*, 258–59.
4. Ibid., 261.
5. Newton, *Raising Hell*, 180.
6. Huxley and Skinner, *Behind the Music*, 144.
7. Ibid., 156.
8. Ibid., 171–72.
9. Ibid., 156.
10. Ibid., 108–09.
11. Ibid., 156–57.
12. *RIP* magazine, February 1995.

8: THE BACKWARD MASK AND OTHER HIDDEN MESSAGES

1. David Sheff, *The Playboy Interviews with John Lennon and Yoko Ono* (New York: Playboy Press, 1981), 175–76.
2. Jeff Godwin, *Dancing with Demons: The Music's Real Master* (Chino, CA: Chick Publications, 1988), 343–344.
3. Thomas Wedge, with Robert L. Powers, *The Satan Hunter* (Carrollton, TX: Calibre Press, Inc., 1993), 95.
4. William Poundstone, *Biggest Secrets* (New York: Quill, 1993), 225.
5. Wedge, *The Satan Hunter*, 95.

9: "IF 6 WAS 9"

1. Stewart, 377–78.
2. Monika Dannemann, *The Inner World of Jimi Hendrix* (New York: St. Martin's Press, 1995), 44.
3. Dannemann, *The Inner World of Jimi Hendrix*, 48.
4. Ibid., 42.
5. David Henderson, *'Scuse Me While I Kiss the Sky* (New York: Bantam Books, 1983), 251.
6. White, *Rock Lives: Profiles and Interviews*, 254.

7. Geoffrey Giuliano et al., *The Illustrated Jimi Hendrix* (China: The Promotional Reprint Co., 1994), 13.

8. Henderson, *'Scuse Me While I Kiss the Sky,* 174.

9. Dannemann, *The Inner World of Jimi Hendrix,* 152–53.

10. Cavendish, *The Black Arts,* 77.

11. Louis Stewart, *Life Forces: A Contemporary Guide to the Cult and Occult* (Kansas City: Andrews and McMeel, Inc., 1980), 125.

12. Stewart, *Life Forces,* 125.

13. Henderson, *'Scuse Me While I Kiss the Sky,* 403–04.

14. Ray Coleman, *Lennon: The Definitive Biography* (New York: Harper Perennial, 1992), 681–82.

15. Frederic Seaman, *The Last Days of John Lennon* (New York: Birch Lane Press Book by the Carol Publishing Co., 1991), 6.

16. Seaman, *The Last Days of John Lennon,* 32.

17. Ibid., 69.

18. John Green; *Dakota Days* (New York: St. Martin's Press, 1983), 42.

19. Green, *Dakota Days,* 53.

20. Ibid., 122.

21. Sanchez, *Up and Down,* 315–16.

22. Green, *Dakota Days,* 32.

23. Seaman, *The Last Days of John Lennon,* 189.

24. Sheff, *The Playboy Interviews,* 91.

25. Seaman, *The Last Days of John Lennon,* 39–40.

26. Ibid., 220.

27. Jack Jones, *Let Me Take You Down* (New York: Warner Books, 1992), 232.

28. Seaman, *The Last Days of John Lennon,* 234.

29. Barry McCloud et al., *Definitive Country: The Ultimate Encyclopedia of Country Music and Its Performers* (New York: Perigee Books, 1995), 876–77.

30. McCloud, *Definitive Country,* 394.

10: THE CLUB

1. Sanchez, *Up and Down,* 79.

2. Faithfull, *Faithfull: An Autobiography,* 169.

3. Laura Jackson, *Golden Stone: The Untold Life and Tragic Death of Brian Jones* (New York: St. Martin's Press, 1993), 223.

4. Jackson, *Golden Stone,* 224.

5.   Sanchez, *Up and Down,* 158.

6.   Hotchner, *Blown Away,* 298.

7.   Ibid., 293.

8.   Gary J. Katz, *Death by Rock 'n' Roll* (New York: Citadel Press, 1995), 106.

9.   Giuliano, *The Illustrated Jimi Hendrix,* 68.

10. White, *Rock Lives: Profiles and Interviews,* 295.

11. Giuliano, *The Illustrated Jim Hendrix,* 81.

12. Frank Lisciandro, *Morrison: A Feast of Friends* (New York: Warner Books, 1991), 131.

13. Jerry Hopkins and Danny Sugarman, *No One Here Gets Out Alive* (New York: Warner Books, 1995), 314.

14. Hopkins and Sugarman, *No One Here Gets Out Alive,* 313.

15. Ibid., 18.

16. Lisciandro, *Morrison: A Feast of Friends,* 111.

17. Ibid., 65.

18. Ibid., 64.

19. Hopkins and Sugarman, *No One Here Gets Out Alive,* 373.

20. Ibid., 367–68.

21. Ibid., 367.

22. Katz, *Death by Rock 'n' Roll,* 82.

23. Rock Scully, with David Dalton, *Living with the Dead* (Boston: Little, Brown & Co., 1996), 369.

24. Katz, *Death by Rock 'n' Roll,* 46.

25. Cavendish, *The Black Arts,* 76.

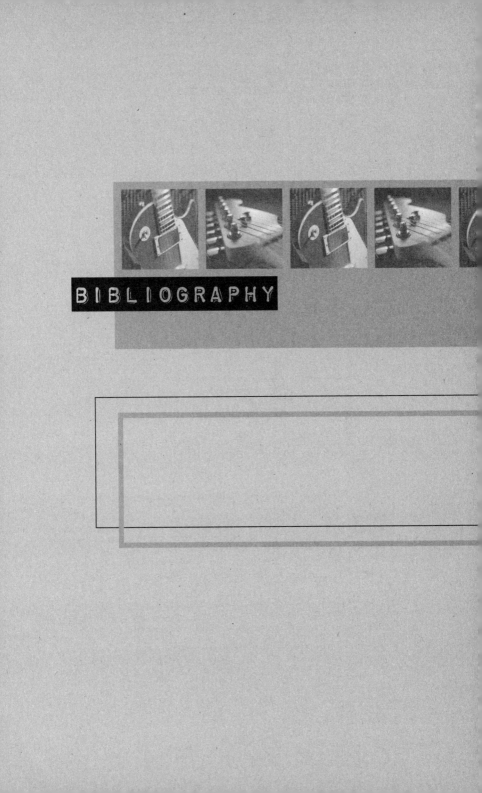

BIBLIOGRAPHY

Amburn, Ellis, *Buddy Holly: A Biography,* New York: St. Martin's Press, 1996.

Barton, Blanche, *The Church of Satan: A History of the World's Most Notorious Religion,* New York: Hell's Kitchen Production, 1990.

Barton, Blanche, *The Secret Life of a Satanist: The Authorized Biography of Anton LaVey,* Portland, OR: Feral House, 1992.

Brant, Marley, *Freebirds: The Lynyrd Skynyrd Story,* New York: Billboard Books, 2002.

Castle, William, *Step Right Up! I'm Gonna Scare the Pants Off America.* New York: Pharos Books, 1992.

Cavendish, Richard, *The Black Arts,* New York: Perigee Books, 1983.

Cohen, Daniel, *Cults,* Brookfield, CT: Millbrook Press, 1994.

Cole, Richard, *Stairway to Heaven: Led Zeppelin Uncensored,* New York: HarperCollins, 1992.

Coleman, Ray, *Lennon: The Definitive Biography,* New York: Harper-Perennial, 1992.

Crowley, Aleister, *Magick, in Theory and Practice,* Secaucus, NJ: Castle Books, 1991.

Dannemann, Monika, *The Inner World of Jimi Hendrix,* New York: St. Martin's Press, 1995.

Davis, Francis, *The History of the Blues: The Roots, the Music, the People—from Charley Patton to Robert Cray,* New York: Hyperion, 1995.

Davis, Stephen, *Hammer of the Gods: The Led Zeppelin Saga,* New York: Ballantine Books, 1986.

Driver, Jim, ed., *The Mammoth Book of Sex, Drugs, and Rock 'n' Roll,* New York: Carroll and Graff, 2001.

Faithfull, Marianne, with David Dalton, *Faithfull: An Autobiography,* Boston: Little Brown & Company, 1994.

Freeman, Scott, *Midnight Riders: The Story of the Allman Brothers Band,* Boston: Little, Brown & Company, 1995.

Friedman, Myra, *Buried Alive: The Biography of Janis Joplin,* New York: Harmony Books, 1992.

Gardner, Martin, *On the Wild Side,* New York: Prometheus Books, 1992.

Giuliano, Geoffrey et al., *The Illustrated Jimi Hendrix,* China: The Promotional Reprint Company Ltd., 1994.

Godwin, Jeff, *Devil's Disciples: The Truth About Rock Music,* Chino, CA: Chick Publications, 1985.

Godwin, Jeff, *Dancing with Demons: The Music's Real Master,* Chino, CA: Chick Publications, 1988.

Green, John, *Dakota Days,* New York: St. Martin's Press, 1983.

Grehan, Ida, *Irish Family Names,* Belfast: Appletree Press, 1985.

Guralnick, Peter, *Searching for Robert Johnson,* New York: E. P. Dutton, 1989.

Halperin, Ian, and Max Wallace, *Who Killed Kurt Cobain?: The Mysterious Death of an Icon,* Secaucus, NJ: Citadel Press, 1998.

Henderson, David *'Scuse Me While I Kiss the Sky,* New York: Bantam Books, 1983.

Herman, Gary, *Rock 'n' Roll Babylon,* London: Plexus Publishing, 2002.

Hopkins, Jerry, and Danny Sugarman, *No One Here Gets Out Alive,* New York: Warner Books, 1995.

Hotchner, A. E., *Blown Away: The Rolling Stones and the Death of the Sixties,* New York: Simon & Schuster, 1990.

Huxley, Martin *AC/DC: The World's Heaviest Rock,* New York: St. Martin's Griffin, 1996.

Huxley, Martin, and Quinton Skinner, *Behind the Music: The Day the Music Died,* New York: Simon and Schuster, 2000.

Jackson, Laura, *Golden Stone: The Untold Life and Tragic Death of Brian Jones,* New York: St. Martin's Press, 1993.

Jones, Jack, *Let Me Take You Down,* New York: Warner Books, 1992.

Katz, Gary J., *Death by Rock 'n' Roll,* New York: Citadel Press, 1995.

Kennealy, Patricia, *Strange Days: My Life With and Without Jim Morrison,* New York: Plume Books, 1992.

LaVey, Anton Szandor, *The Satanic Bible,* New York: Avon Books, 1976.

Lisciandro, Frank, *Morrison: A Feast of Friends,* New York: Warner Books, 1991.

McCloud, Barry et al., *Definitive Country: The Ultimate Encyclopedia of Country Music and Its Performers,* New York: Perigree Books, 1995.

Mann, Alan, *The A–Z of Buddy Holly,* London: Aurum Press, 1996.

Mitchell, Corey, *Hollywood Death Scenes: True Crime and Tragedy in Paradise,* Chicago: Olmstead Press, 2001.

Newton, Michael, *Raising Hell: An Encyclopedia of Devil Worship and Satanic Crime,* New York: Avon Books, 1993.

Nolan, A. M., *Rock 'n' Roll Roadtrip,* New York: Pharos Books, 1992.

Norman, Philip, *Sympathy for the Devil: The Rolling Stones Story,* New York: Dell, 1984.

Parker, John, *At the Heart of Darkness: Witchcraft, Black Magic, and Satanism Today,* New York: Citadel Press, 1993.

Pike, Jeff, *The Death of Rock 'n' Roll,* Boston & London: Faber and Faber, 1993.

Poundstone, William, *Big Secrets,* New York: Quill, 1983.

Poundstone, William, *Bigger Secrets,* Boston: Houghton Mifflin Company, 1986.

Poundstone, William, *Biggest Secrets,* New York: Quill, 1993.

Prud'homme, Jacques Gabriel, *Niccolò Paganini: A Biography,* American Musicological Society Press, 1976.

Repsch, John, *The Legendary Joe Meek: The Telstar Man,* London: Cherry Red Books, 2000.

Sandford, Christopher, *Mick Jagger: Primitive Cool,* New York: St. Martin's Press, 1993.

Sanchez, Tony, *Up and Down with the Rolling Stones,* London: Blake, 1991.

Schaffner, Nicholas *Saucerful of Secrets: The Pink Floyd Odyssey,* New York: Delta Books, 1991.

Scully, Rock, with David Dalton, *Living with the Dead,* Boston: Little Brown and Company, 1996.

Seaman, Frederic, *The Last Days of John Lennon,* New York: Birch Lane Press Book by the Carol Publishing Group, 1991.

Sheff, David, *The Playboy Interviews with John Lennon and Yoko Ono,* New York: Playboy Press, 1981.

Skinner, Quinton. *Casualties of Rock: Behind the Music,* New York: Simon & Schuster, 2001.

Spence, Lewis, *An Encyclopedia of Occultism,* New York: Citadel Books, 1996.

Steffon, Fr. Jeffrey J., *Satanism: Is It Real?,* Ann Arbor, MI: Servant Publications, 1992.

Stewart, Louis, *Life Forces: A Contemporary Guide to the Cult and Occult,* Kansas City: Andrews and McMeel, Inc., 1980.

Thompson, Dave, *Better to Burn Out: The Cult of Death in Rock 'n' Roll,* New York: Thunder's Mouth Press, 1999.

Tosches, Nick, *Hellfire: The Jerry Lee Lewis Story,* New York: Delacorte Press, 1982.

Yorke, Ritchie, *Led Zeppelin: The Definitive Biography,* Novato, CA: Underwood-Miller, 1993.

Wedge, Thomas, with Robert L. Powers, *The Satan Hunter,* Carrollton, TX: Calibre Press, Inc., 1993.

White, Timothy, *Rock Lives: Profiles and Interviews,* New York: Henry Holt & Company, 1990.

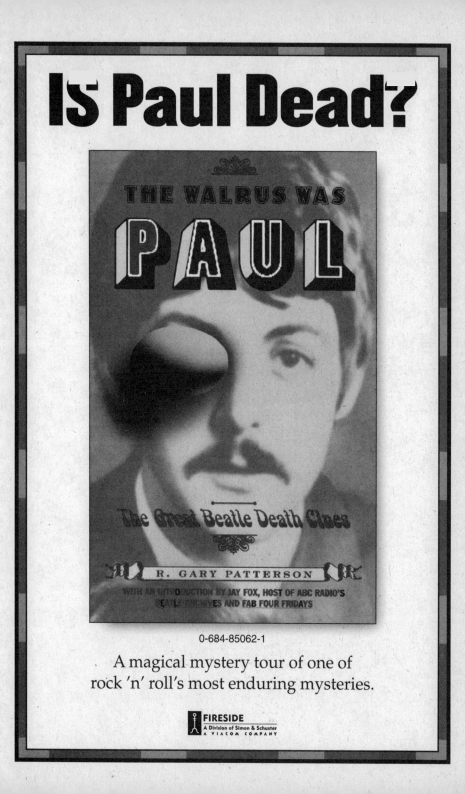